Prac

Published in conjunction with
the British Association of Social Workers
Series Editor: Jo Campling

Practical social work series

celia doyle

working with abused children

from theory to practice

third edition

First edition 1989
Second edition 1997
Third edition 2006

Published by
PALGRAVE MACMILLAN
Houndmills, Basingstoke, Hampshire RG21 6XS and
175 Fifth Avenue, New York, N.Y. 10010
Companies and representatives throughout the world

PALGRAVE MACMILLAN is the global academic imprint of the
Palgrave Macmillan division of St. Martin's Press, LLC and of
Palgrave Macmillan Ltd. Macmillan® is a registered trademark in
the United States, United Kingdom and other countries. Palgrave is a
registered trademark in the European Union and other countries.

ISBN-13: 978-1-4039-1621-1
ISBN-10: 1-4039-1621-7

This book is printed on paper suitable for recycling and
made from fully managed and sustained forest sources.

A catalogue record for this book is available from the
British Library.

10   9   8   7   6   5   4   3   2   1
15   14   13   12   11   10   09   08   07   06

Printed in China

This book is dedicated to my children and to
the memory of their father — my husband, John

Contents

Preface to the third edition

Since the first and second editions of this book, we have entered a new millennium. At the time of the first edition, child protection workers in the UK were coming to terms with the Children Act 1989 and were recovering from upheaval and change in the wake of the Cleveland Inquiry. At the time of the second edition, practitioners found themselves 'refocusing' their intervention after the publication of a raft of government-sponsored research. The discourse became one of a 'child in need' not at risk; 'assessment' rather than investigation; and 'support' rather than responding to abuse. At the time of writing this third edition, child protection workers are reeling from the Laming Report into the torture and death of Victoria Climbié, as well as the Bichard Inquiry following the murders of two young girls at the hands of a predatory sex offender. The discourse of 'need', 'assessment' and 'support' seems somewhat inadequate in the face of the events addressed by Lord Laming and Sir Michael Bichard.

In the new millennium, children continue to be abused, exploited and tortured at the hands of familiar adults, and some children do not survive, as evidenced by the Laming and Bichard Reports – but most do. However, they live on, coping as best they can with their experiences, emotions and memories. It is clearly not enough just to assess, file a report, offer some support to the parents, or even remove the children, and then leave the victims to cope unaided until perhaps they come to the notice of the agencies again. Furthermore, while assessment is important – so is prevention, especially at a societal level by changing the way that children are perceived as being objects and possessions rather than fellow citizens with rights to dignity, justice and protection. Assessment is important – but so is assistance with the healing process given through individual, family or group work. A book on working with abused children, updated by research and reflection, seems as valid today as it did when first published in 1989 – in the previous millennium.

One of the major changes in this edition is the explicit application of theory. There has been a growing recognition that practice needs to be evidence-based. This means that practitioners should understand what, why and how situations, emotions, behaviour and events occur. There are several sources enhancing practitioner understanding. The first is direct information from service users themselves, with an increasing emphasis in their involvement in policy-making and training. The second is indirect information from service users, presented as research findings. The third source of understanding comes through reflective practice. A final source of understanding is provided by theories, which are in the main the systematic observations and reflections of experienced practitioners and researchers. The exact nature of theory is examined in the opening chapter.

As well as increasing the theoretical content in this edition, there is also the inclusion of suggested 'activities' the end of each chapter, under the heading 'Putting ideas into practice'. These are designed to help readers review, consolidate and apply ideas presented in the various chapters. It is important, however, for readers not to make overwhelming emotional demands on themselves when undertaking the suggested activities. Some exercises ask you to remember and reflect on a particular situation that applied to yourself. If you are feeling emotionally vulnerable choose a relatively superficial memory, unless you feel well supported and have someone to turn to in the event of your memories overpowering your capacity to cope.

Another change between this edition and the previous two is my own increased research and understanding of emotional abuse. This underpins all other forms of abuse. Even when it is the sole or main form of abuse, it is arguably the most corrosive because it is an attack on the persona and sense of self of a vulnerable individual. Yet, paradoxically, emotionally abused children are those least likely to be offered a therapeutic service. My research, however, also showed that abused children can be remarkably resilient, and factors promoting resilience are often ones readily available to be harnessed by helping professionals.

Finally, this edition has been informed not only by my own experiences of childhood, coping with the disability of undiagnosed 'dyslexia' and a varied cultural heritage. It has also been informed by parenthood – and widowhood, which has given me insights into the impact of loss on young children. My understanding of play work has been extended by my role as trustee of a play therapy charity and a small amount of direct work has enabled me to ensure that the suggested activities are feasible and can be managed by hard-pressed practitioners.

As with previous editions, I conclude this preface with a note on terminology. Words have the power to increase or challenge discrimination and to create positive or negative concepts. I have chosen words and terminology with all due care but recognize that some concepts and terms that currently are appropriate will alter subtly in meaning and become unacceptable over the next few years. I hope that later readers will mentally insert the more appropriate contemporary terminology, which I currently cannot anticipate.

CELIA DOYLE

Acknowledgements

A debt of gratitude is owed to those many colleagues who have inspired me over the years. Not everyone can be named, but early mentors include Dr Margaret Oates, David N. Jones, Andy Perrins and Maddy Collinge, while more recent ones include Sally Romaine, Chris Durkin, Lesley Best, Robert Gunn, Rosemary Wilcox and Eunice Lumsden.

Among the most important people to thank are those survivors, Helen, Sarah, Roy, Lloyd and Marie (whose names have been changed to maintain confidentially) who so generously shared their accounts. Additionally, the children with whom I have worked have made an essential contribution to the understanding and knowledge I have attempted to share in this book.

This book would not have seen the light of day without the encouragement and advice of Jo Campling, Catherine Gray and colleagues. I would therefore like to take this opportunity to thank them.

As ever, family and friends are an incalculable source of support. My brothers and sisters-in-law, Mick, Peter, Jenny, Elaine and Jacky are always on hand to provide guidance, sustenance and recuperation. The greatest 'thank you' is reserved for their nephews – my younger sons Peter, Charles and Richard. Never has a group of teenagers coped with their mother's foibles with such fortitude, tolerance and good humour.

CELIA DOYLE

Introduction

The inspiration for this book comes from the life and death of a small boy, Darryn Clarke. He was killed by his mother's partner and was the subject of a public inquiry (Clarke, 1979, in Appendix). Shortly after his death, as a participant in a child protection training course, I was asked to present the report as though I were Darryn himself giving evidence to the inquiry. For the first time I saw the events through the eyes of the abused child.

This caused a profound change in the focus of my work. Previously I had concentrated on helping the parents. It was, after all, easier to communicate with fellow adults. Moreover, I could largely dismiss the pain felt by the children if I concentrated on the parents' needs. Their distress was considerable, but not as poignant as that of their children. But having relived Darryn's last weeks, albeit in a very rudimentary form, I could no longer ignore the plight of the maltreated child.

From then on I tried to look at abuse from the children's perspectives. I sought ways to communicate with all young people, from the smallest infant to the most sophisticated and cynical of adolescents. I slowly began to understand how best we might give them real and lasting help. This book is the product of those years of striving to focus on the abused child.

It is also the product of not only working directly with abused children but also of training other helping professionals and of receiving formal and informal training myself. This has resulted in a need to explain and have explained why and how certain interventions appear to be beneficial and others less so. These explanations become 'theory'. The nature and issue of theory and its relationship to practice and reflective intervention is discussed in the first chapter.

The next three chapters are designed to place intervention in context through an attempt to understand the perspectives of abused children and the psychological processes that will inevitably influence their development, emotions and behaviour. The sociological and social policy contexts within which children live, and helping professionals work, are also explored.

The subsequent four chapters explore direct intervention with abused children through individual work, family and group work, and through indirect intervention, whether by the provision of substitute care or by promoting those factors that increase resilience.

Linking with the theme of resilience, the final chapter revisits some of the children who gave an account of childhood abuse in the second chapter, in order to examine the effects of abuse in later life, as well as exploring ways of helping adults abused as children.

Crucially, this is not a book covering all aspects of child abuse. In particular, it does not explore assessment and investigation in any depth. In the UK comprehensive government-sponsored guidance is provided (Department of Health, 2000) while Calder and Hackett (2003) and the contributing authors explore assessment in a wide variety of contexts.

This focus of this book is on practical ways of helping children, but the practice is based on theoretical understanding. Some of the ideas are drawn from other areas of social work such as bereavement counselling and work with children with disabilities. Conversely, many of the models and methods of intervention suggested here might be useful for practitioners working with client groups other than abused children.

The book also challenges the idea that only highly-trained specialists can offer direct help to abused children. Undoubtedly, some of the victims of abuse have suffered such deep emotional trauma that only in-depth, long-term therapy will have any effect. However, the majority of abused children will derive considerable benefit from help that is well within the scope of a wide range of child-care workers, including social workers, pastoral education staff and health professionals. Furthermore, many non-professionals who have sensitivity and empathy towards children can give vital help. Indeed, one of the most underrated and underdeveloped sources of help for children in general, and maltreated ones in particular, are social 'aunts' and 'uncles'.

In the interests of confidentiality, all identifying information and names in case material have been altered unless the case has been the subject of a public inquiry. This is indicated by the publication year of the inquiry report appearing after the child's name. The references for these documents can be found in the list of inquiry reports in the Appendix.

Finally, some of the material in this book is emotionally challenging. Many readers may find the material distressing. This may be because childhood abuse is part of their direct experience and/or because they have an enhanced ability to empathise with the vulnerable and oppressed. Whatever the reason, it is helpful to identify people who can give you support and 'a listening ear' if you experience distress. Furthermore, feel free to take a pause from reading or engaging in the activities at the end of each chapter whenever you feel the material is putting you under undue emotional pressure.

1 | Theory into practice

Working with children requires more than a wish to help, an ability to communicate with them, or even a willingness to respect their views – all essential attributes. It also requires an understanding of how, why and when particular forms of assistance and intervention are appropriate. Such an understanding is based partly on reflection upon one's own experiences and observations, and partly on 'theory', which is, in a sense, other people's reflection on their experiences and observations.

The nature of theory

'Theory', according to the New Oxford Dictionary, is 'a supposition or system of ideas intended to explain something, especially one based on general principles independent of the thing to be explained' or a 'set of principles on which the practice of an activity is based'. The important concept in these two definitions is that of 'principle'. A principle is 'a fundamental truth or proposition that serves as the foundation for a system of belief or behaviour or for a chain of reasoning'.

The issue here is, what is 'fundamental truth'? For some, 'truth' emanates from the divine, through sacred scriptures or the pronouncements of gurus, prophets, saints and other holy people. These truths, often associated with organised religion, regulate human behaviour, including what to eat or drink and how to relate to other people. Throughout the ages and in many cultures, philanthropic and social welfare intervention has been based on principles emanating from these revelations of how we should treat members of our society.

For others, 'fundamental truth' is based on reason. This is the version of truth most closely associated with the natural sciences. Here, truth is discovered by close observation leading to a set of propositions, the soundness of which is then tested through repeated observation, logical deduction or experimentation. Since the eighteenth century, much Western welfare intervention has been based on these ideas. For example, rational observation and deduction dictated that welfare provision for disadvantaged sectors made economic and military sense when, during the Boer War, the UK government discovered many young men were too enfeebled by illnesses associated with poverty to be conscripted into the army.

Frequently, 'theory' is equated with this perspective on truth. 'Scientific' theories emanating from an observation of phenomena then refined and tested by quantitative, preferably experimental, methods are seen as the only sound, reliable theories – and therefore the only 'real' truth. Many theories used by helping professionals are built on this version of truth, and evaluated against scientific ideals and concepts such as 'positivism', 'rationality', 'reason' and 'modernism'.

Fascinatingly, the challenge to this rational concept of theory was based partially on the observations of the pre-eminent scientist, Albert Einstein. His theory 'says that *all* frames of reference are equally valid, and that there is no absolute reference frame' (White and Gribbin, 1992, p. 28). So this third perspective contests both of the concepts of truth, divine revelation or human reason described above. Generalizing from Einstein's theory, 'truth' is viewed as being relative, and situated in a particular time and place. Therefore, what might be 'normal' human development in one cultural context might be 'abnormal' or inappropriate in another. Some recent philosophical, social science and social welfare theories are based on this relative or 'postmodern' perspective. For example, it is argued that concepts, even ones that seem rooted in biology, such as 'mental health', 'adulthood' and 'child', are relative and constructed by people living together in a particular society. The same is true of 'child abuse', as Corby (2000) explains:

> Child abuse is a socially defined construct. It is a product of a particular culture and context and not an absolute unchanging phenomenon . . . what is considered to be abusive in a particular society alters over time. Place is another factor. Anthropological studies show clearly that what is viewed as abusive in one society today is not necessarily seen as such in another.
> (p. 66)

If theories are based on so elusive a concept of truth, do they have any value? The answer is that, inevitably, anyone intervening in the lives of others will be basing their intervention, whether consciously or unconsciously, on 'a set of related propositions that suggest why events occur in the manner that they do' – that is, forms of theory (Hoover and Donovan, 1995, p. 38). Well-founded theories, albeit not perfect, will be better than unthinking mechanical input or mindless prejudice, which will fill the vacuum in the absence of theoretical approaches.

One reason why practitioners may struggle with the application of theory is that there are different types of theory.

Some are *descriptive* theories offering explanations about *what is happening* and metaphorically 'open the eyes' so that practitioners become more aware of phenomena. Often they provide a framework of understanding. Elizabeth Kubler-Ross's (1970) work on loss and mourning has provided invaluable insights for those helping people in a state of grief.

Others are *causal* theories and explain *why things happen*. For example, social learning theory suggests that people learn violent behaviour by watching others behave violently (Bandura, 1973).

Yet others are *interventive* theories indicating *what should be done* about what has happened. Examples here include theories of crisis intervention (Golan, 1978; Thompson, 1991; Aguilera, 1998) and task-centred work (Reid and Epstein, 1972; Doel and Marsh, 1992).

Some theories have all three functions. Psychodynamic theory, for example, *describes* human functioning including the role of the unconscious, *explains* why people behave in certain ways and *provides guidance* about how people can be helped.

Most theories relating to human beings are founded on, and developed from, one of several approaches. These are:

● *biological*   based on observations and interpretations of the behaviour of animals and investigations of their physiology and genetic composition;
● *behavioural*   based on observations of manifest behaviour of animals and humans;
● *cognitive*   based on conscious thought revealed mainly though behaviour with some verbal expression, and through computer simulation and artificial intelligence;

● *humanistic* based on conscious thought revealed mainly through verbal expression;
● *psychodynamic* based mainly on unconscious functioning revealed predominantly through verbal expression;
● *systems* based on an analysis of the interaction of one unit with another, whether inanimate objects, living organisms, human beings, social groups or institutions; and
● *sociological and environmental* based on the observed behaviours of social groups, institutions and structures.

These various approaches are not mutually exclusive, and many theories are combinations. For example, John Bowlby was a psychoanalyst and this influenced attachment theory, but he integrated insights from the work of biologist Konrad Lorenz (1970) and his work on 'imprinting' in small animals.

In addition there are a number of perspectives through which the different approaches are developed or interpreted. There is, for example, the economic and class theme exemplified by Marxist thinking. Another major influence is the range of feminist perceptions. Feminist thinking in a variety of forms offers both a critique and an interpretation of theories, and fits well with anti-discriminatory practice because 'a feminist stance endorses egalitarianism across all social dimensions' (Dominelli and McLeod, 1989, p. 2).

Integrated models and ecological theory

Increasingly, it is recognised that 'child abuse and neglect cannot be explained by a single factor, it is a consequence of complex interactions between individual, social and environmental influences' (Browne, 2002, p. 57). Theories that locate the cause solely within parental dysfunction fail to account for the fact that abuse is over-represented where there are environmental stressors such as poverty and unemployment. However, purely sociological theories cannot explain why many socio-economically disadvantaged parents do not abuse their children. This accounts for the increased acceptance of ecological theory, which highlights the complex interplay of psychological and sociological factors.

Ecological theory is a systems approach based on concepts advanced by Bronfenbrenner (1979). According to this theory, the child is located within a series of nests. The first, the *microsystem*, comprises the child's immediate family and close contacts. The second nest is the *mesosystem*, containing the microsystem and embracing wider contacts such as a playgroup, school or immediate neighbours. Next is the *exosystem*, whose components are beyond the child's direct contact but whose influence has an impact on the child, such as the parents' workplace and friendship network, the wider neighbourhood, or distant extended family. Finally, all these systems exist within the all-encompassing *macrosystem*, comprising the political and cultural context.

It is worth noting that ecological theory underpins the approach and structure of this book. The next three chapters consider psychological and sociological explanatory or causal theories, while those on intervention are organised on the basis of working with the smallest to the largest systems.

Evaluating theories

Smith (1998) warns that 'In all areas where there is a fairly structured and extensive body of thought in a particular social science, we can witness a reluctance to question bedrock assumptions' (p. 187). Because no theory is the absolute 'truth', each will have both strengths and limitations. They may be useful in helping to explain why or how things occur, but there are dangers when they are used uncritically. All theories need to be questioned and appraised. The next section provides an example of the evaluation of one profoundly influential theory.

Attachment theory is vitally important in the appreciation of the relationship needs of young children and the understanding of the relationship patterns of people in older life (Howe, 1995; Howe *et al.*, 1999). The theory emerged from the work of Bowlby (1951; 1969) and hypothesised that on the basis of babies' interactions with their mother they develop an 'internal working model' of what might be expected from relationships in general. Young humans need to explore their environment and develop independence, but to do so successfully they need a secure base to return to for comfort and reassurance when under stress. This base, essential to future mental health according to Bowlby, is 'a warm, intimate and continuous relationship with his mother (or permanent mother-substitute – one person who steadily 'mothers' him) in which both find satisfaction and enjoyment' (Bowlby, 1969, p. 13). In the same work, Bowlby outlines the role of fathers thus: 'fathers have their uses even in infancy . . . [providing] for their wives to enable them to devote themselves unrestrictedly to the care of the infant and toddler' (p. 15). The evident concern here is the potential oppression of women, and indeed of men, with the implied requirement for mothers not to delegate care of their children to others and the relegation of fathers to a remote secondary role.

Other criticisms include the theory's failure to explain why poorly attached, abused children do not inevitably go on to be unsatisfactory parents, yet an internal working model based on early abusive relationships would suggest they should. Furthermore, the theory does not take into account all the family dynamics, especially sibling relationships (see the work of Judy Dunn – for example, Dunn, 1995) and extended family members, such as aunts (Doyle, 2001), nor does it fully acknowledge the social factors impinging on family relationships (Papalia *et al.*, 2003). In fact, Bowlby (1969) and Ainsworth (1969) explicitly reject a consideration of environmental factors, believing that such consideration 'hinders understanding to the extent that it is a flight from the recognition of the importance of interpersonal relations' (p. 198).

Ainsworth developed Bowlby's theory (Ainsworth *et al.*, 1978) devising an experiment in which a baby is left with a stranger for a short period. Depending on the baby's reactions, she identified three forms of mother–child attachment: 'insecure–avoidant', 'insecure–ambivalent' and 'secure', with secure being generally regarded as the optimal one in terms of future relationships.

Criticisms of Ainsworth's work include, first, the unethical nature of deliberately putting a child, who cannot give informed consent, in a situation of stress without clear benefit to the child; second, the artificial nature of the experiment; and third, the negation of factors such as temperament. Parents with several children know that from birth their children have different characteristics, and this common-sense observation has been validated by a number of studies (Thomas and Chess, 1977; Rothbart *et al.*, 2000, 2001). For example, some children appear to be anxious from birth and show fearful, shy behaviour throughout childhood (Kagan, 1997). Physical and physiological differences between these children and more outgoing ones have been identified (Arcus and Kagan, 1995) indicating a biological basis for their anxious demeanour, rather than unresponsive mothering.

Studies have shown that babies in some cultures have far higher levels of non-secure attachments than others. For example Miyake *et al.* (1985) found Japanese infants show much higher levels of insecure attachments compared to American ones. Using meta-analysis, Von Ijzendoorn and Kroonenberg (1988) found among British children 75 per cent had secure attachments and 3 per cent resistant ones, whereas in China 50 per cent had secure and 25 per cent resistant attachments. Anthropologist Margaret Mead (1962) expressed concern that Bowlby's theories did not take into account those many non-Western societies that cared successfully for children through multiple nurturing figures, and argued that 'satisfactory' child-rearing practices differ from one culture to another depending on the societal requirements. Ainsworth dismisses this with the statement 'her [Mead's] final criterion seems to be the cultural appropriateness of patterns of behaviour. Although this is a common criterion in cultural anthropology, it can be challenged. Can we not differentiate between societies that facilitate and those that handicap the health growth of personality?' (Ainsworth, 1969, p. 209). This assertion is not particularly helpful for social workers trying to practise in a non-judgemental and non-discriminatory way.

Certainly, the concept of attachment is a valid one to the extent that, from Sigmund Freud onwards, most theorists agree that early relationships can influence adult functioning. But there is no reason why other theories cannot be as valid as attachment theory in explaining human relationship development. Alternatives include: Erikson's (1965) stage theory, which highlights the need in infancy to establish 'basic trust'; Maslow's (1970) need theory with its emphasis on the basic need for security, and Rogerian concepts (Rogers, 1967, 1980) of 'non-judgemental positive regard'.

Any theory, if applied uncritically or taken to extremes, can become equally unhelpful. Therefore, there is a need to approach the use of theory with a degree of critical evaluation and reflection.

Dogma into practice

Some theories and principles are elevated to dogma – that is, 'principles laid down by an authority as incontrovertibly true' (Oxford English Dictionary – OED). Often their origins can be traced to good practice but they have been applied indiscriminately. Philpot (1995) explained:

Sacred cows have no place in child protection work. Where practitioners have become inseparably attached to a particular theory or preconception, we have been left with cases where the truth has been pushed out of reach and children's experiences have been shrouded in confusion . . . Social workers must reject sacred cows and stop taking refuge in spurious certainties.
(p. 1)

This section examines a number of past and present theories, and principles that have been applied without proper understanding or reflection and have consequently become dogmas that have had an adverse influence on child-care practice.

The 'fresh start' theory

Pat Bastian (1994) joined a Children's Department in January 1955. Looking back forty years later, she recalled 'All of us subscribed to . . . the "fresh start" theory where children could be divested of their previous identity and given a new (and better) one' (p. 70).

During the first half of the twentieth century children came into care for a range of reasons, especially illegitimacy or extreme poverty. Throughout the Victorian era the concept of the ideal middle-class family had been promoted, so poor, working-class families were often deemed 'unfit', and this unfitness, along with illegitimacy was a major disgrace. Child-welfare workers were determined that the children in their care should not suffer from such a stigma. The advocates of the fresh start idea were well-intentioned and in some ways anticipated researchers and theorists who highlighted the insidious nature of negative 'labelling'. On being taken into care, children could lose the label 'illegitimate' or 'indigent' and take on a new identity as a member of a respectable upper working- or middle-class family.

This policy persisted for nearly a hundred years. It was not until in the 1970s that there was a perceptible change. Then Janet Hitchman, in her book *King of the Barbareens* (Hitchman, 1960) described how her many moves in care and attempts to give her a 'fresh start' each time had led to her lifelong search to establish her identity. Bastian (1994) recalls:

The revelation came to me, as it did to many others, as a blindingly obvious fact and it is hard for the present genera- tion of social workers to realise that we hadn't understood this before. The children who could not cope with life in whatever setting were those who did not understand who they were, why they were there and what was happening to them. (p.72)

The blood-tie

The Second World War saw the massive disruption of families throughout Europe. In England, many children were evacuated from the main cities, which caused distress to both the children and their parents. After the war, there was a desperate search by refugees and concentration camp survivors for blood relatives and family members. Meanwhile in England the death of one child, Dennis O'Neill, shook the foundations of the establishment. Tom O'Neill describes what happened to his seven-year-old brother six years after he was taken into care: 'On 9 January 1945 my brother, Dennis O'Neill, was beaten to death by his foster-father in a lonely farmhouse in Shropshire . . . At the time of his death Dennis, whose stomach showed no traces of food, weighed just over 4 stone at thirteen years of age' (pp. ix–xi). Then six years later came Bowlby's work on the importance of attachment to one mother figure and the deprivation that ensued from separation from her.

All these events lead to an emphasis on the importance of the blood relationship and for children to remain with their birth mother if at all feasible. The 1948 Children Act set up in the wake of the death of Dennis O'Neill stressed the importance of returning children wherever possible to their birth parents.

On 6 January 1973, another child, Maria Colwell, was killed. She was eight years old. She was 'beaten to death by her step-father in a council house in Brighton . . . At the time of her death, Maria, whose stomach was empty, weighed a mere 36 pounds' (O'Neill, 1981, pp. ix–xi). She had been happily settled for nearly all her childhood with her aunt and uncle, who fostered her. Then her mother and stepfather demanded her return – only to abuse system- atically and eventually kill her. The blood-tie with the birth mother prevailed over all other considerations. A report by the local author- ity, in whose care Maria had been, reflected, after her death:

'The blood tie' is a term often applied to the belief held strongly by many people that there is a strong physical tie between a child and his parent by virtue of his physical inheritance and the fact of conception and child-bearing. The term 'natural parent' somehow implies that any kind of substitute for the parent is to a degree unnatural . . . There can be no question of automatic assumptions that a child is better off with any particular category of person, whether parent or parent substitute. It must depend on the circumstances of each case individually.
(Appendix, Colwell, 1976, p. 87)

Despite criticisms of the over-emphasis on the blood-tie, a deep-seated belief in its importance continues to influence policy and practice.

Anti-discriminatory practice

This may appear to sit uneasily in this section because it is difficult to see how anti-discriminatory practice can be anything other than beneficial. Anti-discriminatory practice challenges discrimination and oppression wherever it is encountered and at all levels, including among professionals themselves and in the systems used by them. At the forefront of antidiscriminatory practice is anti-racist practice. This is defined as:

developing a model of strength and empowerment in social work.   It is based on the self-definition of black experience, needs and aspirations and therefore involves the acknowledgement of black people's views values and concerns, it involves dismantling pathological assumptions and cultural stereotypes in favour of an approach that is sensitive to cultural pride and differences.
(Gambe *et al.*, 1992, p. 10)

The emphasis on anti-discriminatory and anti-racist ideologies has, however, had some negative consequences for intervention. The removal of black children by white workers who condemn child-care practices they do not understand has been rightly condemned as discriminatory. Nevertheless, Ahmad (1989) and Owusu-Bempah (2003) both point out that it is equally discriminatory to do nothing to protect children from minority cultures when there is evidence of abuse. For fear of being seen as racist, child protection workers have tended to shy away from their duties of protecting black children from abuse. Similarly, Corby (2000) reminds us of the culturally relative nature of child abuse, which means that social workers have an obligation to challenge the imposition of the standards of the majority culture on minority groups. Nevertheless, Corby warns against the 'extraordinary degree of tolerance' (p. 67) – in the name of anti-discriminatory practice and cultural sensitivity – shown by social workers towards unequivocally abusive behaviour, which has led to the deaths of a number of children.

During the 1970s and 1980s there was mounting concern about the problems of black children in white foster (or adoptive) families, which included identity confusion and little guidance about how to cope with racism. Gambe *et al.* (1992) explained that 'black families can offer [black] children an added dimension, over and above a loving environment, covering such things as continuity of experience, contact with the relevant community and understanding of a pride in the child's particular inheritance, and skills and support in dealing with racism' (p. 69). In response, in the 1980s several local authorities imposed a ban on black children being placed with white substitute carers. Because the drive to recruit more black foster carers lagged behind these policies, some black children lingered in residential care or were placed with mismatched black foster carers (see, for example, Lau, 1991).

One of the most iniquitous practices in the name of anti-discriminatory practice has been the treatment of dual-heritage children. Their white heritage has been denied as they have automatically been defined as 'black'. Researcher Charles-Hoon (2003), the black mother of a dual-heritage child, explains that this labelling of dual-heritage (black/white) children harks back to the days of slavery when, to ensure that the maximum available number of slaves was maintained, children who had 'one drop' of black blood were defined as 'black' and therefore, unless born of free parents, were automatically slaves. Dual-heritage children should not be labelled as black or white, but should be allowed their own specific identity.

Comment

These, and other dogmas, are or were rooted in theories of good practice. However, when promoted from theory to a dogmatically imposed ideology they have been applied inappropriately, insensitively and without proper analysis.

Foundations of good practice

Whatever the theoretical bases of intervention, there are some basic requirements expected of helping professionals. These will be common to those working with adults as well as those in child-care, and while not specific to working with abused children, it is worth providing a brief reminder of the essentials.

Evidence-based practice

This means ensuring that any intervention is based on the facts and information available. There needs to be a careful factual assessment of the issues in the case, as well as other external contextual information, including research findings. The importance of this is illustrated by the situation in Britain in the 1980s, when specialist social workers became aware of the research findings of Abel *et al.* (1987) and Finkelhor (1984) into the repeat offending and grooming behaviour of sex abusers. They often found themselves powerless to influence case conferences and courts which, unaware of the research, accepted the abuser's protestations of the offence being 'a one-off' and 'out-of-character', and left children in the home unprotected.

Reflection

Thinking theoretically without any form of reflection becomes rigidity of thought, which leads ultimately to unthinking intervention, whereas reflection without any sort of theoretical basis is woolly thinking, which also leads ultimately to unthinking intervention. Unthinking intervention becomes habitual intervention, which in turn leads to ineffective practice.

Reflection covers every aspect of practice, but includes in particular:

● an explicit awareness of personal values, including bias and prejudice, plus a recognition that other people will have opposing views or very different values;
● acknowledging the impact of the self on others and appreciating power differentials;

● being aware of feelings aroused in them by other people or
situations. They might, for example, analyse why they feel
threatened when visiting a particular home, and how realistic is
the perceived threat;
● evaluating the effectiveness of intervention. For example, the
worker feeling under threat might avoid raising a necessary but
sensitive topic with a particular family; and
● identifying the theoretical bases for the intervention, and questioning how appropriate they are.

Boundaries

Establishing boundaries is essential to all care professionals, but is
particularly important in child protection work. A chummy friendship with parents can leave a child exposed to danger. Failure to
establish boundaries when exploring sexual abuse with a child
resulting in the touching of private parts (yes, it does still happen)
will lead the worker to face charges of sexual assault.

Workers also need to try to be firm about establishing work and
private life boundaries. This is easier said than done, and employ-
ers often fail to recognise the counter-productive nature of forcing
their employees to overwork, which leads to illness and burnout.

But workers can also draw too tight a boundary and refuse to see
beyond the immediate focus of their work. The case of Stephen
Meurs (Meurs, 1975, in Appendix) was one in which helping
professionals were visiting children in the household who were
being fostered by Stephen's mother. They took little interest in
Stephen's welfare and he died of neglect despite their visits.

Supervision, mentoring and consultation

Effective supervision is essential for those working in the field of
child protection. As one student reflected:

It is important to be able to step back and reflect and not be
blinkered. Supervision enabled me to view situations from a
different perspective, and to realise that my original perspective could sometimes be naïve and often plainly wrong.
(Watson *et al.*, 2002, p. 161)

Some professionals find that their supervisor has had little experience of child protection work, and feels unable to offer any real

assistance with the complex issues of abuse cases. Here, workers might try to negotiate a consultation with more knowledgeable colleagues.

Walton (2002) points out that there are usually two tasks in supervision – one managerial and the other mentoring. The use of power distinguishes these two components. In the first, the supervisor has the greater power, whereas in mentoring 'power is mainly with the person being mentored and the purpose of the relationship is to encourage their professional development. Mutual trust [Erikson again] is important in both relationships' (p. 565). Some supervisors are unable to share their power and so only the managerial function is fulfilled. Again, if possible, the worker could benefit from a strategy that meets his or her needs for mentoring either by helping the supervisor change approach or by finding an alternative mentor.

Recording

Time and again, inquiry reports (see the Appendix for list of reports) into the deaths of children have commented on poor record-keeping and communication. Good records are essential if the accurate information is to be shared with other colleagues, agencies and courts.

It is advisable when writing up records to avoid general terms such as 'the house was dirty' or 'her clothing was inadequate'. First, these convey very little meaning to others because one person's 'dirty' house is another person's 'lived in' one. Second, when parents and children have access to their records, terms like these can be emotive. Far better is to use an accurate description or if a judgement has to be used then concrete examples given. An example is the Malcolm Page case (Page, 1981 in Appendix), where for months the social worker and health visitor had been recording general comments such as 'some improvement', which proved meaningless. The police officer investigating Malcolm's death gave a purely factual, if stomach-turning, description of the state of the house, leaving the reader in no doubt that it was unfit for any child to live in.

Writing records is time-consuming and there are a number of illustrative methods that can prove to be more effective than wordy statements. Methods include:

● *Flow charts*:   these are lists and dates of all the injuries or abusive incidents to a child. In a separate column other important events are recorded in a way that matches dates, incidents and events. It is a simple exercise but can be remarkably effective in demonstrating patterns of abuse. Practitioners, on seeing these charts, have made comments such as: 'The incidents seem to occur at regular intervals' or 'I didn't realise she had had so many hospital admissions in only sixteen weeks'.

● *Ecomaps*:   circles are drawn, one each for the child and the main relationships and influences in the child's environment such as parents, siblings, relatives, school, other helping professionals, friends and even pets. The nature and importance of the relationships can be indicated by differences in the lines attaching the circles – for example a bold line for a strong positive relationship, a wavy line for an ambiguous one, a dotted line for a weak one.

● *Geneograms or family trees*:   rather than attempt to describe in words all members of the family, it is useful to draw up a family tree. This does not need to be the detailed, formal creation of the genealogist. However, it is advisable to use symbols others can recognise. As with the ecomap, it is also helpful to indicate, through the connecting lines, the nature of the relationship between the child and members of the family.

● *Growth charts*:   children who have been abused sometimes fail to put on sufficient weight and height, despite the fact that their families are of average build and there is no growth-impairing disease or explanatory physical condition present. A child's physical progress can be monitored through the use of growth charts. Medical staff, who can interpret them correctly, and who have access to the same scales and measuring devices every time, are best placed to maintain them but a copy could usefully be kept on the key worker's file. Jasmine Beckford (Beckford, 1985, in Appendix), aged 4, was returned from care only to be killed by her stepfather. Her weight rose in care and fell on returning home. The inquiry report states: 'The failure of Area 6 to take particular note of Jasmine's weight over the three years of a Care Order is perhaps the most striking single aspect of child abuse that was fatally neglected' (p. 114).

Values

All helping professionals are required to maintain the values and ethics of their profession. These values are often made explicit by their regulatory bodies and usually embrace areas such as confidentiality, avoiding discrimination, respecting difference and not abusing any power, privilege and authority the professional may possess.

However, maintaining professional values may not be conflict-free. When there is a particular 'moral panic' against societal 'folk devils', then legislation against a particular disadvantaged group may become very restrictive and punitive. Professionals may find that their values of respecting people's right to self-determination are undermined by the restrictive legal framework in which they have to work.

Professionals can also find that there are conflicts between one value and another. So there is often a clash between the individual's right to self-determination and the professional's 'duty of care' to both the individual and to other vulnerable people. When clinging to one value it is important to ensure that it is not undermining another. So when refusing to share information on the grounds of maintaining confidentiality of one person, it is important to reflect on whether or not this is failing in one's duty of care to another.

Finally, there may be a conflict between a professional's personal values and his or her professional ones. Here, reflection and the use of supervision, consultation and counselling are important.

Anti-discriminatory practice

This is an essential value that should be at the heart of the practice of all professionals. Not only do they have to exercise their own power in a way that does not discriminate or oppress, but they also have to be aware of other means through which people are being oppressed and disadvantaged.

Anti-racist practice and the challenging of policies and practices that disadvantage black, Asian, dual-heritage and other minority ethnic groups is at the forefront of anti-discriminatory practice. However, professionals are aware that there are other discriminations, including ageism, disablism and homophobia. Women in particular are oppressed in relation to child protection policies. Milner (1993) writes about the way that fathers have in effect been allowed to evade responsibility for the protection of their children. Similarly, Doyle (1998) found that in instances of emotional abuse in registered cases the mother was held accountable most frequently for the abuse, but when survivors of emotional abuse were questioned the majority (whether sons or daughters) felt that their fathers were the more blameworthy parent. This imbalance could support the view that society is more likely to hold women accountable for child abuse, when in reality women are probably no more culpable than men.

Power in practice

Power can be a positive force, as Foucault (1980) explains: 'it transverses and produces things, it induces pleasure, forms knowledge, produces discourse' (p. 119). But power can be corrupted, and maltreatment and oppression occur if people with power abuse or misuse it. In the macro environment – that is, society or the nation – oppressions (for example, the former South African apartheid) are officially sanctioned by those 'in power', even if they are the minority. Conversely, 'force' of numbers can mean that the majority often oppresses minority groups in society. In the micro environment (for example, small institutions, family homes) abuse occurs when there is a power imbalance and those with the greater power misuse it. In order to practice in a truly anti-discriminatory way, and to help those who are abused, social workers and other helping professionals need to understand and be able to analyse the power dynamics.

A number of commentators have recognised that 'power' is not a single entity but rather that there are different forms of power. Handy's (1985) analysis is perhaps one of the most useful because it is very comprehensible and transfers readily from the world of business and organizations, for which it was originally devised by Handy, into the social and welfare environment. Handy identified six forms of power and here they are applied to child abuse:

Physical power   This is clearly apparent in the domestic setting and relating to physical abuse, with the larger physique of adults compared to children, and of many men in comparison to women.
Position power   This again is seen most clearly in physical abuse. In some countries, simply by virtue of their position as parents,

adults are allowed to assault child in way that would be illegal if inflicted on another adult.

Resource power   The failure of parents to use this power in terms of material resources is clearest in cases of physical neglect. But resource power can also be love, praise and encouragement, all of which are often denied in cases of emotional abuse.

Expert power   Sex offenders often use their knowledge of what attracts children in order to seduce them into sexual activities.

Personal power   This is personal magnetism, charisma and charm. Again, this is often used by sex offenders to beguile both children and potentially protective adults.

Negative power   This is the ability to be subversive and to stop things happening. Often abusers use this power in order to impede an investigation. They may, for example, repeatedly use the complaints procedure to block progress and ensure that the investigators have to focus on defending their actions rather than concentrate on the investigation.

When working with abused children, helping professionals need to be aware of the power dynamics in the situation. This includes awareness of their own power, which is often considerably less than the literature would suggest, especially in the case of social workers. Having only a degree of position and resource power, social workers often have to rely substantially on their expert power. But often this is not recognised and they find themselves overruled by other professionals who are seen to be more expert. Some people with whom they work will have very little power indeed, hence the requirement to empower vulnerable 'clients'. However, many abusers do not require empowerment; instead, some need to be disempowered while others could usefully be shown how to use their power differently.

Empowering children

Coulshed and Orme (1998) identify components of empowerment as the giving of a 'voice' and conferring rights. Children can be given a voice by having adults act as advocates for them. In child protection case conferences, while the parents have a right to be present, the children are usually absent, yet they should have an inalienable right to be present or to choose a person to speak for them. Children can be given a voice by being actively involved in research (Iwaniec and Pinkerton, 1998; Greig and Taylor, 1999). Parental consent requirements should not be used as an excuse to 'gag' children, who have a right to express their opinions. Similarly, there is now an emphasis on service users being involved in social work training. This must include the most vulnerable of service users, particularly maltreated children, as not to do so will further disempower them. Universities and placement providers need to devise imaginative ways of embracing the views of these children, such as by the use of videos or young people preparing their own training materials and Powerpoint presentations.

Definitions

This book is influenced by the view that truth is relative, and many, if not all, concepts are socially constructed. There is therefore a need to explain the way that various key terms are defined.

Child abuse

The term 'child abuse' refers in this book to the physical or emotional mistreatment and neglect of children or their sexual exploitation, in circumstances for which the parents can be held responsible through acts of commission or omission.

This emphasis on parental maltreatment does not mean that abuse outside the family is not important. However, for most children during their dependent years society has identified their parents and immediate family as their primary protectors. Children who are abused within their family are therefore especially vulnerable. In societies willing and able to afford a welfare system, it is professionals working for the system that are charged with the protection of these particularly vulnerable children. It is to those professionals that this book is addressed, hence the appropriateness of the definition.

Maslow's (1970) 'hierarchy of needs' is a theoretical framework providing a means by which 'child abuse' can be conceptualised. Abuse constitutes a failure by a parent to meet the children's needs. Therefore, unmet physiological and safety needs constitute physical neglect. Physical, sexual and emotional abuse is a failure to meet safety/security, esteem, belonging and love needs. All abuse conspires to thwart any sense of self-actualisation or self-fulfilment.

Other key terms

'Parent': includes birth, adoptive, step and foster parents. 'Child' refers to people from birth to seventeen years. The term 'abused child' will often be used not only to mean the primary victim; children who are often called 'non-abused' siblings are here considered to be secondary victims if they have witnessed the mistreatment of their brothers or sisters.

Finally

All family members are important, and all can suffer in cases of child abuse. Parents in particular always warrant respect and consideration. However, the child victims of abuse need understanding and appropriate assistance. A significant proportion of the public inquiries (see Appendix) that have followed the deaths of children, have highlighted the fact that some social workers and other professionals have become so preoccupied with the needs of the parents that they have overlooked those of the children, to the detriment of everyone involved.

The remainder of the book focuses on understanding abused children, and appreciating their perspectives, and on intervening in ways that will help them in both the short and the longer term.

putting it into practice

Activity 1

Choose any theory with which you are familiar. This can be a social science or social work theory if you are already working in a caring profession, or it can be a theory from your other studies if you are new to the caring professions or child protection work. Having chosen a theory, try to list all the positive, helpful features of the theory. Then list all the limitations of the theory that you can identify. Draw a conclusion about whether, on balance, the positive features outweigh the limitations.

This activity is designed to help you evaluate the theories that you are likely to use in practice rather than applying a theory in an unquestioning way.

→

Activity 2

Reflect on any case of child protection with which you are familiar. Draw a circle to represent the maltreated child. Around this, draw additional circles to represent the key people or agencies involved with the child. In each circle identify the types of power held by each person, including the child. For example, the parents or main carers may well have all six forms of power in relation to the child, including substantial physical and personal power. Social workers may have resource, position and expert power, but no (or very limited) physical and personal power. How have the various players been using, failing to use or misusing power?

The purpose of this exercise is to show how important power is to an understanding of child protection issues. Children are protected if parents, family, friends and agencies use power benignly and effectively. Children will be abused if they lack effective power and that held by significant others is misused or not used effectively. Altering the power dynamics can prevent further abuse.

Further reading

There are several important works which provide a broad overview and useful introduction to the key issues for researchers and practitioners in children protection. These works include Jones *et al.* (1987), Corby, (2000), Winton and Mara (2001), Wilson and James (2002), and Beckett (2003). Payne (1997) and Coulshed and Orme (1998) remain the core texts about social work theory and practice. Watson *et al.* (2002) provide guidance about integrating theory and practice in placements and in assignments. Thompson's (2003) guide to challenging discrimination and oppression is helpful and thought-provoking. Theories relating to social psychology are made accessible by Stainton Rogers (2003), while readers seeking summaries of theories on child development will find Papalia *et al.* (2003) particularly helpful.

2 | Voices of the children

A number of abused children can ask for help in a firm, direct manner and are able to describe their experiences clearly and coherently. But these are probably in the minority. Most are inhibited by fear, shame, mistrust or attachment to their abusers. Furthermore, younger children do not have the command of language needed to communicate their distress in a straightforward manner. For these reasons, the perspectives of maltreated children all too often are ignored or misunderstood. Yet child-care workers will fail to give effective help to children unless they can appreciate what the experience of abuse means for the victims. They also need to recognise how a child may attempt to communicate that experience.

Insight into the world of the abused child can be provided by adults who have suffered childhood mistreatment and are willing to describe their experiences. This chapter contains five such accounts, which serve as case examples to increase understanding of an abused child's predicament. For reasons of confidentiality, names and identifying details have been changed.

Marie's account

I lived with my mother, father, brother and sisters. Pauline was the eldest. Barry, my brother, was two years younger than me, and Linda was the youngest. My father was violent to my mother and all of his children.

Until I was eight years old, our family seemed fairly 'normal'. There were rows but I was not aware of any extreme violence. My father was in the navy and away from home for quite long periods until I was aged about five. Despite the apparent normality of the situation there was already an atmosphere of fear in the house because my father was very strict. At bedtime he would look at the clock and whoever's turn it was to go to bed would scurry away.

After my eighth birthday came a dramatic change. My father had played with us – giving us 'twizzles', swinging us around. My eldest sister then went to live with grandma. Us other children were asked a lot of questions by our mother. Father was also away at this time. When he came back there were lots of rows and we were not allowed to play the games with him any longer. One thing that puzzled me was that my mother gave us a strip wash in front of my father. I didn't know why, but I found it very embarrassing; we had been taught to keep covered up in front of my father.

The situation went from bad to worse. I had the impression that something bad had happened. I heard sexual words like 'climax' for the first time but I didn't really understand what they meant. I remember Pauline being withdrawn and unhappy. A cloud descended over our house. We were not encouraged to have any friends. My father always found something wrong with them. Everything became very secretive. When my father went away to sea we became happy as a big weight was lifted, but we all knew he would be coming back and the void would return.

Our mother used to work hard. She would often cry. At nights I would go to bed then get up later, creep down, make her a cup of tea and stay up with her until three or four in the morning when my father was away. I was very close to her and I knew this was a comfort to her. I was an eight-year-old comforting my mother.

This pattern continued until I was about eleven. Then we moved house. We hoped this would be a new beginning; things were going to be different and get better. But they weren't, and from then on the situation was horrific. At around this time Pauline told me that our father had sexually abused her. He had done nearly everything except penetrate her. She wanted it to stop. He kept saying 'Have you come yet?' to her but she didn't know what he meant. Not long after this conversation Pauline ate a hundred aspirins in front of me. I didn't realise what was happening, I thought she was eating crumbly white cheese. She tried to commit suicide six times after this. I just didn't understand what she was going through. I was totally confused and afraid. When I did realise, I felt it was my fault. I should have stopped her. My mother accompanied Pauline in the ambulance and she kept saying, 'Don't tell anyone why you did it. They will ask you but don't tell them.' These incidents seemed to have no effect on my father; he denied abusing Pauline, apart from the one earlier incident when I was eight.

Our father was often very violent. Frequently, he had been drinking. On one occasion when I was outside the house and everyone else was inside, my father was on the rampage and had his hands round my mother's throat. A next-door neighbour called me over to her house and told me to listen. Through the walls I could hear someone shouting to get the police. The neighbour gave me a lift to the police station. I felt this was all I could do, but I knew how violent my father could be. When the police arrived he tried to pretend it was just a domestic dispute. Us children ran out of the house and hid. The younger two kept singing 'They've come to take him away ha ha, he he!' Although the police arrested him he did not stay away for long.

On another occasion my father wanted money. He started throwing my mother's perfume and all her possessions about the house in a temper because she would not give him any. At the time I had a paper round; my mother told me to hide my money. My father asked me where it was. When I said that I had lost it he started hitting me. He also hit my mother and wrecked her bedroom, breaking up everything as he looked for money.

One Christmas a row started over something trivial. My father smashed a plant, a present for my mother, on to the kitchen floor. It made a mess with the soil and broken pot. He threw a large box of chocolates on top. He then made the younger children take the baubles off the tree and threw them into the kitchen too. My mother aimed an ashtray at my father. It missed but caused a hole in the wall. He, in retaliation, cut her leg with a broken dinner plate. The other children were crying and he slammed out. I was left picking up the pieces and I helped to bathe my mother's leg.

I always used to calm the others and tried to look after them. Pauline would go to her room and became increasingly withdrawn. Linda would switch off and block out what was happening. Barry never seemed to be around; he managed to 'duck out'. I sometimes used to hide with him in the cellar. It was, however, usually my mother, Barry and myself who had the good hidings. Our father used to hit us with anything – his belt, his fist or kick us with his boots. When I was bruised I was kept off school until the bruises faded.

The night times were bad. Us girls shared a room. I used to be awake a lot, particularly because I would try to comfort my mother by going to her to hold her hand. We would hear my father's key, then I would quickly clamber back to bed and pretend I was asleep. My father would creep into our room, ostensibly to tuck us in but he seemed to be trying to see who was in the deepest sleep. Sometimes he would stay by our bedside for two minutes, sometimes for fifteen. At that stage he didn't touch me but there was always the fear, the dread, wondering if it was going to be my turn. If one of the other two woke he would say, 'Shh, you're only dreaming; go back to sleep.' Living in fear was the worst thing. One night he dragged me out of bed at one o'clock because I hadn't cleaned his shoes. He started hitting me and made me clean them in the middle of the night. My mother tried to defend me saying, 'I'll do it, she's got to go to school tomorrow.'

I couldn't mix in school; I used to sit alone. From thirteen years onwards I played truant continually. We were cut off from the other children for fear of letting anything slip. I was dying to tell someone who would take me away, someone kind who would understand. But then I used to think, 'How would my mother and the others cope without me?' I felt it was me who held them together. We always appeared clean and tidy. We were not allowed to wear make-up or be fashionable, and we felt different from everyone else. We knew too much. I felt so very alone, totally alone.

You can't concentrate at school while wondering what will happen when you get home. I was very wary of all the male teachers. I couldn't learn from them because of the need to put up all the defences. I assumed that underneath they were all like my father, and I was hostile to them. I tried to be helpful to the women teachers. I used to sit wondering if they were battered at home too. I also wondered what other children's lives were like at home. I once went to another girl's house and I couldn't believe how nice her mum and dad were, and thought 'why aren't mine like that'?

We would swing from a semi-normal life when my father was away and we could have friends, including boyfriends, to a state of fear when he came back. It was difficult to have friends because they couldn't understand why I was friendly one moment and suddenly distant the next. It was easier not to have friends, so I became isolated. I couldn't tell people what was happening at home; they wouldn't believe me or they would misunderstand what I was saying. I began to try to predict what my father would do, try to get to know the enemy and stay one jump ahead of him.

As we grew older we used to devise signals. For example, if our father was out we would leave the outside light on for our boyfriends. If the light was off then they must come nowhere near the house. We explained to the boys that we just had a rather over-protective father. Our mother knew everything. I could tell her anything. She would be frightened for us. She had a terrible time, stuck in the middle. Mother stayed with our father because she loved him. She did leave him once but not for long. I feel there is nothing lovable about him. In some ways I'm angry with my mother for staying while knowing what he did to us.

Pauline and I often wondered how we did not end up in an asylum, having to live with all that fear and violence and the constant threat of sexual abuse. My main feeling was to try to make it easier for everyone else. I used to clean the house from top to bottom, do all the ironing and get the youngsters out of the house as much as possible to be away from my father. He was really hard on Barry, who could not stand up to him. Barry kept starting fires and stealing. Father used to just give him a good hiding.

I was sexually abused by my father when I was 21 years old. I had married but my husband was violent and sexually abusive so I went back to live with my parents. It was then that my father attempted to have sex with me although he did not manage to penetrate. I could hardly believe what was happening. I had escaped during childhood then all of a sudden my nightmare came true.

Lloyd's account

My father was away a lot and when I was conceived he was else-where, so in fact I was illegitimate and my father was not my biological one. I think I am a constant reminder for both parents of mum's infidelity and I guess this is why I was mistreated. My broth-ers, who were my father's own children, were not ill-treated in the same way.

I was given no love by either parent. I was an outcast. A typical scene when the family was watching TV was for my oldest brother and mother to sit close together and my youngest brother and father to sit together, with me isolated on the floor. When it came to birthdays and Christmas, the other two had presents and parties; I was lucky if I had a card. If I fell over I was hit and told to get up. I was given no sympathy and shown no kindness. My older brother copied my parents and was abusive and bullying towards me. My younger brother would try to be kind, but only in secret.

My mother's cousin died in a house fire so my parents fostered the children. One of them was a boy aged sixteen, and from the age of nine years I was being sexually abused by him. He gave me cigarettes and drink in exchange for sex. My parents knew but did nothing. There were no other family members to help me.

In primary school I settled quite well, especially as one teacher found out I was really good at maths and spent time with me. This made me feel special, so in some ways it made me think that I was treated differently at home because I was special and clever, and not because I was unwanted.

But then we emigrated. In my next school my appearance and accent meant I was immediately subjected to negative stereotypes. I was seen as a 'trouble' and because book learning came so easily I was labelled lazy. At that point I gave up and picked fights with teachers and other pupils – they expected me to be a troublemaker – so I was. The sexual abuse also made me worry about being a boy. I had to prove I was not a girl so became very tough. My brothers fared better because they were good at sports so were more accepted.

In my teens I more or less left home. I was lifted by police when I was eleven for smashing up an American's camper van. I was having to sleep rough and they were staying overnight in a field, my field. I became angry and thrashed out. I felt jealous of all they had.

My misery was so great that when I was about fourteen or fifteen years old I tried to hang myself, but the rope was not long enough and I twisted my ankle. My family never knew. I also tried to overdose a couple of times, but I vomited and slept it off. I was escaping through drink and drugs much of the time.

I did not have many friends, although Bevis, a local yob turned good, taught me martial arts and showed an interest in me. I also had one good friend of my own age, Gilroy. I had a fight with him and because neither of us could win, we decided to be pals. From about the age of twelve we beat up all the other children together. When I was about fifteen I had a row with him on the Friday. I told him to 'Fuck off and die.' I didn't see him again. Gilroy drowned (by accident) on the Sunday. I felt responsible and very guilty, but I could not talk to anyone about this.

Helen's account

I should perhaps have been a happy child – after all, I lived in a big house with plenty of food, toys and pretty clothes. I had a father who enjoyed being with me, a mother whom I loved and a brother whom I thought wonderful.

Frank, my brother, was five years older than me and was a quiet, studious boy. My father was warm-hearted and jovial, but he was not at home very much because he would commute daily to London, spending long hours at his office, or would be abroad on business trips. My mother did not go out to a paid job but she was always very busy. She spent much of her time supporting children's charities.

My mother seemed to be devoted to children. She expended so much energy on fund-raising for deprived and cruelly-treated children. But I knew that she didn't love me. That must have been, I concluded, because I was such a horrible, unlovable child. It never occurred to me that perhaps the problem lay with my mother, who was attracted to the sentimental image of children but could not abide the real thing. It was only gradually that I realised that she did not like Frank very much either.

I used to try so hard to be good so that she would love me. She used to tell me how lucky I was to have a nice house and pretty clothes. I longed to be poor. I thought I might be more lovable if I was destitute. I used to wear only my oldest clothes. My mother had a struggle to make me wear any of my newer, more attractive dresses. I used to deny myself sweets and would not spend my pocket money on myself. I used to pretend whenever possible that I was poor. I would hide from school friends that fact that we had a car, holidays abroad and other trappings of affluence. I was ashamed of our big house and would not invite friends home in case they saw that I was not poor.

Wearing shabby clothes in fact irritated my mother because she was a smart woman obsessed with neatness, order and cleanliness. I could not really play freely in the house or garden because everything had to remain tidy and spotless. Even my dolls had to be arranged in serried ranks. If my mother found a toy out of place she would confiscate it. The only doll she never bothered with was Penny, my scruffy rag doll with only one arm and a bald head. I loved Penny dearly because she was really mine. All the others I regarded as my mother's to take and give back as she chose.

If, when I was young, I was so ill that I had to stay off school my mother was very angry with me. It meant that she either had to cancel a meeting to stay with me, or pay for a baby-sitter. I tried very hard not to have days off school so that when I had flu I would sit sweating and nearly fainting in the classroom, and shivering uncontrollably in the playground at break-time. When I did have to have days away from school I had to stay in bed and sleep or read all day. When the baby-sitter was used I would hear my mother come back home after a meeting. I would cry out to her. I just wanted to see her yet she would not come upstairs. I eventually stopped calling for her and just sobbed quietly. My brother would often bring me my tea. Eventually, sometime during the evening, my mother would come in and ask me angrily what I had been making a fuss about.

At night I had to go to bed, switch off the light and go straight to sleep. Often I could not go to sleep immediately, but I would not dare to get out of bed and switch the light on. I would lie there terrified because I could hear the floorboards creak outside my door and I was sure that a man with a gun was coming in to shoot me. I sat staring at the door for ages waiting in fear for the man to come.

My fears were relieved a little when I was about six because Frank started to come to my room in the evening to cuddle me. We did not switch on my light but could see dimly by the glow of a lamp shining through my window. I loved Frank's reassuring embraces and felt so grateful to him. I thought that the man with the gun would not come in with Frank there. I looked forward to his visits. I knew that I was being naughty because I should have been asleep. I also sensed that Frank thought he was doing some-thing wrong because when he heard our parents come upstairs he would dash out. The toilet was next to my bedroom so that if they saw him coming from the direction of my room they would assume he had been to the toilet. Often he would have time to flush it.

As time passed, the cuddles became closer. Frank would take off my nightie and come in wearing just his dressing-gown, which he would also take off. He would rub me between the legs. I liked this and he made me feel special. Then he started to practise different ways of kissing me, which I didn't like so much. He also simulated intercourse rubbing his penis between my legs. He told me it was alright because it was what 'Mummies and daddies do to get babies'. I still didn't like it. I felt the weight of his body squashing mine and I could smell his excited sweat as I struggled to find a breathing space in the gap under his armpit between his arm and his chest.

One problem that emerged at this time was that Frank seemed to get excited and wet my bed a little. I used to cover the patch with a towel so that I did not have to go to sleep lying in the damp part but I was always apprehensive in case in the mornings my mother or father pulled back the sheets too far and saw the towel or the patch. I realised that the sheets were messy so I began to volunteer to help make the beds including my own and would change my own sheets at the weekends.

As we grew older, Frank's demands increased. He started to attempt full intercourse. It hurt me so much but I could not scream out loud in case my parents heard. I just had to scream inside my head. I had a recurring nightmare of screaming and screaming but knowing no one could hear me or help me. Frank also wanted to experiment in other ways, anally and orally. I hated this but he threatened to spank me if I refused. I didn't realise that this would probably not have been possible in the circumstances, all I knew from the occasional spankings my father had given me that they were noisy, painful, humiliating affairs that I wanted to avoid at all costs. I also wanted Frank to love me, which could be best achieved by pleasing him.

I began to realize that what we were doing might result in pregnancy. Frank explained that that would not happen until I started having monthly periods. These started when I was thirteen. Frank then stopped coming to my room, partly because it coincided with his leaving home to start at college and partly because he now had a girlfriend, something he had not had in his earlier teens because he had been so painfully shy, uncertain of himself and isolated. He had been unloved by our mother and put under pressure by our father, who had high hopes for his only son. In some ways I felt sad and rejected when Frank stopped coming to my room. I had wanted some of the sexual activities to stop but he had made me feel special and important to him; now he took little notice of me.

I was terrified for both myself and for Frank in case our secret was discovered. I would not let anyone get close to me in case they 'saw through me' and found out what I was really like – a dirty, rude little girl. My father still wanted to cuddle me when he was at home but I held him at arm's length, in case he came so close that he saw how dirty I was. Once, as I backed off from him, I caught the hurt look in his eyes. I felt unworthy of his affection.

At school I appeared to be reasonably popular. I was naturally very good at most sports, therefore my class mates always wanted me in their team. I learnt to strum a guitar, which also helped in my teens. But inside I felt so isolated, I was different from the others. I had done something so wicked that I deserved a dreadful punishment. I tried to be good and work hard in order to avoid any punishment. I could not bear being given a bad conduct mark at school as it only served to confirm how dreadful I was.

I also tried to work hard because I thought that by getting high marks my mother would love me, because she was always delighted when Frank did well academically. As a teenager my isolation increased. My fellow pupils used to jeer at me because I was regarded as so naïve about sexual matters. The others would gather in little groups to read the juicy bits of various salacious novels, I did not join in because I was frightened that I might let something slip and show that I knew too much. I also didn't have boyfriends because I could not abide the feeling of being experimented upon by an inexperienced youth.

Even after the sexual abuse stopped I still carried a weighty secret and felt unclean and guilty. I wore clean clothes every day. I tried to eat very little. The reasons for this were various. I needed to be in control of my own body and forbidding myself food was a form of punishment. Moreover, I feared being sexually attractive and being molested again. Finally, I suppose I was still trying to make myself into one of those emaciated children for whom my mother seemed to feel such affection.

Sarah's account

I actually decided fairly early on that I didn't like my father, which is a big decision for a child. It was because I was frightened of his strict discipline and use of corporal punishment, but I also hated the way he treated my mother. My younger sister, Barbara, and I used to compete not to sit behind him in the car because we could not bear to be that close to him.

I used to get spanked a lot. He was a headmaster and I went to his school. The role of father and headmaster became muddled, but

I didn't realise anything was wrong; I just thought that what he did was what all teachers did. I was isolated and had no comparison of my family life with any other.

My father used to tell me not to put my hands in my pockets because it was, in his opinion, slovenly. Once I was at my grandparents' when my father arrived. He caught me with my hands in my pockets. He saw this as an act of defiance, although in fact I had been playing happily and hadn't realised what I was doing. He grabbed me, bundled me into the car, took me home and beat me. My grandmother had cried and pleaded with him not to hurt me, but he brushed her out of the way. After he had beaten me, I was heart-warmed to find my other grandmother sitting on the stairs weeping because of the way I had been treated.

He bullied everyone, either in a straightforward way or by using a judicious combination of good looks, charm and manipulation. He was used to having his own way. I accepted the fact he had a right to hit me. The beatings hurt and I wanted them to stop. The pain didn't leave a lot of space in my mind for any other thoughts. I was very miserable afterwards, feeling rejected, cast out, punished, not worthy. The effect of this situation was to make life such that, because punishment might happen at any time, no day was a safe day, a good day, until it was over. I resented not owning my life.

Besides the beatings my father used other strange ways of punishing us – for example, he would put us in the car then drive very fast to teach us a lesson. I can remember the liberation that came when I was eighteen and was so unhappy that I didn't care whether I lived or died. This meant that when he drove fast he could no longer frighten me. I found that experience almost exhilarating.

One New Year there was a party next door. Both my parents drank heavily. I came back with my father and sister but the following morning my mother still hadn't returned. There was thick snow on the ground. My father told me that my mother was probably dead and sent me out to look everywhere, under all the hedges, for her body. I still carry the horror of that episode. She had in fact stayed overnight with the people next door, but I didn't realise that, and believed my father.

I always felt that if anything happened to my mother I wouldn't know what to do. Whatever kindness came from our home was from her. I always thought of her as my father's first victim and myself as his second. I was distressed by the way I had to witness his treatment of my mother. He would constantly undermine her – for example, she was once enjoying music on the car radio when my father decided to stop the car and get out. He switched off the radio, saying that he had to save the batteries. Even as a young child I realised it had nothing to do with batteries. Another time, on holiday, my mother sat on a wall and standing up had some tar on her skirt. My father shouted 'God, woman, you've sh . . . . d yourself as usual'. Yet he constantly told us how beautiful she was and how lucky we were to have her as a mother. This, however, struck me as false.

I felt protective towards my mother. She was fascinated by my father and even when they finally separated she never became a whole person again. She needed to be fighting disasters and crises. She couldn't accept herself and turned more and more to drink. She was so unhappy that a lot of me parented her; I tried to cheer her up. It was only as a parent myself that I became angry that she never protected us. I have never told her how angry I felt.

I remember truly hating my sister. My father used to say to me, 'Why can't you be like your sister, she's gregarious, has lots of friends and is cheerful? You are just a sour puss.' I was jealous of her. I did not realise he said the same to her about me, making her jealous as well. I could not afford to protect her. When I eventually decided to leave home, my father threatened me with the fact that Barbara would be made to suffer because I was not there. But I had to close my mind to that. I used, however, to draw his fire because, when I dared, I stood up to him. I now only have a superficial relationship with my sister. He made me have my hair cut very short like a boy, so I wore headscarves. He said by doing this I was trying to look like 'a duchess', trying to show that I was better than the rest of the family. Once, when we were having a picnic, he made me sit some distance from the family in a field by myself to eat. I cringed up inside. He always made us feel he was in the right. In order to escape I used to daydream. One place that could be mine was inside my head, but he even resented this. We were in the car when I was imagining the dog I would give my grandmother for a present. I was hauled out of my reverie by father shouting, 'Look at that bloody, snotty cow in the back, too hoity-toity to talk to the rest of us.' His verbal attack was vitriolic. Another time when I wore a new bathing costume and felt quite proud of it he shouted across a quiet beach, 'Hold your belly in, woman, you look like a pregnant cow.'

I was eleven years old and the only girl in my father's school. As the headmaster's daughter I was not popular. I felt very isolated but in a desperate attempt to gain popularity I became involved in some sex play with the boys. When I heard that my father had found out I fainted with fear. I was also frightened of one of the boys and so I withheld his name from my father who, when he discovered this, made me change into some of his thin rugby shorts. Then he caned me really hard. Half way through he showed my mother my bottom and she was sick, then he carried on caning me. A fortnight later when my mother jokingly patted my bottom I cried out because the pain was still so intense.

I asked my mother if I would have to go away after this incident. She said, 'Yes, perhaps.' I thought I would just be thrown out of the house into the proverbial darkness. I wondered if I could live in a cave that I knew about in the mountain and hoped someone would put out food for me. In fact, I was sent to boarding school although it was the summer term. I was very unhappy. I cried so much at bedtime that the staff had to intervene. They thought I was home-sick, missing a loving family, but I was crying because I felt rejected and did not seem to belong to anyone. Because I started in the summer term friendships were already made in that year and yet by the next term I did not belong in the new intake. I made no real friends. My father kept telling me that if I didn't achieve high academic results I would be sent to a state school, implying that I would be virtually 'chucked in the bin'. I spent my time on the fringes, wishing I had the confidence and the time to socialise. My father kept me short of money so I could not join in any school activities that cost money. I tried to tell some of my schoolmates about my home life, but generally they did not believe me. My father was handsome and charming and when he came to school the pupils would all try to catch a glimpse of him and say how lucky I was. I was so grateful to one friend who stayed with us for a while and, realising what I had been saying was true, told me she believed me. I used to look forward to going home for the holidays because I always hoped that this time the nightmare would end and we would be an ordinary family.

As a teenager I was subjected to sexual bullying. He used to take me out, making comments such as, 'People will think you are my girlfriend.' He would have a lot to drink. On the way back he would stop the car and fondle me. I could smell the drink on his breath. I did not believe I could say 'No' to him, so I just used to freeze. When I tried to refuse to masturbate him he said that I shouldn't get married because I was frigid and any man who took me on would be getting a poor deal. I wished he wouldn't do it and I felt guilty because I thought that I was letting my mother down and committing an infidelity. He would describe to me the merits of various women with whom he had affairs.

When I was seventeen I met a man many years older than myself and fell deeply in love with him. Perhaps in an attempt to escape from home I became engaged to him. He was a man very like my father. He found another girlfriend. The engagement was broken. I was devastated. But other people didn't let me down. Aged eighteen, I decided to leave home for good. My father threatened me in order to keep me from leaving. My mother rang my uncle and aunt. I took a bus to their home and my uncle met me at the bus stop. They took me into their home and made me feel valued and cared for. When I was ready to move on they let me go.

Roy's account

I did not have any brothers or sisters. Mum was pregnant with another baby after me but she carried cement around the garden and lost the baby. My father constantly told me I was useless and worthless. I would not make anything of my life. I was a waste of space, a 'fat slob'. He would stand over me forcing me to eat food I did not like. I would have to sit in front of it for ages until I managed to eat it. It used to make me sick. But I began to overeat things I did like for comfort, and I became very fat. Dad would also make me sit and write until I managed it perfectly. He kept screwing up the paper and put it in the bin. This could go on for two or three hours. If I wanted to watch television I was only allowed to do so if I could name the programme correctly. Mum was too frightened to stop Dad treating me in this way.

I witnessed a lot of marital violence. Dad used to beat mum up although he did not hit me. But I used to feel very angry. I desperately wanted to hit out at Dad but knew I did not stand a chance. Once he put a stiletto heel through my mother's skull. Another time

I was upstairs, mum was downstairs and Dad was carving the chicken. Suddenly he started, and she went at him with a fork. She stormed out, taking me too, and went to the police. But she had him back on a six-month trial, which made me feel very bad. Both Mum and I were nervous wrecks. On one occasion, Dad told Mum to 'write your will out' just as she was going into hospital for an operation. This made me see red and I threw a hot cup of tea at Dad, who looked completely stunned. After this my father stopped hitting Mum for a while.

Dad also had an interest in very young girls; he was into gymslips. When Mum went in hospital for a hysterectomy he was in bed with a girl. At first he had an affair with her mother, who had an abortion because he made her pregnant. Then he started knocking off her daughter; she was about twelve years old at the time.

After years of abuse, Mum left home for good, taking me with her. I had to grow up so quickly when my mother left Dad that I pushed things to the back of my mind.

I tried to understand my father. His mother, my grandmother, walked out when his father had an affair. My grandfather remarried and Dad's stepmother was really cruel. She would beat Dad until her hands were blue and my grandfather did nothing protect him. My mother was born illegitimately and brought up in a children's home. Neither parent had many relatives but those that there were supported Dad. They felt it was normal for a man to beat his wife and children. My mother had a best friend I called 'Aunty', and she would always say nice things about me and was always ready to listen. I also had a pet cat, Tallulah, who was always a good companion.

In school I was quiet and very withdrawn. I did not have many friends. In fact, I was so fat that I was bullied a lot. I was off sick much of the time, but this was a problem when Dad was at home. There was one teacher who encouraged me and I was able to talk to him a bit about things at home. But at the next school I started to play up and was threatened with expulsion. I never told the teachers there about home.

I left school when I was sixteen and started an apprenticeship. I was still fat, over 19 stone. Then one day I was really upset by a cutting remark and I stopped eating. I lost weight, went down to 6 stone and was told I had less than a year to live. Hospital did not

help much, but then I went to a day centre where there was counselling and other people with problems. It was really the other
patients who gave me support. I was nearly twenty, however,
before I managed to gain a reasonable weight and eat normally.
Mum was not able to help much as she had so many problems of
her own.

Comment on the accounts

One of the key features of the five accounts is that although the
children were all clearly suffering at the hands of family members,
on the whole they were 'suffering in silence'. The accounts show
how assiduously children will hide the abusive situation at home
and how difficult it is for them to disclose any maltreatment.
Helen went to great lengths to conceal both the emotional and
sexual abuse she experienced. Sarah, on the other hand, tried to
tell her school mates what was happening but was not believed.
Even when there was overwhelming evidence of something amiss,
the extent of the family problems was not recognised, as shown by
the cases of Roy and Marie whose family members were hospitalised, and the cases of Marie's sister and Lloyd who both made
suicide attempts.

The accounts also show how very damaging is the experience of
abuse. The depth of the children's suffering is clear. As well as the
suicide attempts, there was evidence of eating disorders, behavioural problems, drug-taking, criminal offending on the part of
Lloyd and Marie's brother, educational underachievement, and
massive damage to children's sense of self-esteem and self-worth. It
is, however, important to note that, despite the harm, maltreatment
does not always lead to permanent damage. The five survivors will
be revisited in the final chapter, where it will be shown that, with
help, abused children can achieve fulfilled adult lives.

Cries for help

The five accounts in this chapter were all given by adults. It is
generally harder for children to talk so directly and clearly about
their experiences. The reasons why this should be so will be examined in the next chapter. However, children indicate their distress
in a variety of ways and many of these are outlined below.

Verbal communication

Small children who have learned to talk but who cannot fully appreciate the consequences of what they say may describe their abuse spontaneously. This can, however, go unrecognised. 'Daddy tickles me with his hammer' may be dismissed as childish nonsense. Sometimes children do not have the words to describe their experiences so they make words up. One little boy kept saying that 'Uncle Harry gooed on me.' It was only with careful questioning that he was able to indicate that he had been sexually abused and had been trying to describe the way the perpetrator ejaculated on him. A small child often has difficulty indicating the degree of the abuse, so a child may say, 'Mummy smacked me and made me sad' which could equally mean that the mother administered a mild slap or that she lashed out harshly and recklessly for no good reason. Small children may also lack clarity in their enunciation, leaving adults unsure whether the child is saying something like 'Daddy showed me his willie' or 'Danny showed me his wellie'.

Older children may be able to articulate what has happened to them, but are more aware of possible consequences. They sometimes start to tell somebody in a manner that gives them a way out if they change their mind and also tests the reactions of the person in whom they confide. They may therefore start with a question such as, 'What is meant by intercourse?' or by a statement such as, 'I don't really want to go home this afternoon.'

Certain disabilities may make verbal communication, or its signing equivalent, particularly difficult. Speech may be impaired so that what the child is saying is indistinct and misinterpreted. Complex concepts, embarrassing incidents, confusing experiences are difficult for enough for children well able to manipulate the language of the majority. Seeking help becomes all the more difficult for those with a restricted or minority language. Furthermore, as Kennedy (2002) explains, children who use alternative communication such as word boards may only be understood by a couple of key people, who may in fact be their abusers.

Children, with or without disabilities, may find that they are not believed, as happened in the case of Sarah, who had a superficially charming father. They rarely totally lie about abusive experiences within the family. However, like adults in emotionally difficult situations, they may not be absolutely truthful either. For example, one girl accused her stepfather of sexually abusing her. Investigations eventually revealed that the abuser was not her stepfather but her grandfather. She had been desperate for help but had wanted to protect her much-loved grandparent. Children may make up stories about their home background, as exemplified by Helen, who pretended that she was poor. However, if these stories are negative ones they may well indicate some form of abuse, albeit not the mistreatment described.

It is not unusual for children to retract their allegations. This does not necessarily mean that they were originally lying. A common reason is that they cannot cope with the consequences of disclosure, especially if the family is disrupted and its members reject the child. He or she may feel that a retraction will result in the family being reunited and everything 'being all right'.

Non-verbal communication

Not all communication is verbal. Most practitioners will be familiar with theories of non-verbal communication (for example Argyle, 1988). When children's gestures, facial expression, demeanour or other movements are incongruent with their words there is cause for concern, especially if, for example, they say are fine but look nervous or despondent. None the less, some children are very good at compartmentalising their emotions, so that they may say they are fine and look perfectly happy when in reality they are facing distress and abuse.

An important factor to bear in mind is that there are social and cultural conventions about some types of non-verbal communication. For example, in Western cultures eye contact tends to convey interest and sincerity. But in other cultures it may signal status, and subordinates, including children, are expected to lower their eyes, so those who maintain eye contact are seen as rude and insufficiently deferential.

Physical appearance

There are non-verbal, physical indicators of abuse. Sometimes, abused children will draw attention to a physical injury in a straightforward way. They may have had enough and want the abuse to stop, whatever the consequences. Sometimes they may indicate an injury indirectly in the hope that someone will notice their discomfort – for example, refusing to do PE because their leg hurts. More usually, children will try to cover up bruising or weals and, if they are asked about them, will give an explanation, but one inconsistent with the injuries.

Although the cause of many injuries can only be identified by skilled paediatricians, there are some patterns of injury that should alert an observant lay person. Bruises and lesions on different parts of the body, especially of different ages, will not have occurred during one incident, such as falling off a bike. Generally, when common-sense suggests that the injury does not fit the explanation, there is cause for concern. Finally, patterns of absence from nursery or school should be noted if there is any suspicion of abuse because, as happened in the case of Marie, children may be kept at home until injuries heal.

Neglected children may have evident physical signs. A poorly clad, dirty, emaciated child will be readily identified, although neglect may have to be distinguished from the effects of severe poverty. Clothing can often mask an underweight child. Maria Colwell (1974, in Appendix) always wore long, loose dresses and thick cardigans. It was only when the teacher picked Maria up to sit her on her knee that she felt how very much lighter she was than all the other pupils. Babies often have naturally chubby faces, which can belie an emaciated body.

The child's facial expression and body movements can be indicators of abuse. Distressed babies will usually cry; however, some infants who have been persistently attacked will show 'frozen watchfulness'. The baby will have a fixed smile and her eyes will follow adults around in a wary manner. She will not laugh, cry and gurgle in a spontaneous way. Older children may look apprehensive, and again lack spontaneity in the presence of adults.

Behavioural signs

The reactions of children to abuse can vary to a considerable extent. It is therefore difficult to list the full range of behavioural symptoms of abuse. For disabled children, behavioural difficulties may be attributed to their impairment rather than the emotional impact of abuse (Kennedy, 2002). However, a sudden change of behaviour can be significant; for example, the normally outgoing child who becomes withdrawn. Extremes of good or bad behaviour may also be an indication of mistreatment at home. Helen was so concerned not to be thought of as bad that her behaviour in school was exemplary, whereas Lloyd felt he had nothing to lose by behaving badly. Many abused children, like Marie, truant from school because they feel so different from other children. They are ashamed of what is happening and want to hide away from the world. Sometimes they are forced to stay away to look after younger siblings.

Small children who have been sexually abused may act out their experiences with other children or toys. Nursery staff often recognise when children are going beyond the normal games of 'mummies and daddies'. Older children may become promiscuous or, as in Helen's case, show extreme naïvety and lack of interest in sexual matters. Children who are subjected to physical or verbal violence in the home may well show aggressive behaviour and bully other children. Conversely, they may be very passive and seem to invite the attentions of the school bully. Lloyd and Roy exemplify these two alternatives.

The signs of post-traumatic stress may be apparent, particularly in children who have been subjected to, or witnessed, abuse, terror and violence (Dwivedi, 2000; Ford et al., 2000; Cohen et al., 2003). This is discussed further in relation to adults in Chapter 9, and all practitioners should be familiar with the theory relating to post-traumatic syndromes. Children may show signs of repetitive play associated with the trauma, nightmares, or complete avoidance of anything associated with the abuse. They may also show signs of increased arousal including sleeping difficulties, irritability and outbursts of anger, difficulty concentrating, over-vigilance (being alert all the time, especially to the mood and behaviour of adults), and an exaggerated startle response.

Eating disorders may be a sign of abuse, as exemplified by Helen and Roy. Self-harming often has its roots in maltreatment, and for some children life may become so intolerable that suicide is attempted, as illustrated by Marie's sister and Lloyd.

Finally, children may show no extremes or oddities of behaviour because they compartmentalise their lives. They metaphorically put the abuse into a separate box and forget about it during the times when it is not occurring. Nevertheless, there will be faint clues, as most abused children feel isolated, unworthy and afraid. Perhaps the child will daydream a lot, be forgetful – the memory blanks out bad experiences – or be tired as night-time abuse and nightmares take their toll.

Although there are many signs of abuse, as numerous public enquiries into child deaths have shown, recognising that maltreatment is occurring, and being aware of the extent and severity abuse, is by no means easy. There are many obstacles to recognition. One of the key ways of overcoming these obstacles is by increasing your understanding of theories that explain why and how children relate to others and cope with adversity. This understanding is the focus of the next chapter.

putting it into practice

Activity 1

Choose one or two of the stories of abuse outlined in this chapter. Identify who the main players in the case are, including professional agencies such as schools or the police. Who held what sort of power? How might shifts and alterations in power have alleviated the situation? Could the victim have been helped by empowering either the children or other people in their lives? Might it have been useful to 'disempower' or limit the power of any of the significant people?

This activity is an extension of the second exercise in the previous chapter. It is designed to help you to identify the importance of power dynamics in relation to working with cases of abuse. It is also designed to help you consider the issue of 'empowerment', which often results in the limitation of the power of other people.

Activity 2

According to the stage theory of Erikson (1965), a child needs to establish and maintain a sense of basic trust as a foundation for the positive completion of other developmental tasks. In each of the cases described in this chapter, Marie, Lloyd, Helen, Sarah and Roy identify how far they were able to trust the people (including those in agencies such as schools) they encountered. How far might their sense of trust, or the breach of trust, have enabled or prevented them from seeking help or escaping from the abuse?

This activity is designed to help you apply theory to specific cases. It also demonstrates how an understanding of some basic theoretic approaches can enhance our appreciation of the actions of victims of abuse.

Further reading

Accounts by former victims of child abuse abound and give valuable perspectives; for example, Cameronchild (1987), Spring (1987), Ben (1991) and Yen Mah (2002). Insight into the impact of sexual abuse on black children is provided by Angelou (1984) and Rouf (1991a, 1991b). Boys as victims and accounts of children sexually abused by female perpetrators are provided by Bolton *et al.* (1989), and Elliot (1993). The significance of domestic violence in relation to child protection is explored in Humphreys (2000) and Thangam and Mullender (2000).

3 | Understanding abused children

Practitioners will encounter abused children who are only too happy to be rescued from their homes, but they will meet others who defend their parents, hide their injuries, guard the family secret and try to avoid removal from their home. This chapter continues the examination of abuse from the child's perspective, and will I hope throw some light on the apparent paradox of victims who resist 'rescue'.

The child as a family member: attachment and related theories

The family is an important unit in most societies. It has played a significant role in politics and in the exchange of property, and therefore children from a variety of cultures are brought up to have a healthy respect for their families.

The 'blood-tie'

There is a strong belief in the blood-tie. 'Blood is thicker than water' is a familiar saying. Before the comparatively recent introduction of forms of social security benefit, weaker family members relied on the stronger ones for survival. In many countries, demographic and economic conditions mean that ageing parents depend on their offspring for material support. The older generation therefore has a vested interest in emphasizing the importance of loyalty to family members and the obligation owed to blood relatives.

In all societies, the less strong are vulnerable to abuse. It is not surprising that adults fearful of the new generation of fit, strong, young people have sought to protect themselves in their declining years by emphasising the requirement to 'honour' parents and older people in society. This has usually been elevated to the commandment of a deity and revealed though the scriptures: 'Honour your father and mother' (The Old Testament; Orchard and Fuller, 1966,

p. 63); 'Honour the mothers who bore you' (The Koran; Dawood, 1990, p. 60); and 'Shall I kill my own masters, who though greedy of my kingdom are yet my sacred teachers?' (Sanskrit poem, *The Bhagavad Gita*; Mascaro, 1962, p. 48).

One way of reinforcing messages to children is through folk tales and nursery rhymes. A study of fairy stories worldwide shows that where a child is mistreated, this is generally at the hands of a non-family member or a step-parent. From their infancy, children learn that they may be mistreated by people who are not really part of their family, but if they suffer at the hands of their parents it is either because they deserve punishment or because the parent is acting in their best interests. For the adopted, fostered or step-child there is still the spectre of the blood-tie, because in its absence they may feel unable to take the care of substitute parents for granted.

Inheritance and identity

Familiar phrases such as 'like father, like son' and 'a chip off the old block' reflect the belief that aspects of personality are inherited. Children are reluctant to think of their parents as weak, cruel or evil, because these characteristics reflect on the children themselves. Jocelyn Peters (1966), referring to children with a range of family difficulties writes, 'In a close-knit family community, distress and deprivation will draw the members more tightly together. Disapproval of a parent means to a child disapproval of himself' (p. 74).

Playground talk often consists of boys and girls boasting that their parents are stronger, braver, richer or cleverer than those of their school mates. Children therefore have a vested interest in, for example, interpreting their parents' violent behaviour as a display of strength. This desire to be the child of someone virtuous is again reflected in, and reinforced by, those fairy tales that tell of good children of apparently poor or wicked parents turning out really to be the progeny of rich or benign ones.

Sarah, whose account was given in the previous chapter, came to dislike her father early in childhood. She recognised that this was, in her own words, 'a big decision for a child'. Echoing the words of Jocelyn Peters, Sarah's disapproval of her father led, inevitably, to self-disapproval. This resulted in a loss of self-esteem, which meant that she submitted to physical, emotional and sexual abuse because she felt she had no right to resist.

Attachment behaviour

Bowlby (1951, 1969) contended that the primary caregiver for babies is their mother. Research indicates that infants of only a few days old prefer their mother's face to other faces (Carpenter, 1974), their mother's voice to other voices (Mills and Melhuish, 1974), and can distinguish their own mother's milk from that of other women (MacFarlane, 1977). Researchers (Waters *et al.*, 1995) using a more recent qualitative Q-sort method found across a diversity of cultures that babies tend to rely on their mother as a secure base. Rutter (1981), however, argued that a group of consistent carers provides this attachment, and subsequent studies have confirmed that babies are likely to have a similar attachment to their fathers (Lamb, 1987; Geiger, 1996). It is therefore probable that children develop strong attachments to parents and other caregivers even if the attachment from the adult to the child is weak.

Despite the criticisms of Ainsworth's attachment classification noted in Chapter 1, her great contribution was to identify that, while nearly all children have an attachment to at least one primary carer, not all such attachments are beneficial. This recognition led other researchers (Main and Solomon, 1986) to the identification of a further, less than satisfactory, attachment pattern – the insecure-disorganised.

Some abused children live in such physically, socially or emotionally isolated families that there seems to be no alternative to the inadequate parent. They cannot redirect their attachment behaviour, because a substitute is not available. They have little option but to continue to focus all their energies on trying to attract the abusive parent. For others, their maltreatment does not start until after they have developed an attachment to their parents. Furthermore, a strong attachment can be formed with the non-abusing parent and other members of the family. Children may not want to leave home or upset the family because of the love they feel for the non-abusing parent, their siblings or even a pet.

The natural world has provided for small animals to survive by being looked after by substitutes in the absence of their biological parents. Similarly, children can become attached to alternative caregivers. This ability to redirect attachment behaviour is the basis of successful adoptions and step-parenting. However, it again means that the child may attach to a foster, step- or adoptive parent who has little affection for the girl or boy in question. Children whose attempts to be cared for by their birth parent have been thwarted will be all the more desperate to cling to substitute caregivers once they have given up hope of being nurtured by their natural parents.

The child as a victim: the Stockholm syndrome theory

Bowlby (1969), discussing attachment theory, wrote:

> The attachment of children to parents, who by all ordinary standards, are very bad is a never-ceasing source of wonder to those who seek to help them. Even when they are with kindly foster-parents these children feel their roots to be in the homes where, perhaps, they have been neglected and ill-treated and keenly resent criticisms directed against their parents.
> (p. 80)

This section explores the reasons for this apparent defence by maltreated children of their abusers. This attachment and defence behaviour is not confined to abusive parents. It can sometimes occur when the offender is another family member or even someone outside the family.

Hostages, kidnap victims and concentration camp prisoners can, despite their suffering, demonstrate loyalty and affection towards their persecutors. An examination of the circumstances in which this may arise will provide some understanding of the child/abuser attachment.

In kidnap and hostage situations, negotiators recognize that captives frequently develop positive feelings towards their captors and show hostility towards any rescuers: 'Even in the face of an armed officer of the law, the victim would offer himself as a human shield for his abductor. As absurd as this may seem, such behaviour had been observed by law enforcement officers throughout the world' (Strenz, 1980, p. 147).

This paradoxical phenomenon has been termed the 'Stockholm syndrome'. Its name derives from the events in Sweden in August 1973, when four employees of the Svergis Kredit Bank were held hostage for 131 hours by two bank robbers. It became clear that, during the siege, the hostages, despite being law-abiding citizens, were more afraid of the police than they were of their captors, and subsequently defended the robbers.

There are a number of similarities between the victims of hostage situations, concentration camp prisoners and abused children (Doyle, 1985, 1997a). All are innocent, unsuspecting victims imprisoned and mistreated emotionally and/or physically by aggressors who feel that they have to hold the balance of power and have to be in total control of the victims.

Sarah Davidson, an Israeli housewife, was on the Air France airbus flight 139 which was hijacked and flown to Entebbe, Uganda in 1976. She kept a diary and in it noted how upset she was by the way her fellow passengers would agree with the suggestions of a hijacker called Bose, clapping every time he made a speech. Reflecting on what was happening, she wrote:

> All these years I could not comprehend the holocaust. Year in, year out, I read what is written on the subject, and I see the films and hear the horrifying testimonies, and I don't understand. Why did the Jews enter the gas chambers so quietly? Why did they go like sheep to the slaughter when they had nothing to lose? I needed the nightmare at Entebbe to comprehend . . . The German man adopted a pleasant manner. He was a concealed enemy, pretending, tempting his victims to believe his good intentions . . . If he had said to march in a certain direction where his colleagues were awaiting us with machine guns, ready to mow us down, we would have gone.
> (Dobson and Payne, 1977, pp. 226–7)

There appear to be a number of psychological factors that enable a victim to cope with the stress of the situation, and which may explain the Stockholm syndrome.

Frozen fright, denial and isolation

At a time of disaster and terror in which there is some possibility of escape, individuals may panic, scream and run. However, in most hostage situations the captors ensure that the victims are trapped with no means of exit. This results in what Martin Symonds (1980) has termed 'frozen fright':

> This superficially appears to be a cooperative and friendly behaviour that confuses even the victim, the criminal, the

family and friends of the victim, the police and society in general . . . the victims narrowly focus all their energy on survival, exclusively concentrating on the terrorist. This reaction is enhanced by the criminal terrorist's intent to totally dominate the victim. The terrorist creates a hostile environment and thwarts any efforts that would reduce this domination. The victim then feels isolated from others, powerless and helpless.

(pp. 131–2).

All this is reminiscent of the frozen watchfulness of the battered infant, and the feelings of helplessness and isolation recounted by many victims of child abuse.

Another early emotion is denial. It is more reassuring to believe that the captors intend no harm, than to recognise that they may well be prepared to maim and kill. One hostage of the hijack of TWA flight 355 in 1976 expressed the belief that the bombs held by the hijackers were fakes even after one of the bombs had killed or injured four bomb disposal officers. Chodoff (1981), who studied concentration camp survivors, noted:

It appears that the most important personality defenses among concentration camp inmates were denial and isolation of affect. Some form of companionship with others was indispensable, since a completely isolated individual could not have survived in the camps, but the depth of such companionship was usually limited by the overpowering egotistical demands of self-preservation.

(p. 4)

This is an echo of the isolation felt by child abuse victims. The relationship problems caused by the need for self-preservation was illustrated in the last chapter by Sarah, in relation to her sister, Barbara.

Fear and anger

Fear and anger may be repressed or turned, not against the captor because in the hostages' impotent state that would be too uncomfortable, but against the rescuing authorities. There is a sense in which both captors and captives feel united against the outside world. The threat 'within' is transferred to an external menace.

This does not disappear as soon as rescue is achieved. Victims may:

> remain hostile toward the police after the siege has ended. The 'original' victims in Stockholm still visit their abductors, and one former hostage is engaged to Olofsson. South American victims visit their former captors in jail. Others have begun defense funds for them. A hostile hostage is the price that law enforcement must pay for a living hostage. (Strenz, 1980, p. 149)

This fear and anger is sometimes seen in abused children. It is not uncommon for practitioners to find that the children they are attempting to help view them with hostility, mistrust and resentment.

Hope and gratitude

Having coped with anger and fear of their captors, victims will search for evidence to confirm their hope that the captors are really acting in their interests. Acts, such as the captors arranging for the provision of food or allowing the victim to make himself more comfortable, are seen by the captives as proof of the hostage-takers' kindness and concern for their welfare. Hostages and abused children have in common the fact that, although they are in the power of someone who may threaten their safety, they cling to him or her because they are dependant on the captor/abusing parent to provide life's necessities.

There is also a sense in which the hostages feel that they owe their lives to their captors. Charles Bahn (1980) explains that, in the case of hostage situations when a threat to life is not carried out, there is a build-up of intense gratitude. Similarly, concentration camp prisoners may believe they will survive if their guards are, under the surface, caring and interested in their welfare. The prisoners will therefore attach great importance to any slight gesture of kindness. Solzhenitsyn (1974), recalling his time as a Russian concentration camp prisoner, describes the deep indebtedness felt towards a jailer who greeted the prisoners with a friendly 'good morning' (pp. 541–2).

When adult hostages and prisoners can react with such gratitude and lack of resentment, it is less surprising that children should feel grateful and forgiving towards parents who, although seeming to threaten their lives, do not (in most cases) actually kill them. All children, but particularly abused ones, can believe that their parents could kill them. Dorothy Bloch (1979), after years of working with children and studying their fears and fantasies, concluded:

> Children are universally disposed to the fear of infanticide by both their physical and their physiological stage of development and the intensity of that fear depends on the incidence of traumatic events and on the degree of violence and of love they have experienced . . . Why shouldn't children be afraid of being killed? To begin with consider their size. Is there anyone more killable?
> (p. 3)

Despair and acceptance

Once captives have convinced themselves that their abuser is good and worthy of gratitude, they reach the inevitable conclusion that they are suffering because they are bad and therefore deserve to suffer. This can lead to anger being turned against the self, and overwhelming feelings of depression and despair.

The child psychiatrist Bruno Bettelheim (1979), who was himself a concentration camp victim, observed prisoners' stages of adaptation. First, they would regress to the state of a dependant child. This was induced partly by camp rules, such as those that resulted in prisoners soiling themselves. They became increasingly compliant as they realised how dependant they were on the goodwill of the guards. Eventually, many went beyond compliance and began to accept the values of the guards. Some long-standing prisoners took pride in copying the verbal and physical aggression of the guards towards fellow inmates, and would try to make SS uniforms for themselves.

Another study of adaptive behaviour in the camps noted that, after the initial response of shock and terror, apathy set in. This 'was often psychologically protective and may be thought of as providing a kind of transitional emotional hibernation' (Chodoff, 1981, p. 4). A camp survivor, Sherry Weiss-Rosenfeld recalled: 'The feeling was something indescribable; it was a feeling of total despair . . . And I said to myself, even if I were to sprout wings all of a sudden I could not fly out of here' (Dwork, 1991, p. 225). A similar apathy can engulf some abused children so that they no longer look for any escape and simply accept their mistreatment.

'Psychological contrast' was the term used by Solzhenitsyn to describe the 'good guy, bad guy' tactics used in many interrogation situations and by hostage-takers:

> For a whole or part of the interrogation period, the interrogator would be extremely friendly . . . Suddenly he would brandish a paperweight and shout 'Foo, you rat! I'll put nine grams of lead in your skull! . . .' or as a variation on this: two interrogators would take turns. One would shout and bully, the others would be friendly, almost gentle.
> (Solzhenitsyn, 1974, p. 104)

This is reminiscent of the experiences of abused children. Their abuser may be violent, threatening or coldly callous one moment and then, perhaps feeling remorseful, be loving and tender the next; alternatively, one parent may be persistently cruel whereas the other parent is kind and caring.

In *The Gulag Archipelago*, Solzhenitsyn (1974) lists the various tortures used to weaken the resistance of prisoners. Many of these are reminiscent of the behaviour of abusing carers. Psychological methods include the use of night-time, when the victim lacks his daytime equanimity. Marie, it will be recalled, described being pulled out of bed at one o'clock in the morning to be interrogated by her father about his uncleaned shoes. Foul language and humiliation are often used in torture situations; these were very much part of Sarah's account of her father's behaviour. Inducing confusion, intimidation accompanied by enticement, promises and 'playing on one's affection for those one loved' were other psychological methods of torture cited by Solzhenitsyn and illustrated by Marie's account. Physical torture methods include: burning with cigarettes, tickling, beating, locking in a bed-bug infested room, not allowing victims to sleep, and forcing them to stand or kneel for long periods. All such methods are familiar in the field of child abuse. It is therefore hardly surprising that mistreated children, like prisoners subjected to torture, will become compliant and offer little resistance to the demands of their abusers.

The roots of resistance

Many, but not all, victims of hostage situations, concentration camps or child abuse show compliant behaviour or respond positively to their aggressors. Those that show some resistance often have a strong value system or an alternative model of behaviour to which they cling tenaciously. Solzhenitsyn himself condemned the treatment to which he was subjected. Chodoff (1981), in his study of Holocaust survivors, noted that certain political and religious groups were exceptions to the general response of denial and isolation. Similarly, children who are subjected to mistreatment at the hands of a newly-arrived step-parent, or who have other positive influences, may resist and complain because they know there are alternative forms of parental behaviour.

Strenz (1980) noted that the Stockholm syndrome is likely to be absent when captors showed no kindness towards their victims:

> Those victims who had negative contacts with the subjects did not evidence concern for them . . . some of these victims had been physically abused by the subjects. They obviously did not like their abuse and advocated the maximum penalty be imposed.
> (p. 143)

It seems that if children live with two constantly abusing parents, they will not have the same sense of loyalty and concern for the parents. The same is true if one parent is actively abusive and the other indifferent to the children's plight. Dorothy Bloch (1979) noted, 'In no case did the child feel loved by either parent . . . with these children the abusive and hating parent seems to be unworthy of respect and in some instances "didn't deserve to live", and the other parent seemed at best, passive and neutral' (p. 237).

The victim as a child: Erikson's stage theory

Many hostage, kidnap and concentration camp victims are adults who have experiences of life from which they can draw strength, plus a fully-developed intellect they can use to rationalize their experiences. Abused children do not have these advantages. They are imprisoned by overwhelming emotions and, in cases of long-standing abuse, by an abnormal learning process.

There are many emotions leading abused children to believe that they are in the wrong and the abusing adults in the right. It is interesting to note how the key emotions mirror the developmental process identified by Erikson (1965). He argued that the healthy person progresses through eight positive stages that result in the establishment of a sense of basic trust, autonomy, initiative, industry, identity, intimacy, generativity and ego integrity. The alternative progression results in the acquisition of a sense of basic mistrust, shame/doubt, guilt, inferiority, role confusion, isolation, stagnation and despair.

Fear and mistrust

Feelings of fear and mistrust are closely related. Abused children are unable to trust those who are meant to be protecting and caring for them. In their state of mistrust and uncertainty they are beset by a number of worries. In some cases the fear is quite straightforward and is caused by apprehension about future harm, or that abusers will carry out threats (for example, Angelou, 1984). Sex abusers are particularly adept at playing on a child's fears in order to secure his or her silence. Often, children are not so much afraid for themselves as for their loved ones. Marie kept quiet about her father's behaviour because she was worried about what would happen to her mother and siblings if she was removed from the family. Some children feel impelled to submit to abuse without resistance in the hope that this will keep their siblings or a pet safe (for example, Fraser, 1989). One boy wanted to stay with his abusive step-father even when his mother left because he was worried about his aviary full of birds that would have been too large to move to his mother's new flat.

Fear of alternatives is another common and understandable anxiety. Many young children assume that, if their parents mistreat them, it is because every parent behaves in that way. Sarah believed that all headmasters and fathers beat the children in their care. She would have resisted any attempt to place her with foster parents because, in her inexperienced eyes, they would probably have been as bad if not worse than her father. Many abusive families and abused children are isolated, with little opportunity of observing alternative family models. Mistreated children, lacking basic trust, may well take a long time before they can accept that other adults are well-intentioned.

Fear of being killed is a more complex concept. Dorothy Bloch, as noted in the previous section, concluded from her clinical experience that children fear they may be killed by their parents. Although Freud dwelt at length on the tale of Oedipus murdering his father to marry his mother, he did not mention the first part of the story, which tells of the attempts of the parents to kill the baby Oedipus. The fear of infanticide held by children has its roots in reality, and will be all the more intense for children who have been abused, attacked and threatened. Their hope of survival lies in parental love overcoming parental aggression, so they have to make themselves lovable and valuable to the parent. This may be achieved by accepting abuse without resistance and without causing problems:

> In most instances the patient convinced himself that his
> parents wanted to and were capable of loving him but that it
> was his worthlessness that made them hate him and even
> want to destroy him.
> (Bloch, 1979, p. 11)

Some abused children instinctively recognise that they will survive if they can find a useful role for themselves in the family system. This may explain why some children accept being made the scapegoat or take over the parental, caring role.

The sibling of an abused child or a child abused by siblings may well harbour the same fear of being killed and will therefore develop the same mistrust, sense of unworthiness and need to win parental love, whatever the cost. Dorothy Bloch (1979) noted that:

> It did not need to be necessary for the child himself to be the
> target . . . It was sufficient if the parents committed violent
> acts of any kind . . . towards each other, or towards another
> child or even towards an animal . . . Violent and habitually
> attacking older siblings were experienced as agents of the
> parents; where the parents didn't intervene effectively to
> protect the child, he assumed they wanted him killed.
> (pp. 6–7)

Neglected children, similarly, have a realistic fear of death. Small children can die from starvation and from diseases associated with unsanitary conditions and malnutrition. Children who are ignored are in danger; consequently, they may behave badly in order to attract attention. If they can feel a beating or hear a rebuke they know that they are alive and that someone is taking notice of them.

Finally, as the previous section on hostages indicated, victims can become paralysed by fear. A baby's 'frozen watchfulness' is one example. Erin Pizzey cites another:

> Ever since he was tiny, James has watched his mother suffer burning with a red hot poker, cigarettes stubbed out on her face, her legs slashed with knives, and his sister beaten before it was his turn. James is 9, and has been attending hospital for three years for depression. James is not a stupid child, he is just paralysed with fear, so he can barely read or write.
> (Pizzey, 1974)

This paralysis will result in the child's inability to resist the abuser or seek assistance. Some will grow so quiet, almost mute, that they are literally unable to cry for help.

Doubt, shame and guilt

Abused children, riddled with fears, not only mistrust others but also question their own capabilities. They are trying to win their parents' love but as long as the abuse continues they seem to be failing. Consequently, they distrust themselves, the safety of their environment, the ability of other people to rescue them, the ability of substitute parents to love them, and the ability of the rest of the family to survive without them.

Shame is another enduring emotion besetting abused children. First, there is the shame associated with being bad and deserving punishment. Smacking, scolding and sending to bed without supper are all common ways of punishing misbehaviour. According to the straightforward logic of children, if they are severely beaten, continually shouted and sworn at or locked for ages in a room without food it must be because they are very wicked. Bad behaviour and punishment are associated with disgrace and therefore a sense of shame overshadows the lives of abuse victims.

Children who are intimidated or distressed can find it difficult to control their bowels and bladder and, once old enough to be toilet-trained, will be ashamed of wetting or soiling themselves. To compound matters they are often told they are lazy, dirty and disgusting for doing so.

Other abusive practices can induce a sense of shame. In most cultures, children learn from an early age that being naked or playing with private parts is seen as rude. A child who is smacked on the bare bottom or coerced into sexual activities may therefore become very embarrassed and humiliated.

Sexually abused children often feel that they are to blame for the abuse. Sometimes they enjoy the sexual activities or willingly accept the advances of the perpetrator because they are lonely or succumb to bribes. The rest of the family, wishing to preserve the integrity of the perpetrator, may also blame the victim. Even some material designed to prevent sexual abuse may have the effect of compounding the guilt. 'Danger-stranger' protection strategies can have an adverse effect because children are told to say 'no' to a sexual advance. If they fail to do so, they may feel they have disobeyed instructions.

Infants cry and, unless grossly neglected, are fed and tended to. They seem to have magical powers to control their environment. Consequently, small children begin to feel responsible for whatever happens: 'With his concept of the magical nature of his thoughts, wishes and feelings, he may also assume responsibility for an extra-ordinary range of unhappy events' (Bloch, 1979, p. 5). Older children may have to contend with the feeling that they were old enough to have done something about events. All this adds to an abused child's feelings of guilt.

Children can also feel responsible for others. If they tell someone about the abuse their parents may be prosecuted or the family split up. The reason for so many retractions lies in the guilty feelings weighing on a child whose disclosure has led to such distressing events. Those removed into care may be unable to enjoy their freedom from abuse because they believe that it was achieved at the expense of other family members. Guilt may also be induced in the child if the parents are abusive one moment and caring the next:

> When the parent is good the child feels guilty for the hatred
> [he or she] feels during the periods when the parent is bad.
> This is further complicated by strong feelings of compassion
> and pity because the parents look helpless and in need of the
> child's love and affection. When the parent is bad the child
> becomes full of hatred and contempt for the parent and for
> himself for being fooled yet again by compassion.
> (Pizzey, 1974)

Finally, children may be blamed for having provoked the abuser. There is still a strongly held belief in 'Lolitas' – that is, prepubertal or adolescent girls seducing 'innocent', unsuspecting males. In relation to physical abuse, there is the concept of over-chastisement: the child has deserved punishment and provoked the parents so much that they have lost control. A constantly crying baby is regarded as provocative. In all these cases, the child is seen as the agent of abuse, the person to blame, while sympathy is reserved for the adult who claims to have been pushed beyond the limits of endurance.

Towards despair

Inferiority

Abused children develop a sense of unworthiness because of the feelings of shame and guilt evoked by mistreatment. This results in a sense of inferiority, reinforced by the child's seeming inability to win parental approval and love. It follows that abused children may be reticent about seeking or accepting help; they conclude that if their parents do not think that they are worth protecting and loving, there is no reason why any other adult would do so.

Role confusion

The fifth of Erikson's stages is identity versus role confusion. Inappropriate role adoption is a recognized aspect of child abuse. Children may accept the role of family scapegoat or victim in order to be of some value to the parents. They may, moreover, cling tenaciously to their role, fearing rejection, even annihilation if they lose it. This explains why abused children sometimes resist change and rescue. They know no other role and, if removed from the family, attempt to establish themselves as scapegoat and victim in their substitute families.

Role confusion also occurs when the child becomes responsible for family members and takes on a parental function. Summit (1983), discussing the way that children adapt to sexual abuse, writes, 'the child, not the parent must mobilise the altruism and self-control to ensure the survival of the others'. This means that the victims may feel bound to keep the family's secret whatever the cost in order to ensure the family is not split up. They may then be unsettled in care, worrying about what is happening to absent parents and siblings.

Isolation

A sense of isolation, the sixth of Erikson's stages, is apparent in the accounts given by many abused children. They often feel different from their school fellows. They may be ashamed of their families or their condition. Furthermore, abusive parents tend to discourage friendships. Abused children cannot be intimate with anyone outside the family because of their feelings of guilt and shame. They will suspect genuine kindness because of their inability to trust and their sense of their own unworthiness, and so they keep people at arm's length, carrying the burden of their secret alone.

Stagnation and despair

Children who feel mistrustful and isolated will be heading towards stagnation and despair rather than being full of ideas for change and hope for the future. They will resist disclosure and removal from home because they may, in their despair, doubt that the situation will ever improve for them. Even when settled in a loving foster home they may expect things to deteriorate and will try to provoke the foster carers into abusing and rejecting them rather than wait for the inevitable (they believe) abuse and rejection to occur.

Abnormal learning

The theory of 'learned helplessness' is associated with despair. It is a term coined by psychologist, Martin Seligman (1975). His experiments showed that if animals, and possibly people, attempt to escape but are unable to do so they will eventually give up attempts to escape even when given the opportunity. Some victims of abuse seek help indirectly. If, time and again, adults fail to understand the children's messages, they will give up hope of any help being forthcoming. Alternatively, some children are able to ask for assistance directly but often they are not believed or nothing happens because the parents are unable to change, and the legal grounds to force a change or protect them are absent. Children are then in a worse situation, as now they will despair of receiving help. Subsequently, they may resist offers of help even when, eventually, someone with the power to intervene tries to assist.

Behaviourist theories teach us that training children is a simple matter of conditioning. Children are taught how to behave by being given rewards for good behaviour and punished for bad. They will seek pleasure and avoid pain. But this can be deceptive, as life is rarely so straightforward. Abuse victims may accept pain and suffering rather than lose something less tangible. Helen accepted the pain of attempted intercourse rather than lose the attention of her brother, and she went hungry and uncomfortable in an attempt to win her mother's love. Those outside the family may not understand why victims choose to remain at home even though they are likely to be beaten, molested or go hungry. But for the child some things such as security in what is familiar, or the chance to win parental love, are more important than mere avoidance of pain and discomfort.

Neglected children can fail to develop because their environment lacks stimulation (Iwaniec, 1995), and emotionally or physically abused children may be prevented from exploring their world and satisfying their curiosity, because if they go beyond very tight limits or cause any disruption they will be punished. Eventually, it becomes more expedient not to reach out, not to try anything different, not to seek a change in their circumstances.

Finally, victims may not seek help or removal from home because, despite advancing in years, the abuse results in their remaining emotionally like dependent infants. In some cases, especially those of neglect and physical abuse, brain damage might be a factor. But, more often, any developmental or learning problems are of a less tangible nature. Hostage situations and concentration camp imprisonment result in regression in adults. A similar situation such as the abusive home is likely to produce regression or, if the child is too young to regress, failure to develop. Abused people sometimes remain emotionally dependent, infantilised and clinging to their parents. If they do manage to leave home, they may become dependent on a partner who, like their parents, alternately cares for and abuses them. They also depend on their own children to meet their emotional needs and become frustrated when their offspring fail to do so. Therefore a proportion of abused children (but not all – see Herzberger, 1993) becomes the next generation of abusive parents.

The following chapters examine ways of working with children in order to overcome or alleviate some of the more negative emotions and perceptions that result in children becoming imprisoned in abusive situations.

putting it into practice

Activity 1

Think back to Chapter 2 and the case stories of Marie, Lloyd, Helen, Sarah and Roy, then review the ideas presented in this chapter. List, in each of the cases, any obstacles to recognising the severity of the abuse that professional workers are likely to have encountered.

The purpose of this activity is to help you to identify the factors that might prevent even skilled, committed and well-trained professionals from recognising that a child is being abused. For example, Helen came from a 'respectable' family, with a mother committed to the welfare of children. Furthermore, her thoughts, feelings and behaviour exhibited aspects of the Stockholm syndrome; she craved affection from her family while denigrating and despising herself.

Activity 2

In three of the cases in Chapter 2 – those of Roy, Sarah and Marie – there was clear evidence of emotional and physical abuse by one parent figure against the other parent. Terminology describing this form of oppression is evolving, but 'domestic violence' is a commonly used term at the time of writing. Consider what you know about these three cases and what you have learnt in this chapter about the Stockholm syndrome. How far do you think that the Stockholm syndrome might be at least a partial explanation of why victimized parents, like the mothers of Marie, Sarah or Roy, have difficulty leaving their partners?

The purpose of this activity is to help you think about how the Stockholm syndrome can entrap anyone, adults or children, in an oppressive situation. It is a positive psychological and often adaptive response to dangerous, threatening situations, but unfortunately there can be negative outcomes, which further entrap victims of abuse. The other purpose of this activity is to help you think about the links between child abuse and domestic violence (including emotional aggression, such as that suffered by Sarah's mother). This double-faceted oppression can substantially increase the complexity of working with abused children.

Further reading

Concepts in relation to the emotional entrapment described in this chapter are discussed more fully in Doyle (1985, 1994, 1997a). Strenz (1980) gives a clear description of the Stockholm syndrome. Further details of post-traumatic stress disorder among children are given by Wolfe *et al.* (1994) and Dwivedi (2000). Parkinson (1993) also examines the topic and includes notes on the Stockholm syndrome. A wonderful book by Orr (2003) gives the perspective of a child with multiple disabilities, albeit not an abused child. Kennedy's writings (for example, 1990, 2002) on children with disabilities who have been abused are always informative.

4 | Children in society: policy and prevention

The preceding chapter identified some of the psychological factors having an impact on the child victims of abuse, and influencing ways of working with abused children. This chapter examines the sociological, environmental and social policy issues that will have an effect on family functioning, and on the ways that helping professionals intervene in the lives of maltreated children.

Because of the short-term suffering and the possible adverse long-term ramifications of maltreatment, it is preferable to prevent maltreatment occurring in the first place. If that is not possible, then the avoidance of further abuse becomes the imperative. The social policy and other societal contexts relating to prevention will also be explored in this chapter. Prevention is addressed in this relatively early chapter rather than towards the end, to indicate that it should be at the forefront of thinking rather than tacked on the end, almost as an afterthought. The term 'safeguarding' is used in this chapter to indicate the triple response to child protection of intervention, to:

- alleviate the effects of abuse;
- prevent further mistreatment after abuse has occurred; and
- prevent abuse from occurring in the first place.

The origins of the modern-day concern for the welfare of children can be traced back to late-nineteenth-century philanthropy. The emphasis was on rescuing the child and punishing the parents. Nigel Parton (1985), in his historical perspective on child abuse, writes, 'Families were expected to take full responsibility for their members and if this was not possible the state would intervene in a harsh, controlling way' (p. 36).

The earlier part of the twentieth century saw a gradual change in this attitude: the state came to be seen to have some responsibility for the welfare of its citizens, including the youngest. State support for 'poor but honest' parents became an additional ingredient, although rescue of neglected or mistreated children remained the main protective intervention.

The evacuation of poor city children to more affluent country areas during the Second World War brought home to a much larger and more influential section of society the widespread nature of child poverty and deprivation. It was recognised that rescue and punishment was no longer a feasible means of managing family problems. In addition, the death of Dennis O'Neill (1945 in Appendix) at the hands of his foster father demonstrated that removal from 'inadequate' parents was not always the answer. Therefore, for the majority of cases, 'reform' of, or support for, parents was seen to be more appropriate.

The emphasis of the next three chapters is on releasing the children from the morass of potentially destructive emotions that ensnare them in an unhappy situation, however caring the nature of their new substitute home or their 'reformed' original families. Nevertheless, the scope of any intervention will be heavily influenced, not just by the assessment of need, and the ability and availability of the relevant helping professionals, but also by the policy and social contexts, which impinge on the families and the services provided. Intervention will also be influenced by prominent social theories and constructs. The next two sections explore the policy contexts of child welfare, protection and prevention services.

Policy contexts

Harding (1997) is one of the leading UK commentators on child care policy and has identified four main perspectives, namely laissez-faire, state paternalism, modern defence of the birth family and, lastly, children's rights. Her framework addresses child care policy specifically rather than as part of a more general approach to welfare and as such it offers useful perspectives on the context in which child care professionals operate. Here her framework has been adapted to highlight the implication of each policy approach to safeguarding children.

Laissez-faire

According to Harding, the laissez-faire approach to social policy need not incorporate a patriarchal structure, but in practice the two have largely coincided – for example, in the West in the nineteenth century, and in its re-emergence in Britain in the later 1980s.

Fundamental to this view is a distrust of the state and an awareness of the dangerousness of its powers. It is associated with capitalist societies, where it is felt that the state should keep out of personal relationships and the private areas of citizens' lives. The home is a private area, a retreat and the domain of women. The public arena in which individuals associate and interact is the domain of men. The physical power of adults over children, and men over women, is socially and legally structured and determined.

Safeguarding children

This approach assumes that parents will do what is best for their children, bringing them up in the way they see fit. In extreme cases, if as a result of death, illness or extreme abuse, birth parents are no longer able to look after their children, then ideally they should be placed with substitute carers who should, similarly, be left to look after them undisturbed. Harding pointed to the studies by Dingwall *et al.* (1983) which revealed that social workers tended to operate within this perspective, showing reluctance to use any coercive powers while interpreting events in a way most favourable to parents. This suggests that it is important for current child-protection workers to reflect on how far they are influenced by this policy perspective.

Under the laissez-faire approach, prevention is not high on the political agenda, although voluntary and private agencies might be permitted or even encouraged to provide services to support parents.

State paternalism

The state paternalism approach, in contrast to the laissez-faire one, envisages a substantial role for state intervention in order to protect children from cruelty or inadequate care. The approach makes the assumptions that optimum child-rearing can be defined, but birth parents do not always reach an adequate level. Children have a right to receive a good standard of care and protection, and parents have a duty to provide this. Where parents do not do so, the force of law, even to the point of removing the child, might have to be used. Adult interests have to be sacrificed to those of children, who are dependent and vulnerable, and with needs that are different from those of adults.

Among criticisms of this perspective is the charge that it contains an insidious class element, with predominantly middle-class professionals judging poor, working-class families who, through poverty and disadvantage, may not be able to achieve middle-class standards and, in any case, have their own equally valid standards. A similar concern is expressed in relation to cultural diversity and the imposition of white standards on black or Asian parents. There are also criticisms from a feminist perspective – parenthood is viewed as self-sacrificing, but because women are often the main carers it is women who make all the sacrifices.

Safeguarding children

Unlike the laissez-faire proponents, those espousing state paternalism hold that the state has a duty to intervene to provide help and prevent maltreatment. Furthermore, the state is capable of providing better care than inadequate or abusive parents. Associated with this view is Mia Kellmer Pringle (1974) whose writings coincided with the outcry following the death of Maria Colwell. She identified the needs of children and was very critical of the societal emphasis on biological parenthood.

The modern defence of the birth family and parent's rights

This perspective holds that the birth/biological family is of supreme importance for both children and parents, and should be maintained wherever possible. Biological bonds are essential, but if children cannot be cared for by their biological parents, they should nevertheless have as strong a link as possible with their family of origin. It is believed that class, poverty and deprivation underlie much family disruption and incapacity, and therefore the state should intervene in a supportive role.

The European Convention on Human Rights also reflects this perspective. Adopted in 1950, it was influenced by the problems of family separation resulting from evacuation, death and refugee status. It therefore aimed to strengthen the natural family, and only gave rights to children in so far as they were compatible with parental rights. The Convention sees the family as a unit and fails to recognise the competing rights of child and parent (Masson, 1995).

Those who take issue with this perspective pose the question as to why some disadvantaged families lose their children to the care system whereas other equally disadvantaged ones retain full care of their children. Another objection is that proponents of this view seriously underestimate birth parents' capacity to abuse. A third related objection is that the disadvantages of care are often compared to the advantages of being nurtured in a caring, non-abusive birth family, whereas many of the children in care would be living in unstable, volatile situations were they to be returned home.

Safeguarding children

There is a sympathetic view of abusing parents, with the belief that their problems are largely a result of social deprivation and stress. Parents need a materially favourable environment in order to meet the needs of their children. There is therefore an extensive role for the state working to prevent abuse by giving help to disadvantaged and burdened parents.

Children's rights and child liberation

There are a number of different perspectives within this approach. The main unifying belief is that children are entities separate from their parents and their wishes are important. Children are seen as being stronger and less vulnerable than the supporters of the previous three perspectives believe. Therefore, children should be free of both state and adult control, or at least they should be enabled to express their own views, wishes, feelings and choices without these being imposed by adults who 'know what is best' for them.

A more radical position is one that opposes any system of child-care, because such state intervention is a way of controlling children. Moreover, there should be no need for special child-care provision, because children should have the protection afforded to all citizens.

Objections to this perspective includes the charge that its proponents ignore what is now known about human growth and development, especially human learning. Leading theorists and researchers such as Sigmund Freud, Piaget (1983) and Vygotsky (1978) see a distinct difference between the capacities of children and those of adults. Similarly, according to the behavioural model, children have to learn over time how to participate fully in society, and in that sense cannot be expected immediately they are born to exercise the rights and responsibilities of full citizens.

Another objection is that, if children have full adult rights to self-determination, then logically they should equally bear adult responsibilities. Supporters of children's rights responding to this would point to the fact that many children do, in fact, cope with enormous responsibilities, such as the child carers of sick family members, including those with HIV/AIDS (Dearden and Becker, 1995; Francis, 1995; Rickford, 1995); children of needy abusing or substance misusing parents who have to parent their parent (Children's Society, 1995); and children who intervene between warring parents to prevent them damaging each other (National Children's Homes, 1994; Allen *et al.*, 2003).

Safeguarding children

Objections to children's rights only hold true of the most extreme proponents of the perspective. Children do not have sufficient experience of life to give informed consent, so they need to be protected from sexual exploitation. Small children cannot easily feed and care for themselves and need to be kept from harm. Therefore the state has a protective function in relation to children, but equally they need to be empowered wherever possible, just as society attempts to empower vulnerable adults while addressing their individual needs for care and protection. Above all, children should be given a voice, to be active participants in research and, as service users, in service provision and in professional training.

Policy and prevention

Whereas Harding examined the policy approaches to child welfare in general, Hardiker *et al.* (1991) considered the precise relationship between policy and prevention. The implementation of preventative measures depends heavily on the political and popular will of any particular society. Hardiker and colleagues point out that different forms of prevention are linked to different approaches to welfare policy. They identify four approaches:

● *residual*: state welfare is minimal and the only prevention is in the form of strategies to avert repeat abuse in confirmed cases;

● *institutional*: state welfare supplements family and voluntary support in cases of need. Prevention is targeted towards clear 'at risk' cases;
● *developmental*: state welfare is available to all and social injustice is challenged. Prevention occurs because there is good support for all, and so families will receive help before, or as soon as, difficulties arise; and
● *radical/conflict*: the victims of injustice themselves challenge society. Prevention is automatic, because all formerly disempowered people will be empowered.

Although one of these social policy models is likely to be dominant, in many societies several approaches are combined. In Britain at the end of the twentieth century, for example, all four models were in evidence, but the residual model seemed to prevail (Sapey, 1995): this model holds that state spending on welfare and prevention will be minimised: the state will only be involved when a child is in a life-threatening situation, and then the prevention will be tertiary or quaternary. Stevenson (1995) commented, 'The British public has been brain-washed by constant references to public expenditure as somehow undesirable, even wicked' (p. 4). But the institutional model (encapsulated by the main Barclay Report, 1982) is still evident in many of the provisions of the Children Act 1989, such as the duty of local authorities to 'safeguard and promote the welfare of children within their area who are in need' (S.17. 1a). Moreover, the findings of the government-sponsored research (Department of Health, 1995) suggests more emphasis should be given to children in need, rather than merely providing crisis investigations.

Meanwhile, the developmental approach underpins many social work values and anti-discriminatory practice. It is illustrated by Appendix A of the Barclay Report (1982) and remains an important aspect of social work training. But the radical model is also reflected in certain aspects of anti-oppressive practice espoused by social workers. Not only should professionals be challenging oppressions such as racism, sexism, homophobia, 'disablism' and poverty, but they should also be empowering the victims of these injustices to challenge them directly: 'The voice of the "expert" should not substitute for that of the oppressed' (Gambe *et al.*, 1992, p. 99).

The task of primary and secondary prevention can more readily be implemented and maintained when the prevailing welfare models are 'developmental' or 'institutional'. Attempting to prevent abuse when the 'residual' model holds sway could well be a frustrating and dispiriting experience, because workers in the statutory agencies will find such activities are not viewed as being a legitimate part of their workload. Meanwhile, those who are operating independently or in voluntary agencies will fare little better because, while the ruling powers will countenance their preventative enterprises, there will be no tangible state assistance.

Historical perspective

Table 4.1 gives a brief outline of the major legislative and policy developments relevant to child protection since the eighteenth century.

The table relates to developments primarily in the UK. The key legislation refers expressly to English and Welsh provision. The law in Scotland and Northern Ireland is specific to those countries. Nevertheless, the key developments will be reflected not only in the UK but in those areas of the world where child protection has increasingly become recognised as a major social concern.

Environmental and economic factors

The contribution of poverty and environmental factors to child maltreatment is a complex issue and has been the subject of considerable debate (Gil, 1970; Parton, 1985). But impoverished circumstances appear to contribute to abuse (Doyle, 1997b) and therefore more adequate provision is likely to help in the prevention of abuse, particularly physical abuse and neglect.

The account of Becky and her children illustrates a range of environmental and economic conditions encountered by some families The names are fictitious but the events are not. Becky was in her late teens, the single mother of Kensa, her baby daughter. They lived on the fifth floor in a tower block complex in large city in Britain. The complex was a depressing, grey, rabbit warren, filthy with litter and excrement. Becky's flat was damp and the community heating scheme provided only erratic heating. The walls of all the flats were thin, and traffic streamed past the complex, so life

Table 4.1 Government policy and legislation in relation to protecting and safeguarding children

From the Middle Ages to the Industrial Revolution there was an appreciable shift from social communality to the prominence of the family unit. Child protection law was minimal. The state rarely intervened in the domestic setting.

1601	Poor Law Designed to prevent the poorest children dying from starvation and neglect.
1822	First Anti-Cruelty Bill Giving a measure of protection to farm or domestic animals.
1824	Foundation of the Society for the Protection of Cruelty to Animals Granted a royal charter in 1840 to become the R(oyal)SPCA.
1833	Factory Act The beginning of the concept of child protection, but only from danger and exploitation in the workplace. Plight of abused children highlighted by authors such as the Brontës, Dickens and Kingsley, as well as philanthropists such as Thomas Coram and Samuel Smith.
1884	Foundation of the NSPCC Based on the New York Society for the Prevention of Cruelty to Children, established in the wake of the case of Mary Ellen. Mary was severely abused by her carers, and animal protective legislation was used as the basis for intervention to protect her.
1889	Prevention of Cruelty to Children Act First UK legislation incorporating concept of protecting children from mistreatment in the domestic setting.
1870	Education Act The first of a series of acts making education compulsory for all children, initially aged 5–10, but later up to 14 and eventually 16. Compulsory education is a significant development in the protection of children. As they were

→

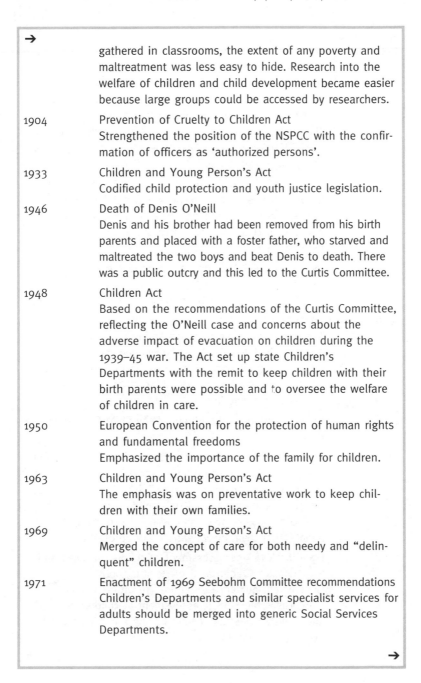

→

gathered in classrooms, the extent of any poverty and maltreatment was less easy to hide. Research into the welfare of children and child development became easier because large groups could be accessed by researchers.

1904   Prevention of Cruelty to Children Act
Strengthened the position of the NSPCC with the confirmation of officers as 'authorized persons'.

1933   Children and Young Person's Act
Codified child protection and youth justice legislation.

1946   Death of Denis O'Neill
Denis and his brother had been removed from his birth parents and placed with a foster father, who starved and maltreated the two boys and beat Denis to death. There was a public outcry and this led to the Curtis Committee.

1948   Children Act
Based on the recommendations of the Curtis Committee, reflecting the O'Neill case and concerns about the adverse impact of evacuation on children during the 1939–45 war. The Act set up state Children's Departments with the remit to keep children with their birth parents were possible and to oversee the welfare of children in care.

1950   European Convention for the protection of human rights and fundamental freedoms
Emphasized the importance of the family for children.

1963   Children and Young Person's Act
The emphasis was on preventative work to keep children with their own families.

1969   Children and Young Person's Act
Merged the concept of care for both needy and "delinquent" children.

1971   Enactment of 1969 Seebohm Committee recommendations
Children's Departments and similar specialist services for adults should be merged into generic Social Services Departments.

→

→

1973   Death of Maria Colwell
Maria was removed from stable foster care to live with her mother and step-father, only to be severely maltreated and killed by her mother and her partner. Subsequent Inquiry reports pointed to deficits in the child protection systems. These led to the development of child protection registers, case conferences and inter-disciplinary procedures.

1975–87   A series of inquiries into the deaths of children, from Stephen Meurs to Jasmine Beckford and Tyra Henry
This showed that any type of parent could neglect and abuse their children, and led to the refinement of procedural systems.

1986   Cleveland crisis and subsequent 1988 Cleveland Inquiry Report
This focused on the management of sexual abuse cases.

1989   Children Act
A major piece of legislation collating the law on most areas of child welfare. It acknowledged the multicultural nature of British society, and catered for the child 'in need' as well as children requiring state protection or care and accommodation.

1989   UN Convention on the Rights of the Child (ratified by the UK in 1991)

1995   'Messages from the Research' (Department of Health 1995)
The publication of extensive research into the workings of the child protection systems. This led to the 'refocusing' debate. It was argued that child welfare services should emphasise 'assessment' and 'responding to need' rather than 'investigation' and 'protection'.

2000   Framework for the assessment of children in need and their families (Department of Health, 2000)
Government guidance for child-care professionals emphasises the holistic assessment of children in need and their families rather than having a narrow focus on investigation and protection.

→

→

2000	UK adopted Human Rights legislation
2000	Death of Victoria Climbié Victoria was an 8-year-old girl, born on the Ivory Coast but brought to France, then Britain, by her aunt, who promised her parents that Victoria would have greater educational opportunities in Europe. Victoria suffered months of extreme torture, physical abuse and neglect at the hands of her aunt and the aunt's boyfriend.
2003 (January)	Laming Report Publication of the inquiry set up to examine the circumstances surrounding the death of Victoria Climbié. The report emphasised the need for clear accountability about who is responsible at every level for the welfare of children.
2003 (September)	Every Child Matters A government Green Paper identifying five key outcomes for children and young people – being healthy; staying safe; enjoying and achieving; making a positive contribution; and economic well-being. Also outlined proposals for information-sharing systems so that children benefit from universal services.
2004 (June)	Bichard Inquiry Report This was set up in the wake of the deaths of Holly Wells and Jessica Chapman, murdered by Ian Huntley. He had been appointed as caretaker at a school despite a series of serious allegations (although without a conviction) of sexual assault against young females. The Inquiry focused on job-vetting processes and the way that agencies, particularly the police, share and communicate potentially significant information.
2004 (November)	The Children Act This implemented many of the proposals of 'Every Child Matters', and provided a legislative framework to encourage integrated planning, commissioning and delivery of services.

was noisy for the residents. There were few local amenities. Becky claimed welfare benefits but the flats were dominated by a 'protection gang'. She had to hand over all her benefits to the gang, and was sometimes given a little back for food. She paid the bills by borrowing from her mother or friends and sometimes by prostitution, resulting in her feeling, in her own words, 'dirty and defiled'.

Becky's physical care of Kensa was good, despite the fact that she had to hand-wash all the clothes. But Becky broke Kensa's arm when the baby was three months old and, frightened of what she might do next, insisted that her daughter was taken into permanent care. A year later, a second daughter, Nessa, was the victim of a cot death, caused probably by a combination of the erratic heating system, which led to the baby being too warm, the advice then in vogue to lay babies face down, passive smoking and heavy city pollution. By the time her third baby, Tressa, was born, Becky had been rehoused on a well-planned estate, in a detached house with a small garden near a thriving community centre and a range of facilities. She had escaped the protection gang and could manage financially because she was able to keep her own money. There were no problems with Tressa, who flourished and developed well.

Social cultural perspectives

The social-culturalist approach to child protection does not define 'culture' simply in terms of the traditions and inheritance of particular race or nationality, but uses the term to denote the pervading values of a particular society. Social-culturalists argue that the dominant values in a society can either encourage or deter abusive behaviour. Gelles and Cornell (1985) are among the proponents of the social cultural view, believing that there is a level of domestic violence to partners, children and dependent older people which is condoned by the absence of any real efforts to oppose it. Gil (1970) shares this perspective, and acknowledges that the prevention of child abuse requires cultural and legal prohibitions against the physical discipline of children and a change in 'child rearing philosophy and practices' (p. 141).

Physical abuse

The morality of accepting the physical assault of children must be seriously questioned in a society that does not accept physical assault on the majority of citizens. In Britain, flogging is no longer an acceptable method of controlling members of the armed services or maintaining law and order. There is a general revulsion against more powerful groups in society beating dependent or less power ful people, whether it is men justifying the beating women, or white people claiming the right to assault black people (see Fryer, 1984). It defies logic that only in the case of children, arguably the one group too small to hit back and the group most vulnerable to long-term physical damage, is physical attack condoned and even encouraged by society.

Sexual abuse

In relation to sexual abuse, Ennew (1986) highlights the use of women and children as sex objects in society, which is sanctioned unofficially. Child pornography is outlawed, but sexual images of women dressed as children in gymslips or in very short, frilly dresses with big bows in their hair and called 'baby' or 'girl', abound. In this way, the use of children as sexual partners is not discouraged by society. Kitzinger (1994) advances the view that there is 'the need to challenge broader social attitudes towards sexuality and violence' (p. 246).

Physical neglect

Attitudes to neglect in Britain are influenced by the fear of appearing 'judgemental' or restricting parental autonomy (see Stevenson, 1996). This is in contrast to cultures in which neglect is viewed more readily as mistreatment because 'In Arab society there is an emphasis on the parent's sacrifice of his or her needs for the sake of the child's needs. Therefore lack of provision or care for the child's needs is considered as a violation of the social norms about parenthood' (Haj-Yahia and Shor, 1995, p. 1216).

Emotional abuse

The widespread experience of emotional abuse, with a prevalence rate in the UK of about 29 per cent (Doyle, 1996, 1998) can be attributed to the considerable acceptance of verbal abuse, threats, humiliation and denigration towards children that is displayed in public, as observed by researchers in England (Yule, 1985) and America (Davis, 1996). While there is widespread acceptance that children should respect adults, there is no demand for reciprocal respect.

Reconstructing children and childhood

The rich variety and complexities of human existence are such that there is a natural tendency to make order out of apparent chaos. One result is that people with physical and physiological differences are categorised: male/female, black/white, child/adult. But the exact physical demarcation between adult and child is not easy to distinguish and has therefore changed from generation to generation and between cultures. Infancy is clearly a very different state from the relative physical independence of the older child and adults. However, once a child is able to walk, talk and co-ordinate sufficiently well to undertake self-care tasks, the difference for many societies has been one simply of size and experience.

Aries (1962) argues that, in medieval times in the West, only the very youngest and most dependent of infants and young children were regarded as 'children': 'As soon as the child could live without the constant solicitude of his mother . . . he belonged to adult society' (p. 125). Postman (1983) argues similarly that before the development of the printing press in the mid-fifteenth century the divide between children over the age of about seven and adults was imperceptible. Not only have there been different constructs of childhood in the past, but there are differences between cultures. Anthropologists offer insights into different social constructs of childhood in different cultures. Benedict (1955) points to cultures in which the 'child' or young person is given the respect and dignity that Western society reserves for adults. She observed power relationships in some cultures that are not ones of dominance–submission but of reciprocation:

> Travellers report wonderingly upon the liberties and pretensions of tiny toddlers in their dealing with these family elders. In place of our dogma of respect to elders, such societies employ in these cases a reciprocity as nearly identical as may be. The teasing and practical joking the grandfather visits upon his grandchild, the grandchild returns in like coin.
> (p. 25)

The age at which children obtain adult status is markedly different from culture to culture. Some societies do not have a distinct age of maturity beyond the evident incapacity of an infant and toddler; all are treated with respect, and expected to undertake those responsibilities with which they can cope physically and emotionally.

Hendrick (1990, 1994) traces how modern Western childhood has been constructed from different forms since the eighteenth century. The child was viewed as either the depraved inheritor of original sin whose will had to be broken, or as born innately good. This latter view led to a romantic belief in the innocence of children sentimentalised during the Victorian era, but still with reverberations today. The tension between needing to keep children in a state of innocence and yet protect them from exploitation results in ambivalence towards self-protection campaigns.

Negative constructs of children

Pilcher (1985) argues that the positive physiological features of children: health, energy, vitality and enthusiasm, are seen as something they will 'grow out of' (p. 35). With the exception of health, their other features – energy, vitality and enthusiasm – are viewed negatively. Too much energy and vitality is regarded as disruptive. At every turn children are demonised or seen as a destructive nuisance – whether in the shop slogan 'W…'s monster sale. Bring your little monsters', or a railway advertisement 'Little devils go for only £2', or a multi-national chain of toy shops, making substantial profits from children: 'We reserve the right not to admit unaccompanied children'. Hart (1988), writing about the prevention of emotional abuse, urges a 'positive ideology' of children. As long as young people are demonised and seen as a problem, abuse will be justified. Children and childhood need to be reconstructed in a less negative (but unsentimental) light, and their positive features valued.

Children as objects

Pilcher (1995) also notes how children are absent from sociological theory and research: 'Children and childhood have been viewed in an "adult-centric" way . . . the dominance of functionalist perspectives has meant that children have mostly been studied in terms of their *socialization* into adults' (p. 31). Children as active, reactive and interactive individuals who play a part in shaping the social world have largely been overlooked. Similarly in psychology, children's development has been studied as a means of understanding adult functioning. The preoccupation with 'child development' suggests that children are semi-adults – imperfect and incomplete human beings who only reach full perfection on achieving adulthood.

Authors of social science books (including Pilcher, 1995; Hayes and Orrell, 1998; Gross, 2003) refer constantly to a child as 'it', and yet when writing about adults of unknown gender they will use alternative strategies. This is not to condemn individual authors, but rather to highlight just how far children are objectified by society and treated as objects of study by researchers and academics. Practitioners are equally likely to treat the child – inappropriately in the view of Butler-Sloss (1988) – as 'an object of concern' (p. 245) rather than a fellow human being and citizen.

Children as parental property

Another tension that has not been fully resolved (Farmer and Owen, 1995) is between the view that children are the property of their parents and the alternative view that they are people with rights independent of their parents. 'Well into the nineteenth century children were by law defined as the father's property, as of course, were wives' (Gittins, 1993, p. 96). Even today, children still sometimes seem to be regarded as the property of their parents, and should not be 'taken away' or tampered with unless the parents have in some way forfeited their rights over their property. In contrast, the Arab philosopher, Kahlil Gibran (1923) wrote:

> Your children are not your children.
> They are the sons and daughters of Life's longing for itself.
> They come through you but not from you,
> And though they are with you yet they belong not to you.
> (p. 81)

Children as citizens with rights

Pilcher (1995) observes:

It is largely taken for granted that the lives of 'children' (chronologically defined as those under 16 years of age) should be organized in a radically different manner from the lives of 'adults'.

(p. 32)

Children are legally controlled in what they may or not do based solely on their chronological age. Holt (1975) comments that:

we act as if the differences between any sixteen-year-old and any twenty-two-year-old were far greater and more important than the differences between someone aged two and someone aged sixteen, or between someone aged twenty-two and someone aged seventy.

(p. 21)

Many adults are vulnerable, but the basic philosophy with adults is to give them full rights unless it can be demonstrated that they cannot safely exercise those rights. Arguably, it is logical that there should be the same basic rights for children, which can be exercised as soon as the child shows competence, and which should only be restricted where the child cannot safely exercise them.

Anti-discriminatory and anti-oppressive practice

The concept of children's lack of competency and physical immaturity has, according to Pilcher (1995), led to the differential distribution of power, responsibilities and resources between children and adults. With the development of the 'privatized nuclear family' children have increasingly been subject to almost absolute parental authority and control. Hockey and James (1993) also argue that groups of people, such as children and older people receiving pensions, who are largely prevented from participating in the labour market, are seen to have a lesser claim to personhood.

Social workers are urged to embrace anti-discriminatory practice in relation to adults, but the need to do this in relation to children is not fully acknowledged. Although Thompson (2001) discusses ageism, in most works exploring anti-discriminatory practice little mention is made of children as an oppressed group requiring an anti-oppressive approach. It is to be hoped that, just as student social workers would be challenged fulsomely if they defended the right of men to beat their wives or wrote about an adult with learning disabilities as 'it', they will be similarly challenged when they defend the right of parents to assault their children or describe a child as 'it'.

Having examined the contexts relating to child protection, the next three chapters explore individual, family and group work, which can be undertaken by professionals, especially those with only modest training or experience and constrained by limits on time, space or facilities. These chapters are designed to offer practical guidance and encouragement to a wide variety of workers and are not confined to 'experts' in specialised settings. The suggestions have all been tried, tested and found to be helpful by myself and by colleagues, including those in local authority settings.

putting it into practice

Activity 1

Consider the sentence '*Children usually have close bonds with their parents.*'
Now rewrite the sentence in the singular, that is, '*A child usually . . .*'.
Next, consider the sentence '*Parents usually have close bonds with their children.*' Again, rewrite the sentence in the singular '*A parent usually . . .*'.

This is not a test of grammar! Instead it is a test of how you think about children. Do you think about them as fully human? Or do you view them as 'objects of concern'? Look at your two singular sentences. Did you use the personal pronoun 'it' to refer to a child in the first sentence, but use a possessive adjective – that is, 'his or her' – or retained 'their' for a parent. 'It' used with children is extremely inappropriate. Think of sentences where the singular personal pronoun might be used for other vulnerable groups – for example, people with learning disabilities, or asylum seekers. You can see how totally unacceptable it is to use 'it' in a sentence such as 'When an asylum seeker is forced to leave its country . . .' Similarly, children are fellow human beings, and it is discriminatory in the extreme to apply to anyone, whatever their age, the personal pronoun we normally reserve for animals and objects. →

Activity 2

Look again at the section on policy perspectives. Using Table 4.1, try to determine which policy perspectives appear to have informed child-care policies in the past? The policy perspective may change over time. If you are familiar with current child-care policy, you can also undertake this activity in relation to contemporary policy.

The purpose of this exercise is to help demonstrate that work with abused children can be facilitated or constrained by social policy. Appreciation of the impact of policy on practice will help practitioners to tailor their involvement in line with policy or, if possible, challenge policies that appear to be overly constraining.

Further reading

An enlightening book providing a clear social and historical context is Corby (2000), while perspectives on child care social policy are discussed by Harding (1997). Contextual issues are also covered in Foley *et al.* (2001). Children's rights are encompassed by Franklin (2002). Prevention and family support is explored in Colton *et al.* (2001). The involvement of children in the protection process is discussed by Davies *et al.* (1995).

5 | Working with individual children

Abused children are so often imprisoned in a world of fear, mistrust, self-denigration and isolation long after the abuse itself has stopped. They will therefore benefit from work aimed as releasing them from the misconceptions and negative emotions described in earlier chapters.

Victims of abuse who present as severely disturbed will require skilled therapy. It is not the purpose of this book to teach general child-care workers about psychotherapy or similar interventions requiring specific training. Children needing this form of treatment are usefully referred to specialist agencies. However, the majority of abused children and their siblings can be helped through various forms of direct assistance, well within the capabilities of child-care workers.

The word 'therapist' is used here to indicate the person who is offering structured, direct help to enable the child to come to terms with what has happened. This help can embrace a variety of methods based on a wide range of theoretical perspectives. The term should not be confused with the word 'psychotherapist', which usually indicates a purely psychoanalytic approach.

The focus of this chapter is not on the investigative process, procedures, parental perspectives or policy. There are a number of publications looking at these issues (examples include Cleaver and Freeman, 1995; Farmer and Owen, 1995; Gibbons *et al.*, 1995; Calder and Hackett, 2003). Instead, it concentrates on the therapeutic needs of children once an investigation has elucidated the situation. However, investigative and therapeutic work are closely allied, so much so that a well-conducted investigation will begin the helping process. Conversely, therapeutic interviews can become the start of an investigation if, during therapy, a child discloses that the severity or extent of the abuse was greater than first thought. Many of the suggestions will therefore apply as much to investigative work as to therapy.

Working with diversity

Children from all sectors of society can be abused. There is no single type of child who is exempt from maltreatment. Therefore, inevitably, helping professionals will work with a diverse range of people, including those from minority ethnic groups, asylum seekers, traveller children and children with a range of disabilities.

Kennedy (2002) outlines key issues in relation to children with disabilities. There may be communication problems, not all of which are readily anticipated, such as the difficulties she encountered when her own sign language was different from that used by a deaf child she was helping. She recommends a communication assessment at the outset as well as the use of facilitators, and the co-working of disability and child protection workers. She also highlights the emotional impact of having a disability *and* experiencing abuse.

Other issues relating to working with diversity are integrated throughout this chapter.

Requirements of the therapist

There are two opposing views of the type of people able to help abused children. At one extreme, it is held that only 'experts' should be allowed to work with them; while at the other extreme it is maintained that anyone can do so. Certainly some expertise is required, but this can be acquired by workers with skills in other areas that are transferable to child abuse cases. Some professionals cannot relate easily to children, and these should bow out gracefully from direct work. Children can readily sense an uneasy adult and will believe that they are the source of that unease, compounding their feelings of guilt and unworthiness. Conversely, as illustrated by Frank Beck (see Kirkwood, 1993), there are people who are extremely good at relating to children but who readily capitalize on these abilities to exploit them.

Therapists should be comfortable with children and adolescents and should be able to tolerate:

● sitting, kneeling, or even lying on the floor;
● biscuit crumbs and paint falling on their clothes; and
● displays of violent behaviour and strings of swear-words.

A lively imagination, inventiveness and a willingness to learn from the child are additional requirements. Above all, the worker must respect children and acknowledge that they should be given the same dignity, value and right to know what is happening to them as is given to adults.

An ability to communicate with children is obviously required. Simply talking may be adequate when counselling adults but is insufficient with children. As Piaget's theories indicate, younger people need to relate abstract concepts to concrete reality. They communicate through play, spontaneous body language and actions. On the other hand, even young children appreciate the opportunity to talk, ask questions, and listen to explanations. One eight-year-old began a therapy session by asking if he could 'talk first and play later'.

Some children will require the therapist to have specific skills in communication, including those who have physical impairments that restrict speech and hearing. A number of children may not be familiar with the English language. In such instances, advice may need to be taken from specialist workers or people who know the child well, and toys and materials adapted to individual needs. Practitioners also need to be aware of possible undiscovered disabilities such as dyslexia, which may mean that children are unable to read or write as proficiently as their chronological age would suggest.

Despite the recognition that some children will not perform in a way expected of their chronological age, knowledge of normal child development will help in the choice of age-appropriate toys and activities. Abusive parents sometimes have over-high expectations of their children, and workers will only add to the child's self-doubt if they also demand too much. A therapist with a good knowledge of child development will also be able to assess how far development has been impaired.

Working with abused children requires emotional resilience. Some adults may find the child's pain unbearable, resulting in an avoidance of any discussion of the abuse itself and a superficial interview. But this can give children the impression that they have been involved in something so dreadful that it cannot be discussed. Moreover, practitioners unable to bear the pain shown by victims may blame them because the children's suffering seems more bearable if they have 'deserved it'.

Inevitably, there will be a number of therapists who were themselves abused in childhood, and for some the distress of the child becomes their own distress. But if they have been able to come to terms with their experiences, they may have valuable insights to offer. Workers who were not abused do not have this advantage and may have difficulty understanding the victims' perspectives. Nevertheless, their relative detachment can be of value, as long as they are able to use their imagination, powers of observation and natural sensitivity to respond appropriately.

Therapists who are themselves parents may find the mistreatment suffered by children who look like their own offspring hard to cope with. Alternatively, they may over-identify with the abused child's parents, particularly if they come from the same social group or the child behaves in a way that any adult would find difficult to tolerate. However, practitioners who are parents may be more comfortable in the company of children and more readily recognise unreasonable parental behaviour.

Consideration also needs to be given to the cultural heritages of the child and the therapist. Kadj Rouf (1991a), who has a white mother and Asian father, reflected 'I wish someone who understood my culture and abuse could have come and talked to me and my family . . . how being abused affected me in terms of my Asian culture.' The ideal is to give children a choice – whether or not they wish for a therapist of the same culture. But where this ideal is not possible, there are two important principles. The first is that children should not be denied individual work because there is no worker from the same background, and second, workers should be sensitive to issues of cultural heritage, and should endeavour to find ways of addressing these where they are important to the child.

The gender of the worker requires careful consideration. A child abused by a woman may be unable to tolerate a female worker, whereas one who has only experienced female company may be uneasy with a male worker. It is ideal if, in the initial stages, the child's wishes and fears can be met by a choice of a worker of the appropriate gender. Later, the child can be introduced to a worker of the opposite sex, thereby learning that not all people of the feared gender are abusive and uncaring. But when considering the gender of the therapist, cultural issues need to be addressed. For example, in some cultures it is uncommon or even unacceptable for adolescents to spend time alone with a member of the opposite sex.

One fear, especially for male workers, is that they will be accused of molesting the children during therapy. Young people who have learnt that all relationships with adults lead to sexual activities, may misinterpret actions by the therapist. To overcome unwarranted accusations, sessions can be witnessed by a supervisor, using a video monitor or a one-way screen. A video camera, or even an audio recorder similar to those used for police interviews, could be used to tape the sessions. Another option is for a familiar adult to stay in the room with the therapist and child.

Whether the therapists are male or female, young or old, parents or non-parents, new to the work or experienced, they all require a competent, supportive supervisor. This is particularly important because some therapists, who have forgotten their own childhood mistreatment, will start to recall it because a client's distress can be a powerful reminder of their own. Doyle (1986) outlines the problems faced by professionals in this situation and suicidal feelings cannot be discounted. The supervisor should be prepared to listen and discuss with the therapist the impact of her or his experiences, but rather than offering direct therapy could usefully help to identify an acceptable counsellor. A supervisor trying to act as counsellor may create considerable role confusion, while the needs of the client may be neglected in the face of the overwhelming emotional demands of the worker being supervised.

Planning individual work

Invariably, abused children and their siblings will benefit from individual work. This may take place before, or in conjunction with, other forms of therapy such as family or group work. One-to-one work is directed towards:

● listening, showing respect for and understanding the child's views;
● allowing expression of feelings in a safer context than in a family or group session;
● communicating positive messages to the child;
● enabling the child to adopt new roles; and
● 'protective behaviours' – that is, teaching the child he or she has a right not to be abused in future.

Individual work can vary in depth, content and setting. For example, severely neglected children may require many sessions simply learning to respond to stimuli, play with toys and relate to one person before they can cope with any other help. Some older teenagers may welcome counselling and the opportunity to talk with no play element, whereas others may welcome the opportunity to play freely and recapture some of their lost childhood. Individual therapy will therefore have to be tailored to the individual. The suggestions in the rest of this chapter should only be followed after the specific needs of each child have been considered.

Before individual work can start there is the planning stage, which includes such matters as duration, frequency, choice of personnel and location.

Duration and frequency

Duration applies both to the number of sessions and to their length. A single session may well be worse than none. Children who share aspects of themselves about which they feel ashamed may, if no follow-up is offered, conclude that they are so awful that the therapist does not want to see them again. Usually a minimum of four sessions is required, but however many are planned there should be provision for an extra meeting in case the child reveals something unpleasant in the final planned session. The worker can use the additional meeting to show the child that he or she is still liked and accepted.

When the sessions have lasted beyond a few months it is worth assessing whether the child would benefit from the deeper experience of psychotherapy or the wider experience of a therapeutic group.

At least two hours will have to be allocated for each session, although much of this is for preparation and evaluation. An initial period should be set aside for the therapist's mental and emotional preparation. Even if there is access to a proper playroom, time will be needed to ensure that materials appropriate for the particular child are to hand. After the session it will take at least half an hour for the worker to assess, evaluate and record what has happened. He or she should also be allowed some time to relax and unwind before starting on the next task. This leaves approximately one hour for direct contact with the child. This period may be shorter, especially in the early stages if the child is uneasy in the one-to-one situation, or longer for children who need time to settle.

Sessions may also be longer if the worker chooses an activity such as taking the child out for a meal. These excursions can provide new stimuli for neglected children who have not had experience of them, or a relaxing environment for children for whom such activities are familiar. However, therapists need to reflect on whether over-reliance on excursions is an avoidance of deeper communication.

Sessions are usually held once a week, preferably on the same day at the same time. Some children benefit, particularly in the early stages, from more frequent contact, especially younger ones, for whom time passes slowly and who need to build up a comfortable relationship as quickly as possible. Towards the end of therapy, sessions may be reduced, particularly if family or group work is planned to take the place of individual interviews.

Allocating tasks

If transport is needed to ferry the child to the session, it is preferable that the therapist is not expected to drive. It can seem economical for one person to undertake both tasks, but workers need all their energy for the therapeutic session. Some workers report that clients talk to them more readily in the car. This, however, usually indicates that there is something wrong with the interview. This could be that the child does not like a lot of eye contact when talking – in which case, communication can be through a pretend telephone or sitting side by side. Children might feel more secure that conversations will not be overheard in the car – in which case they can be encouraged to test the soundproofing of the interview room or play background music to counter the fear of being overheard.   Apart from evident safety aspects on busy roads, another reason why a worker should not double as a driver is that the session then lacks a proper start and finish. Beginnings and endings are important in all forms of therapy.

A careful decision has to be taken over whether the worker is also to be involved with other members of the family, or with a group to which the children or their relatives belong. The worker may find that there are conflicts of loyalty if he or she helps other family members, but on the other hand there may be conflicts with colleagues if he or she does not.

Location, materials and environment

Sometimes there are good reasons for undertaking individual work in the child's own home. But often it is more appropriate to use an alternative location, because in the family home children may feel the ties of loyalty binding them more tightly, preventing them from disclosing further abuse or from expressing anger against family members. In a foster home or residential setting, the children may wish to distance themselves from their former unhappy experiences and will not want them introduced into their new environment. If work has to be undertaken in the home, then unless children make a specific request to do so, their own bedroom should not be used. They should be allowed to preserve a 'safe space' where they can relax without the intrusion of painful reminders. Workers also have to consider whether interviewing a child in a bedroom could be interpreted adversely, leaving they themselves open to accusations of sexual impropriety.

The interview room should be comfortable, soundproof and not a thoroughfare for other people. The floor should have a clean, soft covering. Easy chairs, a coffee table and cushions are all useful. If play work is to be undertaken, too few toys are better than too many. It is important that the child is not overwhelmed and distracted by an abundance of play equipment. Spare toys and equipment such as computers or televisions, not intended for use, are best kept out of sight in bags, a cupboard or in boxes well out of reach.

Play materials and play space need to be safe. Protections such as fireguards or electric socket covers may be needed, while small parts representing choking hazards will have to be removed when planning for very young clients. Children of any age, in distress, may well start to suck or chew play materials, so lead paint and anything that is dangerous if swallowed should not be used. Children may become very angry or excited, so sharp implements, very hot radiators, fires and similar hazards must be avoided in case the children fall or bump into these.

Jennings (1999) also advises having some aprons, old shirts and smocks available to protect children's own clothing. In addition, dressing-up clothes are often welcomed by children and need not be unduly elaborate.

Equipment and toys need to be appropriate for each child. It is essential to have a mix of black and white dolls and play figures, as well as toy animals, for example, that do not represent any particular colour. Books should be chosen to reflect the multicultural nature of our society. But a play session is not the place to foist political correctness on children. If a black child selects a white doll or a white child chooses a black one to represent themselves, that is their choice and should be accepted without comment. One white, blonde, blue-eyed six-year-old chose a black, brown-eyed action-man figure. This was hardly surprising, because the star player of his favourite football team was black. Similarly, a range of toys traditionally associated with specific genders should be available, and if girls wish to play with cars or boys with dolls, that is their prerogative.

It is important that people with disabilities are not invisible in reading and play material. There are some specialist dolls available but there are also popular brands of play figures with wheelchairs and other visible disabilities. Such toys all need to be available to all children because they may well have in their family or circle of acquaintances people of a different culture or colour or with a disability, and may wish to play-out scenes to include them.

Older children may seek the comfort of playing with toys associated with an earlier stage. It is therefore useful to have a range of materials, including those associated with babies and toddlers, so that they can choose them, free of the fear of being ridiculed.

There should be easy access to a sink and toilet as well as to a room where a familiar adult accompanying the child can wait. This should include wheelchair access and provision for people unable to walk far or climb stairs. It must be remembered that mobility can be an issue for the children or for their carers. Finally, it is also preferable that the same room, looking more or less the same, is used for each session.

Starting the session

When children first arrive they should be introduced to anyone they do not already know, and then be given time to familiarise themselves with the geography of the building, unless sessions are held at their school or other places familiar to them. It is important to check that the children know the whereabouts of a hand-basin and toilet.

The next step is to ensure that the child does not feel isolated and trapped with the worker. This is particularly important in sexual abuse cases, where he or she might have been closeted in a room with an adult, engaging in sexual activity. The similarities between the abusive and therapeutic scenarios might lead the child to fear abuse, this time by the worker. The child can be reassured by people monitoring the situation through a video or screen, although equally effective is the availability of a trusted adult in a nearby room. The child is given permission to go to that adult whenever he or she wants to. If there is no adult available, the best alternative is to show the child the way to Reception, and again give him or her permission to leave the room and go to Reception at any time.

It is useful to start the work of the first session by asking the child to write labels for the doors of the therapy room and of the room where the familiar adult is waiting, or labels showing the way out to Reception. This has a number of benefits. First, it emphasises to children that they can leave the room and will not get lost. A label such as 'Jane's room, please keep out' demonstrates that the therapy room is the child's territory for the duration of the session, which increases feelings of security and of being special. While the children are writing the labels, their ability to use pen and paper can be assessed. Those unable to write can draw a picture of themselves and their familiar adult. One four-year-old said she could write and proceeded to put obscure symbols on the labels. These were pinned to the doors because the child knew what was meant and was happy with them. Another option is to use stickers or stencils for the labels.

Care has to be taken to place the labels on the doors at the appropriate height. Usually this is at the child's eye level. However, one thirteen-year-old who had been neglected and had consequently failed to grow properly was indignant when the label was placed at her eye level and said, 'What are you putting it there for? I'm not a child, you know.'

An important preliminary is an establishment of boundaries. Geldard and Geldard (1997) emphasise that the 'child–counsellor relationship should be safe' (p. 9). They advocate three rules for children, namely that they are not permitted to hurt themselves, the therapist, or any property. It is perhaps advisable to have joint rules. Neither the child nor the therapist will hurt themselves, each other or any property. Another important rule is no touching that makes either participant uncomfortable, such as the touching of private parts. Whether referred for sexual abuse or not, in the safety of the playroom children may start to act out sexually abusive experiences or test out what is appropriate sexual behaviour. If the 'no uncomfortable touching' rule is established at the outset, children can gently be reminded of the rule if they attempt to touch the therapist inappropriately, rather than meeting a sudden, unexpected rebuff.

It is important to ensure early in the first session that the children understand why they are attending, and what they can expect from the worker. It is worth asking them why they think they are coming. A frequent response is 'Don't know', even when it is known that they have already been prepared for the session. This is often because they are rather confused about what is happening and are afraid of giving the 'wrong answer'. It is worth clarifying the reasons by asking questions: 'Have you been feeling sad?' The child nods. 'Do you think that coming here is something to do with feeling sad?' Children who show no desire to offer an explanation can be told in a direct way, but any implication of fault is to be avoided, for example, not 'Because you told your teacher daddy was hitting you and making you sad' but rather 'Because we heard that your daddy was hitting you and making you sad.'

At the beginning of the first session children need time to play freely and explore any toys. This helps them to relax and feel comfortable. Allowing children free play will also show the worker which toys they like best. In the case of those teenagers who do not want to use toys, a general talk about their hobbies and interests serves a similar purpose, helping them to relax and become familiar with both worker and setting.

Provision of a drink and biscuits is another useful preliminary. Making a drink and finding the biscuits can be used in subsequent sessions as an opening ritual which children often find reassuring. Experience shows that sometimes they consume neither drink nor biscuits until the end of the session, but it is worth having them available during the interview. Zarina, who had been moved constantly from one foster home to another, used her drink by pouring it on to the table. She then put a little plastic duck on the 'pond'. Then a towel, the 'drying machine', dried up the pond. The duck had to move constantly to a new pond each time it was dried up.

It is important to ensure that the same toys are available for a particular child from session to session. Zarina played the 'duck and drying-machine' game repeatedly for weeks. She would have been devastated if the plastic duck had been lost, as she searched anxiously for it at the beginning of each session, so care had to be taken to keep it safe.

The preliminaries having been completed, it is time to start the core work. It is often helpful to begin by asking the children to draw their families. Such drawings reveal a considerable amount of information about their view of themselves and their family relationships. The names given to various father figures can be demonstrated in those families where a mother has a number of co-habitees and vice versa. Interpretations must, however, be made with extreme care; a nine-year-old who was not very adept at using pencils drew her mother as being much larger than her father. This was not because the mother was more important than her father, but simply because she had difficulty drawing her mother's shape and kept redrawing the lines until the figure became very large.

Older children may prefer to draw up a family tree. This usually involves going back as far as possible in the family history. This exercise can reveal hidden worries; for example, one teenage boy commented, 'Uncle John was no good. He was sent away from home because he stole money. I've had to leave home so I guess I'm as bad as he was.'

BASIC Ph

Workers are often perplexed when activities that work supremely well with one child fail to engage another. The work of Mooli Lahad (1992) offers some explanation of why this happens, and how failure to engage can be avoided. He has developed a theory and approach to work called BASIC Ph. This has its complexities, and workers would be well advised to attend several days of a training course before using the approach. However, in essence it has a straightforward logic.

From his extensive experience of working with traumatised adults and children, he observed that people have a range of coping mechanisms and these are based on beliefs (B), affect (emotions) (A), social relationships and support (S), the use of imagination (I), cognition (C) and physical activity (Ph). While ideally people will martial all these mechanisms, for most people one or two will be prominent. The practical application of this theory is that, in the initial stages, children will be more successfully engaged if the therapist utilizes the children's own survival mechanisms. A child using imagination and physical activity for coping will quickly engage with a therapist offering therapy through imaginative, active games. Another child, who copes using social relationships and cognitive processes, will be happy to talk issues through with the worker but will feel uncomfortable and possibly alienated by exhortations to engage in imaginative games.

Individual children's prominent coping mechanisms are assessed by helping them to devise a 'six-part story'. This story is usually drawn or painted, but other media such as clay, fuzzy felt or drama can be used. The child is then asked to describe the story, and their words faithfully recorded. The nature of the story and the types of words used indicate the child's preferred way of coping. A decision about appropriate activities and materials for individual sessions is then made on the basis of initially harnessing the child's most prominent coping mechanism.

The difficult aspect of this method is the scoring of the words, because care has to be taken not to make judgements through the use of interpretation, and some words may be difficult to categorize, hence the need for therapists wanting to use this method to attend a training course or refer directly to publications by Lahad (for example, 1992).

The helping process

There are a number of components of the helping process in relation to abused children and their siblings. These include:

● establishing trust;
● the exploration of feelings;
● messages to counter misconceptions; and
● the acquisition of new roles and protective strategies.

Establishing trust

The most important task of the therapist is to watch and listen to the children, allowing them to express, both verbally and non-verbally, their fears and feelings. At first sight this seems a relatively simple task, but there are many factors that inhibit abused children and have to be overcome before they can express any strong feelings.

They may not be able to trust anyone, and here again an understanding of Erikson's stage theory is useful. The worker has to prove that he or she is trustworthy. Being open about what is happening will help. As the Cleveland Inquiry report (Butler-Sloss, 1988) recommends 'Children are entitled to a proper explanation appropriate to their age . . . and given some idea of what is going to happen to them' (p. 245).

The therapist should be introduced by his or her name and job title, not as 'Aunty Y' or 'a friend'. The comments of Fraiberg (1952) are still valid:

> Sometimes, with the uneasy acknowledgement of the differences in the relationship of adult and child clients, we feel that it is necessary to go under an assumed name for the benefit of the child. In this way a social worker may refer to himself not as a 'caseworker' but as a 'friend'. Unfortunately this avowal of friendship may be received cynically by the child.
> (pp. 59–60)

It is worth reiterating that when recording equipment or one-way screens are being used, they should be shown to the children. They have as much right as adults to raise objections and have the equipment switched off or the curtains drawn across the screen. If a child is very interested in, or upset by, the camera or screen, the time spent allowing him or her to play with them may help to satisfy curiosity and allay fears.

The worker also needs to be honest in relation to the issue of confidentiality. The children can be assured that only people who are in a position to help either them or others at risk will be allowed to know what the child does or says in a session. Complete confidentiality cannot be guaranteed, because during therapy children may indicate that they or another child was more seriously injured or mistreated than first thought, and this will require the involvement of investigating agencies in response to the new allegations. The Cleveland Report, again, recommends, 'Professionals should not make promises which cannot be kept to the child, and in the light of possible court proceedings should not promise a child that what is said in confidence can be kept in confidence' (Butler-Sloss, 1988, p. 245).

Another aspect of confidentiality is that some of the work will inevitably be very emotive and bring distressing memories and emotions to the fore. The child may seem calm and unaffected during the session, only to react with substantial distress afterwards. Carers need to be able to understand the reason for and nature of the children's reactions. Workers should therefore give some thought to what information those responsible for the day-to-day care of the child require in order to cope with any subsequent problems.

Exploring emotions

Children need to be helped to describe at least some aspects of their abuse if their emotions are to be understood and their experiences accepted. Assuming the matter has been properly investigated, there will be no need for the worker to extract precise details from the child, but some aspects have to be shared. Children might be encouraged to begin by using a dolls' house or a drawing of their home to say which rooms they disliked and where they felt safe. Dolls or modelling clay figures representing the family may help them re-enact events, or they may prefer to describe what happened through a puppet or cuddly toy. Children can also be persuaded to talk down a 'no-secrets' telephone, which is simply a disused or toy telephone decorated to look special.

'Anatomical dolls', which have representations of genitals, help sexually abused children to reveal their experiences. However, in legal proceedings, they have been viewed as the equivalent of 'leading' questioning, so it is wise to clear their use with the appropriate local authority managers and legal department. If used, they should be introduced, with clothes on, to the child as special dolls that can help children who have had uncomfortable experiences.

Despite the need for openness, workers are wise avoid 'pressing the bruise' – recognising when a child does not want to pursue a particular line and noticing 'the triggers to withdrawal' (Compton, 2002, pp. 406–7). These may be moving to another activity, rushing around, becoming very still and silent, changing the conversation or leaving the room. There is a difficult balance to achieve, because 'Pressing too hard for overt responses may lead to distortion, even lying' (Compton, 2002, p. 407). However, it may be fear, shame or guilt underlying a child's reluctance to share experiences, and these feelings need to be sensitively and gently challenged.

Children may be inhibited by both imaginary and well-founded fears, some of which can be anticipated and allayed. Victims whose abuse has involved their bottoms and other private parts may worry that they will be in trouble for using 'rude words'. Using books like *A Very Touching Book* (Hindmann, 1983), which contains cartoon sketches of naked bodies, can help.

Erikson's theory helps us to understand the prominence of shame, doubt and guilt for many abused children. Workers can demonstrate that they accept such matters without condemnation by playing with a whoopee cushion, sharing moderately rude jokes or by encouraging messy play. Sticky poster paints for hand and finger pictures, or sand and water, provide delightful sensations and can be used to show how the therapist is unperturbed by mess.

On the other hand, if given too much freedom, children may fear that the situation will run out of control. The worker has to demonstrate that some limits will be maintained, by, for example, finishing on time, insisting that the mess is eventually cleared up and being gently firm if the child's behaviour becomes unmanageable. On the other hand, there will be occasions when control is difficult and objects get broken or spoilt. It is therefore advisable to avoid using anything valuable that cannot easily be replaced.

Guilt may also prevent children from expressing their feelings. A non-judgemental attitude on the part of the therapist is essential, and this also needs to be maintained in relation to any activities of the perpetrators described by the child. It is fine for the worker to say, 'You have the right to be angry with her' if the child shows anger against an abusive mother, but not to say, 'I'm really angry with your mum'. This is because the children's feelings towards their abusers may range from the intensely loyal (the Stockholm syndrome theory again) to the ambivalent. Children may believe that any adult who expresses anger against their abuser will think them stupid for feeling affection for that same abuser.

Anger is often a powerful emotion experienced by abuse victims. This may not be directed towards the perpetrator. Often it is turned against themselves in the form of self-denigration and depression. There are games and exercises designed to help children express anger safely and direct it towards those with whom they have a right to be angry. For example, children choose a doll to represent the abuser and are then encouraged to express anger against the doll. Similarly, they can model or draw a representation of the abuser then screw it up, toss it away or throw objects at it. Some children do not find this direct expression of anger easy. One girl, for example, preferred to keep winding a toy turntable round and round, getting faster and rougher as she talked.

Marie, Lloyd, Helen, Sarah and Roy all emphasized how isolated they felt. Through stories, children can be helped to realize that they are not the only children who are abused. Story-telling is an important therapeutic tool. Compton (2002) writes, 'The most influential books are usually those chosen by the individual child and it is useful to be aware of the children's favourite or least favourite texts' (p. 413). Doyle's (2002) research found that among UK 9–13-year-olds, the most popular book choices were ones in which children were initially mistreated or abandoned, including J. K. Rowling's (1997) *Harry Potter*, Jacqueline Wilson's (1992) *Tracey Beaker* stories and Roald Dahl's (1997) *James and the Giant Peach*. Additionally, there are some special texts, designed for children in distress, such as the truly wonderful *The Frog Who Longed for the Moon to Smile* and similar stories by Margot Sunderland (2000). Finally, there is spontaneous story-telling by either therapist or child, such as Lahad's six-part stories. Children can also benefit from acting out or role-playing the stories (see Jennings, 1999, pp. 59–64).

One reason for their isolation is that the victims have been so hurt that they have built up a protective barrier. Here, a hedgehog puppet is useful. They can be shown how the hedgehog is so prickly on the outside that nobody can cuddle him when he feels in danger. But underneath he is soft and if he feels safe he can get close to people.

Another useful exercise helps children to explore their feelings. The worker draws three blank heads. The children are then invited to fill in the faces, drawing expressions to demonstrate how the people are feeling. Often they choose sadness, happiness and anger. The therapist can join in by filling in additional sets of faces with other feelings such as embarrassment, fear and loneliness. When the child has finished, the worker can ask 'What makes you angry?' 'What used to make you sad?' 'What would make you happy?' Where appropriate, the therapists can use their own drawings to explore additional emotions.

Workers familiar with bereavement counselling will recognise that expression of fear, guilt, anger, isolation and confusion is often associated with loss and the process of mourning (see Kubler-Ross's (1970) theories). Abused children are 'bereaved' because they will have lost, at the very least, security, self-esteem and unconditional love. Many games and exercises that help bereaved young people express feelings will also be of benefit to abused ones.

Countering misconceptions

Children are often very confused about what has happened to them, and a child who has experienced a lot of life changes can be helped through a 'life-story book'. This involves recording important information about the child and events in the child's history, illustrated by documents and photographs. Experience has shown that a loose-leaf book is preferable because additional information can be inserted at a later date. Other media can be used, such as a video or audio tapes. This work is a task undertaken as a partnership between child and worker, and therefore the child is given choices such as whether the accounts of events are written in the first or third person – for example, 'My first school' or 'Sean's first school'.

Children's experiences of sexual abuse can be clarified through the use of simple 'facts of life' books. Twelve-year-old Emma, whose father had attempted to rape her older sister, could not understand why there were restrictions on her father's activities. Concepts such as exploitation and the denial of informed consent were difficult for her to grasp. However, she was told, with the help of diagrams and age-appropriate books, how her father's actions might have resulted in her sister having a baby by him. The girl and worker then tried to draw a family-tree including the hypothetical baby. As she saw how difficult it would be for the baby to sort out parents from grandparents or aunts from sisters, she began to appreciate why her father's abuse of her sister had to stop and some of her confused feelings subsided.

One feature shared by most abuse victims is that they have a low opinion of themselves, and low self-esteem is reinforced by the feelings of shame and guilt. There are a number of ways of assessing the extent of the damage to abused children's self-esteem. One way is by asking them whether or not they like their name. It can be useful to explore this theme further by asking if they know why they were given particular names and if they have a family nickname. Sarah's father, to show his contempt for his wife and daughters, gave the two girls nicknames usually given to boys.

Young people who do not like themselves are often reluctant to look in a mirror or draw or model themselves. Slow, gentle encouragement to look in a mirror or to create an image of themselves as attractive is one way of helping enhance their self-esteem. Older, imaginative children may like to draw themselves as trees then explain the drawing. One teenager drew herself as a stark tree with no roots or leaves but with big patches on the trunk. This provided an eloquent witness to her feelings of bleakness, loneliness and of being defiled by the abuse. In later sessions she was able to add leaves, draw in roots and erase the patches. This exercise reflected her progress towards a happier self-image.

Children, including non-abused siblings who witness abuse, often blame themselves for the mistreatment and need to hear they were not to blame. If they are old enough to understand analogies, these can be used to illustrate the concept of adult responsibility. They could be asked who would be to blame if an adult stole some money then bought sweets for them with the stolen cash. This demonstrates that even if the child appears to enjoy or benefit from the activity he or she is not to blame. However, they need to understand that they bear a degree of responsibility if they bully or sexually exploit other children. Ryan (1989) warns of the dangers of taking the messages of not being to blame too far and generalising it to all situations.

When children have managed to draw attention to the abuse, they need to hear that:

● they have done the right thing;
● that by their disclosure they have helped to protect themselves and other children;
● they may have enabled their parent to receive help; and
● it is not their fault if disclosure has led to their removal into care or the disintegration of the family.

Some children believe that they are so defiled by the abuse that they are 'untouchable'. Helen backed off from her father who wanted to cuddle her in a kindly, fatherly fashion because she felt too dirty and guilty to be held by him. People in distress can benefit from physical comfort, and it can demonstrate to abused children that they are not untouchable. But for some victims, gentle touching and cuddling is either unknown and alien, or interpreted as a preliminary to sexual activities. Workers can begin to give physical comfort through the use of puppets. Their hand touches the child's hand, both safely enclosed by the puppet. Sometimes puppets are not needed as the child is able to accept a reassuring squeeze of the hand or shoulder. However, children should always be in a position to move away from any embrace, and therapists need to ensure any physical contact is not intrusive and cannot be misinterpreted.

New roles and protective strategies

In any family or group, members will take different roles – parent, leader, facilitator, clown. When the family or group has problems, individual members become scapegoats, victims or 'invalids'. Abused children usually have a negative role and, like Lloyd, begin to behave in a way that fulfils this. Others, like Marie, take on a parenting role, comforting their mother or father and protecting siblings. If, during therapy, children do not learn new roles they will remain as parent or scapegoat when they rejoin their original family, or join a new one. For example, if their role was a parental one, they need to learn that responsibility lies with adults and not with children. One eight-year-old, Lisa, who had tried to protect her younger brothers and sisters, devised a game for herself. Using a farm set, she put all the baby animals into an enclosure. She then chose two strong carthorses and placed them with the baby animals. She said that it was for the adult animals to look after the babies. The worker was able to endorse this and they played the game over and over again until Lisa was convinced that both she and her siblings had a right to be looked after by adults. Children can also be encouraged to role-play possible situations in which they might be exploited or bullied, learning through these how to defend themselves.

Although children may not be able to resist someone more powerful, they nevertheless have a right to try to protect themselves and to seek help. One game emphasises this right and encourages them to think about the people they can turn to for assistance. The child chooses something, such as a box, to represent a castle of which they are sovereign. With them in the castle are all the people and things they like – their parents, ice cream, going to the cinema, their brothers and sisters, grandma, birthdays. Outside the castle, threatening the child's happiness and security, is an army of all the people and things they do not like – spiders, a certain teacher, ghosts, crocodiles, being hit, 'daddy drinking and being angry'. Between the threatening army and the castle is another army of all the people who can protect them – their parent or grandparent, a favourite teacher, a social worker, the police. This theme can be adapted to concur with the child's interests, such as a farm threatened by wild animals, a planet under attack from aliens, a train with three carriages or a boat under fire from pirates.

Children can be made aware of their rights to be looked after and not harmed. In the case of children who have been sexually abused it is worth ensuring that they understand the difference between benign and inappropriate touch. There is good touching, like stroking a cuddly toy, bad touching such as being pinched and 'not good' touching which makes them feel uncomfortable and embarrassed, especially when it involves their private parts.

Finally, children need to learn that there are different types of secrets, and some should be kept and others should not. If by keeping a secret they, or someone else, is hurt or made to feel uncomfortable, then the secret should be told to someone who can help. If they fear that there will be terrible consequences from telling someone, they can be encouraged to use a trick like crossing their fingers to ward off any evil. Unfortunately, this may not help those abused children who have a realistic fear of being taken away from home or upsetting their parents, but it will help in cases where the threat is unrealistic – for example, where a child is told he will be turned into a frog if he discloses.

Ending individual work

The end of individual work may signify that the child is unlikely to see the worker again. Therefore, care has to be taken to end on a positive note. Sometimes, in the last planned session children divulge potentially damaging information. In these cases the worker needs to arrange a follow-up meeting to demonstrate to the child that she or he has not been rejected, nor has the worker been harmed by anything the child has said. For workers short of time, a brief, informal follow-up or even a phone call is better than nothing at all.

If there are only to be a few planned sessions, the child can be told at the outset that they will see the worker for, perhaps, six meetings. After each meeting there is a reminder of how many sessions are left. If the number of sessions has been left open, then, as the worker feels termination is drawing near, the child should be prepared for the fact that he or she will be moving on to a new stage.

Most children enjoy individual work despite the fact that sessions can be painful for them. Sometimes they become attached to a certain toy, but it is rarely possible for them to keep it. Generally, children accept the fact that play equipment has to stay where it belongs. However, they can be given a photograph of their favourite toy or a memento. Compton (2002) suggests a personal set of coloured pencils for the child, which can be kept by the child when sessions end. Children can also become fond of their therapist. Again, they can be given a photograph or some other memento such as a badge, button or a drawing. Workers may wish to draw a picture of a trophy and give it to the child as a prize for being brave. This exchange is particularly useful if the worker has asked to keep some of the child's drawings.

Finally, individual therapy may help victims cope for a time, but sometimes they need assistance later in life when they reach another significant point such as the birth of their own baby. Such events can awaken long-buried memories and emotions. Children can be prepared for this by being told that occasionally people's problems recur, and when that happens they have the right to seek support again.

Individual work is unquestionably of considerable value. However, it is not the only way of intervening therapeutically. The next chapter explores working with children in the family context which can provide a useful supplement or alternative to individual work.

putting it into practice

Activity 1

This activity revolves around the 'castle' game suggested under the heading 'New roles and protective strategies' earlier in this chapter. The basic principle of the game is that children explore who and what they can draw upon to protect themselves from the people, things and situations that may threaten their well-being. →

Think of any child with whose interests and enthusiasms you are familiar. Then try to devise a version of the game that reflects these. For example, the castle could become Hogwarts for children who love Harry Potter, or a boat threatened by pirates for the sailing enthusiast.

The purpose of this exercise is to show that, when working with children, it is important to tailor games and activities to the child and not expect the child to fit in with set ideas. Most play activities can be adapted to reflect individual children's interests and enthusiasms.

Activity 2

Reflect on the same game. How might the game be adapted to include children in diverse situations? For example, how could you adapt it for a sight-impaired child? How could you ensure that it is relevant to a child from a minority ethnic group? If you have specialist skills, for example working with children with an autistic spectrum condition, could you adapt the game to make it meaningful for them?

The aim of this activity is to illustrate that play work can be offered to nearly all children without huge quantities of specialist materials. Although there are some very valuable, specially designed play items for specific groups, it is often feasible, given understanding and imagination, to adjust general activities so that they are suitable for specific needs, and for children from a variety of backgrounds and heritages.

Further reading

A particularly useful book is by Geldard and Geldard (1997), initially providing a summary of all the theoretical approaches to working with children, referring back to earlier authorities in the field such as Axline (1947) and Oaklander (1978). Story-telling as a therapeutic tool is explored by Sunderland (2000); in addition, she has produced a truly wonderful series of illustrated stories for distressed children. Playwork specifically with abused children is detailed in Doyle (1987) and Cattenach (1993). An appealing 'facts of life' book has been written by Mayle (1973). Children can be helped to express themselves by using the unconventional colouring book by Skinner and Kimmel (1984). Law and Elias (1995) have designed a book for parents and professionals working with children with communication difficulties.

6 | Working with children in the family context

Child maltreatment occurs primarily within the family, therefore it is appropriate to help children in the family context. This chapter is not designed as an in-depth study of family therapy. Instead, it looks at the type of family-based assistance that a social or other welfare worker, with some understanding of family dynamics, can undertake. Dogra *et al.* (2002) point out that, in mental health work with young people, 'Although most workers do not have formal family therapy training, they draw on some of the key concepts to inform their work which is one distinction between family-based work and family therapy undertaken by professionals with specialist training' (p. 244). All the suggestions in this chapter are rooted in the practical experience of 'family-based work'. Those who used the methods described were all busy professionals with many other demands on their time and with few facilities. They did not regard themselves as 'experts' but they acquired an expertise by careful planning, accepting guidance from colleagues, understanding underpinning theories, practising techniques and by always being sensitive to the feelings and needs of the families.

While family work is valuable, Sinead, an adult survivor, cautions against too rigid an adherence to it:

My father was a complete tyrant. By the time I was about five years old and my brother was nine we were completely withdrawn. We would not move or talk without permission. We could not play and were very quiet. My parents were having problems so we went to stay with an aunt. She was so worried about us that she referred us to a psychiatrist. Because my parents would not be included in any therapy, the psychiatrist said that nothing could be done. He would not treat children without their parents. So we were offered no help and just left to get on with life.

Sinead reflected on how valuable some form of play therapy or individual work would have been, and how much she had needed the opportunity to play spontaneously, express her terrors and frustration in safety, and have the attention of an understanding adult without fearing punishment. The ideal is to intervene in the whole family, but if this is not possible the child should not be abandoned; individual or group work is better than nothing.

Working with diversity

In a multicultural society, abused children will be from a range of ethnic backgrounds. Problems are encountered when workers and the family are from different cultural groups and Lau (2002) highlights the value of families having therapists from the same ethno-cultural backgrounds. But that is not always possible. Often, it is a simple matter of statistics. In one area there may a dozen cultural groups, but only a couple of workers able to engage in family work. Moreover, in small towns, the family may not want a professional who is a member of the same small community 'knowing their business'. Furthermore, the families themselves may be comprised of different cultures. But those from minority ethnic groups should not be denied family work simply because they cannot be matched to a worker from the same group. As Lau points out, in 'cross-cultural family work we need to address the areas of tension in the interface between the therapist and family from a different ethno-cultural and racial background' (p. 93). There are differences in race, symbolic and belief systems, family structure and organisation, and language and communication – all of which need to be acknowledged.

Maitra and Miller (2002) also explore many of the dilemmas of working with non-Western cultures in Western society. A worker may seek a consultation with a professional from the same cultural background as the family. However, care is needed because, as Maitra and Miller (2002) acknowledge 'culture is an evolving process, rather than a static one' (p. 128). People from minority cultures and religions are sometimes dismayed by the pronouncements in the name of their culture of others from their group. Those who interpret beliefs more liberally may be deeply irked by the assertions of the more orthodox or fundamentalist members, and vice versa.

There is cultural diversity not just between non-white families or white non-British ones but also within white British families. There are micro-cultural differences between different socio-economic classes and even different geographical areas. For example, working in one coal-mining area we found that we excluded the grandmother (the mother's mother) at our peril. Invariably, these women exerted a powerful influence, whether by undermining any intervention or by offering valuable support.

There are other aspects of diversity. Families in which parents, children or both have a significant disability will have their own unique ways of functioning in order to manage the disability. There may be communication issues, so a co-worker who can use the same communication system may be necessary (Kennedy, 1990, 2002). Consideration has to be given to adapting materials so that they can be used by all family members, and in some families wheelchair access will need to be considered.

Finally, there is a huge diversity of family structures, with not just male/female parents but also two same-sex parent figures or single parents of either sex. The reasons for single-parenthood can be equally diverse and the reason for it will have an influence on family functioning. A much-loved deceased parent will have a different impact on the remaining family than one who has left willingly to find happiness with a new family. There are reconstituted families with numbers of step-parents and siblings. Some children will have two equally important families. Extended family members may be significant, with several generations living in the same home. Account has to be taken of the role and impact of all potential and absent family members before undertaking family-based work.

Benefits and problems

Benefits

Attachment theory teaches us that children can become attached to abusing parents. They often want the abuse to stop but crave the abuser's love. In many cases, abusive parents have a degree of affection for their offspring despite maltreating them, and family work can develop this into a more protective affection. It can transform an 'ineffective' family into one that can provide a 'good-enough' environment. This is in the child's best interests because children have a strong need to belong to a family; a need reinforced by the emphasis on the 'family' in advertising, in school, on television, in magazines and comics.

A further advantage of family work is that, according to systems theory, if there is a change in one member, the system as a whole will be changed. For example, during family work, a parent who has accepted responsibility for the abuse can be helped to express this to the children. This results in the children being relieved of guilt and shame, marking the beginning of a new, honest, open form of family communication.

Treating children without treating family members can lead to problems, because abused children learn to adapt to the maltreatment, and while their behaviour may seem to be 'abnormal' when seen in the family context it is in fact a normal adjustment to an abnormal situation. Jessica Cameronchild (1978) was physically and emotionally abused from her earliest years. As a teenager she attempted suicide. She was hospitalised and given intensive therapy. She wrote:

> The psychiatrist and hospital staff were, in fact, setting up a
> very futile and destructive double bind by putting me on a
> program that required me to give up defenses which were
> vital to my survival at home . . . the course of my treatment
> exacerbated the violence for my brothers at home, condoned
> our parents' past mistreatment of us, reinforced their denial,
> and augmented my futile view of the world in general.
> (p. 148)

Treating the parents without involving the children can be equally unsatisfactory. The aim of treatment for abusive parents is likely to be directed at a change in their behaviour towards their children. This is usually a long, slow process. But the children themselves will have adapted to the parents' abusive behaviour. Marie talked about learning to stay one step ahead of her father. When the parents alone are given therapy, *they* might change but their children can, as a consequence, become more confused and frightened. They were secure with the 'devil' they knew. Now they are insecure as they can no longer anticipate parental behaviour. Children who had a role as family scapegoat or surrogate parent may no longer feel of value to the parents. Consequently, they might react by trying to provoke the parent into abusing them again in order to restore the former, familiar situation.

Patterns and forms of communication are important in families. Parents given help will learn to communicate more openly and directly with the children. But if not included in the therapy, the children will again become confused. For example, an eldest daughter had protected her younger siblings. She had always acted as their spokesperson, bearing the brunt of her father's anger and violence. Intervention resulted in the parents trying to relate more directly to the younger children, who did not understand what was happening and became frightened and unresponsive, whereas the eldest girl felt ignored and rejected. The parents experienced frustration as their new behaviour seemed to make the situation worse. Family work, which teaches all members to learn new patterns of communication together, would have avoided these difficulties.

Problems and pitfalls

Bentovim (2002, p. 464) offers useful guidance about situations where family work is contraindicated. These include families in which there is:

- a complete rejection of the child;
- a parental failure to take any responsibility or acknowledge there are any problems;
- the needs of the parent taking primacy over those of the children;
- a combative oppositional stance to the professionals; or
- severe personality or related problems in the parents.

Even in families without the above features, problems will still be encountered. For the majority of people, the familiar is comfortable, the unknown is feared. Change often means moving from the familiar to the unknown. A sudden crisis may cause a sudden change but without any other intervention the family system will recreate the situation that existed before the crisis. Disclosure or professional intervention in an abusing family constitutes a crisis. The family may change temporarily, but once the crisis has passed the family will try to revert to the former situation. In cases of sexual abuse, the non-abusing parent may bar the abusing partner from the home at first, only to have him or her back once the case conference or legal proceedings have been completed.

A lone child-care worker is unlikely to be able to resist the powerful processes, inherent in all systems, of returning to the status quo – called 'homeostasis'. The main problem encountered by a therapist attempting to intervene single-handedly is the possibility of being absorbed into the family system. Families are adept at finding roles for people who could be a threat. Roles include 'rich uncle/aunt' – the constant provider of material goods, 'family friend' – the confidant who can be trusted to keep family secrets; or 'fairy godparent' – the person who will solve all problems instantly by magic. In some cases, the worker may become clearly allied with the abusing parent, condemning the children's behaviour as 'provocative' or 'seductive'. Because the needs and demands of its members often conflict, a single professional trying to meet the requirements of the whole family is faced with an impossible task. He or she is likely to become emotionally exhausted or will only find sufficient energy to spare for just one or two members.

A major criticism of family work based on systems theories was voiced by MacLeod and Saraga (1988) because, particularly in cases of sexual abuse, the perpetrator avoids responsibility as blame for the abuse is located in the family 'system' and therefore other members of the system – the non-abusing parent and victim – are given equal responsibility. Anyone working with families has to be clear about who has responsibility for what is going wrong; power imbalances have to be acknowledged. Parents are given considerable power over their children and they are required to use this power for the welfare of the children. In a patriarchal society, there is a strong likelihood that the father will hold the most power. If he has exploited this, then he has to take responsibility for his behaviour.

SWOT or SLOT analysis

One of the problems when assessing a family is that it can be 'pathologised' when viewed from the perspective of professionals from different, and usually more powerful, social sectors. This has been highlighted in relation to class (Gittins, 1993) and cultural heritage, especially black families in a predominantly white society (Gibson and Lewis, 1985; Howitt and Owusu-Bempah, 1994; Phillips, 2002). On the other hand, public inquiries (for example, Malcolm Page, Jasmine Beckford) suggest that child protection workers sometimes operate a 'rule of optimism', thereby failing to address family weaknesses (Dingwall *et al.*, 1983). Another risk is that practitioners ignore environmental factors and focus on deficiencies in the family rather than on adverse external circumstances.

A SWOT analysis can counter these oversights. It is adapted from analyses of service and commercial organisations. It explores the family's potential on the basis of its internal strengths (S) and weaknesses (W), while taking into account external opportunities (O) and threats (T). When working with the family it might be more appropriate to think of a 'SLOT' analysis, with weaknesses being conceptualised as 'limitations' (L). In ideal circumstances, the family members undertake the exercise themselves, identifying the strengths and weaknesses or limitations within their own family, and the opportunities and threats of their environment. They are the people most familiar with their family and how the environment affects them.

Undertaking a SWOT or SLOT analysis does not call for elaborate preparation, all that is needed is a sheet of paper divided into four boxes, or four separate sheets. Each box or sheet is given one of the four headings: strengths, weaknesses/limitations, opportunities, threats. Under each heading a list is made of the family attributes in terms of strengths and so on. Sentences, key words or agreed symbols can be used. The diagrams can become more complex as some weaknesses might be redefined as strengths, or threats redefined as opportunities and so on.

Practitioners can assist the family in several ways. First, there may be strengths or weaknesses that an outside observer can identify but which the family cannot see or do not want to acknowledge. Second, the practitioner may have had early warning of law and policy changes or other environmental factors of which the family are unaware. Third, the practitioner can work with the family on ways to build on identified strengths, to diminish the effect of weaknesses, or to turn a weakness into a strength. Finally, the practitioner can help the family to devise strategies to take advantage of environmental opportunities and protect themselves from external threats.

There are some families that, for whatever reason, are unable to undertake this evaluation themselves. In these instances, the SWOT analysis can be used as an assessment tool by the practitioners and fed back to the family. However, even in cases where the family has been unable to participate fully, the opportunity for family members to add their own perspective can be given.

The great advantage of a SWOT analysis is that account is taken of the family's strengths, whether drawn from their traditional culture, extended family members, their past experiences or a combination of the strengths of individual members. Families differing from the mainstream are less likely to be pathologised, because members are given the opportunity to identify strengths. But it also provides an opportunity to be honest and clear about family weaknesses or limitations. Finally, the impact of the environment is acknowledged so that realistic proposals can be explored.

Joint family work

While the advantages of family work appear to outweigh the disadvantages, a major drawback is that a lone worker can become absorbed into the system. There are, however, a number of strategies that can prevent this. Most require some form of joint work – that is, professionals working closely together to achieve the same objective. This is not the same as interdisciplinary co-operation: a family doctor and an education welfare officer (EWO) can work in close co-operation, but the primary aim of the doctor is the good health of the family whereas that of EWO is the proper education of the children.

Various models for joint working will be suggested in this chapter, but it is acknowledged that sometimes local resources are such that there is only one therapist available for the whole family. In these circumstances, other agencies such as the school and primary medical team have a duty to help the family worker by monitoring the situation as far as possible and passing on relevant information. Too often such agencies expect the worker to seek information from them instead of volunteering potentially important details.

Practitioners who are having to work on their own should also have a supervisor able to provide an objective view of the family and of their involvement, thereby helping to guard against over-identification with part of the family, and emotional exhaustion. In instances where the supervisor has insufficient knowledge of both family work and child abuse, the worker should be encouraged to seek the advice of a consultant. The supervisor and consultant will then liaise in order to ensure that their approaches are consistent and are not presenting the worker with further conflicts.

Co-working

Working with a co-therapist is a tried and tested approach to both group and family work, and offers considerable advantages to workers and family alike. Two workers are more able to resist the pressure of the family system. It is more difficult for a family to find roles for two new members than it is to absorb just one.

The needs of all the different members of the family can rarely be met by just one worker. Even where there is a single parent with one infant it is often difficult to give attention to both. A mother who is abusing her baby is likely to be under great stress and make considerable emotional demands. She is unlikely to tolerate the worker spending a lot of time relating to the baby because she needs the attention for herself. Yet the baby will also be distressed by the abuse he or she has suffered, and by the mother's tension. The therapist needs to build up a relationship with the infant, becoming a familiar figure for the baby, who will then accept handling or examination by the worker should this become necessary.

A useful role-play exercise illustrates the problems inherent in the one-therapist-for-one-family approach. Participants represent a family consisting of a single distressed parent with two children who are being neglected, plus a lone social worker visiting the home in order to alleviate the family problems. Invariably, participants report that the visit made matters worse, especially for those playing the parts of the children. If the worker gives most of his or her attention to the parent, the children feel doubly neglected. However, if the worker spends time with the children, the parent feels his or her needs are being ignored or treated too lightly, and thereby experiences more distress. This situation is avoided if two therapists are involved, one attending to the needs of certain family members while the other concentrates on the remaining members. Often the split is between the parents and children, or between the males and females in the family. Sometimes the needs of one person are so overwhelming that one worker concentrates all efforts on that person, leaving a colleague to attend to all other demands.

Co-working, especially where there is conflict between two parents, can provide a model of adult co-operation and open communication for the parents. The two workers can demonstrate to both parents and children that mutual respect and joint decision-making is possible. A further incidental benefit is that, in potentially violent situations, being accompanied by a colleague offers some protection.

The drawbacks of this way of working are self-evident. Both therapists must be competent and confident. A defensive co-worker who becomes possessive of the clients and keeps trying to 'score points' over his or her colleague is a destructive force. Two workers can start to mirror the split in the family, identifying with different factions and thereby reinforcing family conflict. The abused children may not only be criticised and scapegoated by siblings and parents, but also by two workers. One worker absorbed into the family system is bad, two workers thus absorbed is more than twice as bad.

In hard-pressed social work agencies there may not be sufficient staff to allow for co-working. One solution is to link up with another agency such as probation, education or health departments. However, probation officers, community teachers and health visitors may well have different objectives, constraints and priorities, making any commitment to long-term co-work impossible.

A further problem is that of supervision. Co-workers, even from the same agency, may have different supervisors. There are a number of solutions. One supervisor may agree to have a prime role, while the second simply retains an overview in order to satisfy the demands of accountability. Alternatively, there may be periodical four-way supervision sessions. A third alternative is the appointment of a totally independent supervisor just for a particular case.

Where the therapists have the same supervisor there are still problems about whether they are seen individually or together. The best solution seems to be to have individual sessions, with arrangements made for the co-worker to be available for part of the time. Another solution is to alternate individual and joint sessions.

Recording and case accountability also present problems. If the therapists are from different agencies they will keep individual records, but if they are from the same agency then only one is needed. Alternate recording of sessions evens out the workload but can cause confusion. The most practical solution appears to be for one worker to have prime responsibility for recording, booking facilities, liaison with other agencies and all other aspects of case management.

Live supervision

As its name implies, in live supervision supervisors are present during the family session. They are more than mere observers; their task requires active participation (Blakey *et al.*, 1986). Live supervision can take a variety of forms depending on the facilities available. In its simplest form one supervisor sits quietly in a corner of the same room as the therapists. At the other extreme, a group of colleagues can view one or two workers through a one-way screen or video monitor link. Experience shows that both therapists and family members are able to put cameras, screens and additional people to the backs of their minds and concentrate on the task in hand.

An important principle is that all family members should agree to the involvement of the live supervisors. They should understand what is happening and accept that there will be interventions. It is made clear that the live supervisors are there to assist the worker who, in consequence, will be able to help the family more effectively. The family is usually introduced to all the supervisors, although if there is a group watching through a screen or monitor it can be more appropriate to introduce a representative of the group while inviting the family members to meet the rest after the session.

There are planned breaks during the session, when supervisors and therapists can reflect on events so far, and when changes in direction may be suggested. In addition, there will be *ad hoc* interventions by the supervisors if the workers and family members seem to be stuck or unnecessarily avoiding important issues. These interventions can be conveyed by telephone, through earphones or perhaps by a knock on the door. Notes for the session and for case files are usually made by one of the supervisors, thereby leaving the therapists free to focus all his or her energy on the direct work with the family.

This model can prevent therapists from becoming part of the family system. For example, in one case a single male worker was helping a family of mother, father, Martin their teenage son, and three younger children. The supervisors were able to observe how the worker was being made to take over the role of forceful father in relation to Martin instead of enabling all the family members to express themselves and adopt more appropriate roles.

Live supervisors can also ensure that the therapists do not focus on the needs of certain family members to the exclusion of others. In another case, the supervisors observed how the two workers were focusing attention on the parents and failing to see their daughter's anger and distress, which was such that the supervisors entertained the possibility that she might attempt suicide.

There are problems inherent in live supervision, including the threat posed to therapists by the presence of colleagues who are observing and analysing their work. Related to this is the fear of therapists that they will lose credibility in the family's eyes because they seem frequently to be 'corrected' by other people. But experience shows that workers who have supervisors in whom they trust find live supervision reassuring. Once it becomes an established practice in a team, members can come to depend on it to the extent that an unsupervised session can be unnerving. A family can be helped to appreciate this method of working by the explanation that two or more heads are better than one.

Another problem is the time and commitment required of more than one worker. However, it is better in the long run to have effective therapy that achieves real and positive change in family functioning rather than one worker intervening to stave off yet another crisis for a time. There is little point in intervention that does not give effective help to abused children. Live supervision has a further advantage as it is a little more flexible than co-working, because the live supervisor does not have to be the same person each time. It is important to clarify that live supervision and co-working can be combined, with co-therapists being live supervised.

It is perhaps worth highlighting the fact that live supervision is not used exclusively in family work. It can be used with groups, pairs and individuals. However, it is especially valuable, as has already been noted, as a protection against the therapists becoming absorbed into a very powerful but ultimately destructive family system.

Case-team manager model

It has been shown that different family members have differing therapeutic requirements, yet it is difficult for one or even two workers to give effective help to each family member. The danger is that the needs of the quietest, most withdrawn person will be overlooked, yet he or she may be the most distressed individual, who might, in silent despair, attempt suicide. Alternatively, the needs of the youngest member, especially one not yet able to verbalise feelings coherently, will be ignored. A total team approach therefore has much to commend it. But there are problems when several workers are involved. Teams can mirror the conflicts between individuals and sub-groups in the family, thus creating more confusion than already existed. Intervention can become disorganized because there is no clear line of responsibility, and the needs of some members can be ignored.

In order to avoid the obvious pitfalls, a case-team manager can be appointed. He or she has had no direct involvement in the family but has a vital role in co-ordinating the intervention of the individual workers. The case-team manager is responsible for organising meetings of the workers at acceptable intervals. Fortnightly or monthly meetings are appropriate, depending on the stage of the case. During meetings, the therapists outline their involvement subsequent to the previous meeting and report on the situation of the family members to whom they were committed. The case-team manager then:

- helps the workers to reflect on what was happening and to plan for the next stage of the work;
- identifies conflicts between workers, especially when they mirror conflicts within the family;
- is responsible for keeping a record of all sessions and meetings; and
- arranges the date and venue of subsequent sessions and meetings.

When this model is used, the family have to be kept informed of what is happening and are made aware of the involvement and function of the case-team manager, although he or she does not usually meet the family. If the family ask to meet the manager this can be arranged most usefully towards the end of the intervention.

The main objection to this model is that it appears to be costly. However, each worker can be involved in several of these cases concurrently because the emotional demands are spread between a number of different professionals. One worker trying to achieve the same objective on his or her own would have found the task over-whelming and time consuming. Instead of spending several hours each week contacting fellow workers by telephone, efforts are co-ordinated by a fortnightly or monthly two-hour session, with only brief practical telephone calls in between when necessary.

Supervision is another problem, especially if the supervisor of any therapist feels threatened by the case-team manager's influence. It is inappropriate for agency supervisors to attend case manage-ment meetings. Their presence would make the sessions too large and unwieldy. Nevertheless, occasional additional meetings can be arranged at which individual supervisors can voice their concerns.

A final problem that might affect team functioning is that of hidden agendas. For example, one of the team might have been abused in childhood and might not have resolved this background problem. When a case-team manager suspects that there may be a personal issue involved, he or she should arrange for an individual discussion with the worker to sort out a way of helping other team members appreciate what is happening.

Family centres

Joint working is a characteristic of family centres. There are many different projects that are called family centres. In one model, the total family attends a centre on several days a week. The objective is to help family relationships, provide play and structure for the children, and training in parentcraft for the parents. At family centres, the parents may be taught practical skills such as how to cook, budget family finances, maintain hygiene and establish a routine. In relation to their children they learn about normal devel-opment so that they do not have unrealistic expectations of the youngsters and are helped to appreciate their children's needs for stimulation and security.

Facilitating communications

In family work it is important that all family members take part. This means that people beyond the nuclear family may have to be included if they are an important part of the family system. A common example is that of the grandparent who frequently looks after the children and has tried to protect them. It also means that all members who are present at a session need to participate

actively. It is easy for the more assertive family members to dominate the session, while the youngest or quietest are virtually
ignored. There are a number of techniques which ensure that everyone present is included.

Verbal techniques

One way of including all family members in the verbal component
of the session is by using circular questioning. One member is asked
how another member reacts or would react in a given situation.
The accuracy of the answer is checked with the second member.
For example, instead of asking the father what he does when the
children arrive home late after school, the youngest child could be
asked, 'What does dad do when you come home late?' The child
may say, 'He gets angry.' The father is then asked, 'Do you get
angry?' The father might explain, 'Yes, because I'm worried about
them when they are late.' When one family member is very quiet,
another can be asked on that member's behalf. A subdued teenage
girl, Mandy, who had been physically and sexually abused by her
stepfather understandably refused to say anything during the first
few family sessions. The workers, having in vain already asked
Mandy directly, asked another family member, 'What would
Mandy reply to that question if she was able to do so?' She was
then asked if the response was accurate. She only had to nod or
shake her head. Although she could not talk she was able to voice
her opinions through other family members.

Care has to be taken in this form of questioning. Asking about
the feelings of others poses difficulties for family members. The
question, 'How does mum feel when you do that?' posed to a cynical adolescent may well be met with the response, 'Dunno, why
don't you ask her yourself?' It is marginally better to ask, 'How do
you think mum feels?' thereby inquiring about his opinion rather
than directly about another's feelings. When the response, 'Dunno'
is still forthcoming it is important not to make the young person
feel condemned; so instead of saying irritably, 'But I'm asking you,
not her' the most appropriate response might be a move to a new
area of questioning.

Members can also be encouraged to ask each other questions.
The therapist might say, 'Tommy, can you ask mummy what she
would like to happen?' Tommy may refuse. The mother is then
invited to ask Tommy why he does not want to ask her. Yet again,

care has to be taken, especially with children, to guard against making them feel at fault if, because of shyness or anger, they cannot participate.

In some families it is evident that the emphasis has been on condemnation and punishment. One useful exercise is to ask each family member in turn to say something they like about a chosen member. Then the spotlight moves on to the next person, so that each family member has heard something nice said about themselves by every other member. The therapist usually takes a turn in saying something positive about each family member but it is not necessary for the worker to be in the spotlight unless the family makes a specific request to that effect.

Non-verbal communication

One way in which the therapist can influence family dynamics is by changing the seating plan. This is obviously easier to do in a designated interview room rather than in the family's home. In one case where the daughter had taken over her mother's responsibility for her family, father and daughter used to sit together, while the mother and young son sat together leaving chairs in between each dyad for the workers. After a few sessions the workers insisted on the mother and father sitting together, allowing the two children to sit next to each other. One aim of the work with the family was to distinguish between adults who were the parents and children who should be free of parental responsibility. The change in places provided a tangible demonstration of this. When a family member who should have been present at the session is absent, he or she can be included in the session by being designated an empty chair.

Family members can be asked to communicate non-verbally with other members. For example, a child may start crying and the mother, if she does not do so spontaneously, can be invited to put her arm round her child. Again, care has to be taken because if the mother refused point blank to do so the child might feel all the more rejected and distressed.

Exercises, role-play and video

One exercise helps to illustrate the different perspectives of the family. Members are invited in turn to draw either themselves or the family member they consider to be most important first. This can be on a blackboard or a large sheet of paper. Members are then invited to draw the rest of the family positioned on the paper near to or distant from each other depending on how the person creating the drawing sees the family relationships. With a large family it is probably less time-consuming to represent its members as a large dot. If this exercise had been used with Sarah's family, the two sisters might have seen how they both believed that the other sister was closest to their father, thereby dissipating some of the jealousy and misconceptions that they had about each other. Furthermore, the father would no longer have been able to play the 'your sister is better than you' game. He would have had to have drawn each child at an equal distance from him or have specified a favourite. Positioning coffee cups, buttons, coloured cardboard pieces or little play figures can be used instead of sketches.

Mandy, mentioned earlier in this section, refused to join in this exercise. The workers accepted her reluctance. They said that, although they would like her to take part because her opinion was as valid as that of the others, she was perhaps not ready to do so. Later, when everyone else had had a chance to sketch the family, Mandy was again approached with the suggestion that she could tell another member or a worker where to put the family figures on her behalf. She agreed and chose her brother to act as scribe. Soon she was so involved that when her brother did not put the figures in exactly the right place she went over to the flip-chart and started drawing the family constellation herself.

Role-play is useful in helping family members rehearse what they would like to do in a given situation. For example, a family was being helped through the case-team management model described earlier. The daughter, Zoe, had been sexually abused by her stepfather. She was ambivalent about meeting him. She was frightened about being so angry that she would lose control when she met him and either attack him or dissolve into tears. Similarly Mr D was worried about his response when he met his step-daughter again for the first time since disclosure, yet he wanted to apologize to her and tell her that she was not to blame. There was a female worker supporting Zoe and a male probation officer supporting Mr D. Eventually, the workers decided that Zoe could usefully rehearse what she would like to say to her stepfather by meeting the probation officer who would represent Mr D.

Conversely, Mr D met the female social worker to rehearse with her his apology to Zoe.

Video can also be used in a similar way. After the completion of the various role-play meetings, Zoe still felt unable to meet her stepfather, yet she needed to hear him accept responsibility if she was ever to appreciate that she was not in some way to blame. A video recording was made of Mr D assuring Zoe that the abuse was his fault and showing concern for her welfare. Zoe agreed to see the video and was supported by her therapist as she watched it. She was able to see her stepfather's sincerity and was given further important evidence that she was not responsible for the abuse or the consequences of disclosure. It is vital, however, that workers ensure in any sex offender–victim communication, such as video or letter writing, that the perpetrator is not covertly threatening the child.

Finally, therapists can set tasks to be completed by the family between sessions. For example, a very isolated family may be encouraged to invite one of the children's friends to tea one evening before the next session. If the family does not manage this one week they can be encouraged to try again. If they still do not manage to do it, then the workers accept responsibility for setting a task that was too difficult, thereby avoiding giving the family any sense of failure. It is important, however, not to condone the family doing more than was asked – for example, inviting three friends for tea when they were only asked to invite one. Sometimes doing too much reflects over-high expectations on the part of the family, when the therapists are trying to instil a sense of reality into the situation. Furthermore, some families are so sure that they will fail that they attempt more than they can manage in order to ensure their eventual failure.

One slightly paradoxical task, which is designed to succeed through failure but which usually brings some humour into the situation, is to ask the family to behave in a specific undesirable way but only under certain conditions. In a case of marital discord, for example the parents are told that they must have an argument but it must be at 9 p.m. precisely on Monday evening when all the children are in bed and it must take place in the kitchen. Usually, couples find it difficult to argue to order but this exercise helps them to start thinking about the nature of their rows and how, when and why they occur.

putting it into practice

Activity 1

Try to undertake a SWOT or SLOT analysis of a family with which you are familiar. This need not be a family in which abuse has occurred. What are the strengths that the family could build on for the future? Are there any limitations or weaknesses in the family structure, and can these be reconstructed as strengths? What opportunities are available to the family? What environmental threats are they facing? What conclusions can you draw about the functioning of the family?

This activity will help you to practice developing a SWOT analysis. Sometimes it can be difficult to decide where to place certain factors; for example, is the imminent demise of an adored grandparent a weakness, a limitation or a threat? The important principle is that the categorization makes sense to both the family and the worker. As long as everyone involved is in reasonable agreement, then the technicalities of the classification of factors does not matter.

Activity 2

Using the family in Activity 1, imagine a change in its structure and context. For example, if your chosen family has a male and female parental partnership, in your mind change the parental partnership to two female carers, or maybe a single, male carer. You could change the ethnic or socio-economic background of the family members. Now try the SWOT analysis again. What differences are there? How important are these to the future functioning of the family? You can repeat the exercise, making other alterations such as the physical capabilities of the family members, or environmental factors, perhaps placing a rural family in an urban area or vice versa.

The purpose of this activity is to show how a SWOT analysis can be undertaken with a wide variety of families. It will also help you explore how far a change in just one aspect, such as whether the parent figures are heterosexual or homosexual, can substantially change the strengths, limitations, opportunities and threats facing the family.

Further reading

Sutton (1999) provides a useful introduction to family work, while cognitive-behavioural approaches to family work are outlined in Cigno (2002). Works focusing on child protection and family therapy include Elton (1988) and Bentovim (2002). A book by Hagans and Case (1990) for parents whose child had been sexually abused was warmly recommended by a mother whose daughter was raped by a teacher.

7 | Working with children in groups

Group work is a tried and tested method of enhancing the ability of people to function in a variety of settings. It has been used in recent years to help sexually abused children, and those who witness domestic violence or suffer a significant bereavement. Often these children are offered a place in a group *before* they show any symptoms of distress. An assumption is made that children who have been subjected to sexual abuse or witness domestic violence have had a potentially damaging experience warranting intervention. Group therapy is less readily used as a method of helping other abused children unless they have displayed developmental difficulties or behavioural signs of disturbance. Group work could be useful for all forms of abuse regardless of how far the children seem to be harmed by their experiences.

It is worth emphasising that this does not mean that children who have been subjected to different forms of abuse would benefit from being together in the same group. Members need to have enough in common to appreciate each other's experiences. In a mixed group, the range of areas to be dealt with can become too broad for the group to be effective. Children who have been emotionally and physically neglected may have no problems over secrecy but may have to learn about playing with others, whereas those who were sexually abused will need to exchange ideas about appropriate touching, sexual behaviour, the keeping of secrets and ways they can be protected from sex offenders' advances.

In selecting group members there are few hard and fast rules, although it is necessary to avoid the inclusion of a very disruptive child or one who is not ready to cope with group work. McKnight (1972) makes the point that:

> One thing we have found as the result of hard experience is that it is unwise to include an extremely disturbed child in

the group. The inclusion of such a child too early, and too quickly, leads to him becoming the immediate scapegoat, which can be harmful for the child and the group. It takes a very great deal of skilled manoeuvring to retrieve this situation. We tend to work with such a child by means of face-to-face play situations instead. When the child has worked through some of his problems we may transfer him to a group situation later.

(p. 134)

Working with diversity

As with all other intervention, practitioners will be aware that children come from a range of different cultural and racial backgrounds, and have different abilities and personalities. Therefore anyone planning to run a group has to consider group membership and how far any group can meet the unique needs of each child.

Thought has to be given about including a child who seems very different from the rest of the group. One child using a wheelchair or with a visual or hearing impairment will tend to be the focus of attention. Nevertheless, children who are used to coping in other groups as the only one with certain characteristics will no doubt cope within the group – an example is that of a child with a visible disability who attends a mainstream school. A further point is that children with disabilities or other obvious 'difference' should not be denied services, and therefore every attempt should be made to help them integrate into the group.

Consideration has also to be given to the cultural mix of the group. Kadj Rouf (1991a) who was the only black child in her group, recalls 'I would have felt happier if there had been more black girls in the Group'. Nevertheless, she appreciated the group and she has some suggestions for improving her experience, which could have been implemented even if no other black girls were included. Her first suggestion is that the group should address other cultures and religions, and include representations of black people in materials used, such as books and films. Second, racist comments and terms used by other group members need to be addressed. Third, the specific issues she had about her colour and culture needed to be acknowledged. This could have been done by asking all the members to share what particular personal problems they were encountering. For one child it might have been a father's attempted suicide, for another it might be a court appearance as a witness, and for Kadj it would have been coping with the fact that her father was black, leading to her desire to 'cut out the black part of me because it belonged to my dad'.

Mixing boys with girls is perfectly feasible but there will be some difficulties, particularly with the seven-plus age groups, when boys begin to have a poor opinion of girls and vice versa. Consideration has also to be given to those cultural traditions that deem the mixing of sexes unacceptable, particularly in adolescence. There may also be difficulties if there is only one girl in a group of several boys, or vice versa.

Nevertheless, it is important that children are not denied a source of help simply because the ideal is not available. Research (Doyle, 1998) found that while black families received substantial material help, their children were less likely to receive help through individual counselling or group work. The concern is that they were not offered a service because there were no black counsellors or other black children in the groups. In the real world the ideal is often not available, and where this is the case children should at least be given a choice of services.

Benefits and problems

There are a number of benefits and pitfalls associated with group work. Features associated with all groups and group work theories are well documented in a number of standard works (Bion, 1961; Konopka, 1972; Whitaker, 1985; Brown, 2000; Hough, 2001; Brabender, 2002). A focus specifically on groups for children and adolescents is provided by Dwivedi (1993) This chapter will concentrate on those aspects of group work of particular relevance to work with abused children.

The benefits

The five survivors in Chapter 2 all recalled a pervading feeling of isolation. Mistreated children often feel they are the only ones to have experienced such treatment and there must be something wrong with them. By getting to know other children who have suffered similar experiences, they learn that others share their feelings. Participants sometimes admire a fellow group member such as the nine-year-old girl who felt that another girl in her group was very pretty. Through this she learnt that abuse does not necessarily make a child unattractive. So group work can assuage victims' feelings of isolation, of being abnormal, and unappealing.

Groups provide a means whereby positive messages are reinforced. This is particularly true for adolescents, who are often influenced more by their peers than by adults. A teenage boy, told by a therapist that he is not to blame for the abuse, may take the attitude, 'You're paid to say that.' He might, however, be more easily convinced by a group of fellow adolescents all giving him the same message.

Participants who have learnt new roles in individual therapy can practise these in the group. If, for example, they have always been a scapegoat they can try out new ways of ensuring that they do not take the blame for anything that goes wrong in the group. Generally, role-play between peers is more comfortable than between an adult and a child. A further advantage of group work is that the children may feel that they are in a 'safer' environment than they are in individual therapy alone with an adult. This, especially for sexually abused children, avoids recreating the abusive scenario.

Humour is more likely to occur in a group setting than it is in individual or family work. Laughter is a good tonic and can help children come to terms with negative experiences. Marie pointed to humour when asked what helped her survive her experiences. She explained that after incidents such as the destruction of the Christmas presents, her mother and siblings were able to laugh about their father's behaviour. This made the incident more bearable as he was reduced to the status of a clown rather than remaining an ogre.

Problems and pitfalls

The main problem for hard-pressed social workers hoping to establish a group is one of resources. Group work with children, as with adults, requires commitment from at least two therapists. They need to set aside time at regular intervals for the group sessions, as well as additional time for preparation and planning, review and recording. The same room should be used on each occasion, but in many buildings meeting rooms large enough for groups are at a premium. Unless other colleagues recognise the importance of the group, the workers may find that time and again that their room is commandeered for a case conference or a training session.

Transport is sometimes a problem. In order to find enough children who have sufficient in common to make a viable group, members might have to be drawn from a fairly wide geographical area. Children cannot be expected to make their own way to meetings, yet sometimes their caretakers' ambivalence about the group means that they prove unreliable when it comes to bringing the children for sessions. It is, however, unsatisfactory if the group workers have to ferry the members themselves, because they need to be free to devote all their time and energy to running the session.

All participants have to be capable of handling the group situation. A young person must be able to relate to other children and share the leaders with others. Meanwhile, the group leaders have to be capable of working with a number of children at the same time. They require skills in both direct work with abused children and in group therapy, and above all they need to be emotionally resilient. Commenting on her experiences of running groups for small children, Eileen Vizard (1987) writes, 'From the therapist's point of view, however, a lot of experience in doing this work does not protect one against a feeling of sickness when, for instance, as happened to myself and a new co-therapist recently a 4-year-old girl turned to us in the middle of pinning on her name badge and said simply "I was raped" (p. 19). The same author went on to note, 'In theory, many mental health professionals might be able to run such groups . . . However, in practice we know that it takes more skill, and considerably more supervision, than we had originally thought' (Vizard, 1987, p. 21).

When running children's groups, we find that caregivers are often very concerned about what is happening in the group and may put their child under pressure to give details. If they are overly suspicious of what is happening, they may attempt to persuade the child not to attend. Under such circumstances it is probably advisable to provide the carer with sketchy details, thereby satisfying curiosity without breaching the child's confidences. Bannister (2002), writing about group work with abused children, noted, 'it cannot be emphasised too strongly that parents or carers should be carefully prepared for the group and also supported for its duration' (p. 494).

A major pitfall is the assumption that all problems can be helped through group work. This is not the case. A prime example is that of people suffering from eating disorders. Groups help people trying to lose weight, because the element of competition is a spur to greater efforts. Unfortunately, the same process can work in the same way with people suffering from anorexia nervosa. There is the danger that members will secretly compete to see who can lose the most weight. Anorexia nervosa is thought to be linked in some cases to sexual abuse (Oppenheimer, 1985). The idea of a group for teenage girls, who not only have the experience of sexual abuse in common but also share the problem of anorexia nervosa, is an inviting one. But, unless the group is run by someone with consummate skills (and such people do exist, but are rare), it is more likely to compound the problem of weight loss rather than help it.

Variations on the theme of group work

Sometimes there are too few children with enough in common in one area to form a viable group. Furthermore, the problems outlined in the previous section may prove too daunting for professionals who might otherwise have used group therapy. There are two methods of intervention that provide many of the advantages of group work yet avoid some of the main problems. These are 'pairing' and 'family groups'.

Pairing

As its name implies, 'pairing' refers to work with two children, who are not siblings but have much in common. Usually, they will have already had some individual help. They reach a stage where they need to know for certain that other children are abused, and consequently feel less isolated. They may also need to act out their experiences and practise strategies both for avoiding the victim role and for asserting their right to be safe and properly cared for, which is more easily accomplished with a peer rather than an adult.

One abused child is invited to meet another who has had similar experiences to him or herself. If one declines the invitation, he or she is evidently not ready to cope with the situation and should not be pressurised into doing so. If both agree, the group can go ahead. Where the same person has provided individual work for both children, he or she will probably continue as the group therapist. In cases where each child has had a different worker, a new therapist can be designated for the group work or the two original workers can become joint leaders.

Once the children are introduced and feel comfortable, they can be invited to draw up rules for the group. In individual work they may each have had different limits and expectations of themselves and the worker. For example, one child may have been used to entering and leaving the interview room at will, whereas the other child may have felt it important to ask the worker's permission. One group of two girls aged seven and nine plus one adult devised and wrote out a list which (with no apologies for the spelling) reads:

> Rools of the group
> no swaring
> only leave the room if ask
> no smoking
> no breking toys
> no hiting
> no secrets.

The last point about 'no secrets' required much discussion. The members had to draw a distinction between being honest with each other and yet having the right to some privacy. They also talked about not telling people outside the group what members had said. They agreed that if they really had to tell someone else about events in group sessions, they must discuss who they were telling and why with the other group members. This gave the worker the permission she needed to protect the children and their siblings in the event of their making further disclosures during group sessions. It also had the advantage of alerting the worker if at any stage either girl was placed under pressure by their caregivers to give an account of what was happening in the group.

In small groups with only three or four members, the absence of a couple of participants will be keenly felt. However, in the case of pairing, when one child cannot attend a session the leader can revert to giving the other an individual interview. As individual work should already be familiar, this is usually a relatively positive experience. There is, however, considerable difficulty if after a short time one child withdraws. The remaining member may feel that he or she has done something wrong, compounding the sense of rejection. It is therefore better to plan a limited number of meetings, perhaps two, to begin with. Assuming these are successful, the leaders can suggest two further meetings, repeating this process until they sense that the members are so committed to the group that longer-term planning is feasible. Alternatively, the leaders may feel that one child is reluctant to attend, in which case they can terminate the group in an ostensibly planned way.

Pairing is useful not only in alleviating the isolation of older children but also in helping younger children who have been physically or emotionally deprived and restricted. Some may have been so neglected or so inhibited by punitive parents that they have yet to learn to play, explore and experiment. Once they have learnt to play with toys and materials under the guidance of adults, the next big step is to play with other children. Pairing can bridge the gap between the comfortable but limited nature of individual play and the daunting prospect of participating in larger groups.

Family groups

Work can be undertaken with a group of children from the same family where there are three or four children within an age range of about five years. Once these children feel fairly comfortable about their situation they can be matched to a similar set of siblings. This results in a group of between six and eight children. It is difficult to assimilate three or four children from the same family into a group where all the other members are individuals rather than sibling groups, but in this way the two sets of children have a richer experience than they would otherwise have had if they were only offered help in their own family group.

One advantage is that there is an almost ready-made group. There is little of the initial awkwardness associated with half-a-dozen strange children meeting one another for the first time. The time required for the usual preliminaries such as learning each other's names is cut by more than half. Another important advantage is that the children learn that theirs is not the only family with problems of abuse.

One possible drawback is that the two different families will remain separate and the group will not coalesce; however, in practice this does not seem to happen. After a brief initial period new alliances are made that cut across the two families. Nevertheless, care has to be taken to ensure that the families are compatible and their structure suitable. It would probably not be appropriate, for example, to link a family with only one girl with another family with all boys, leaving the one girl without a female ally.

Groups for younger children

There are many principles of groups that apply to all groups whatever the age of the participants. These again are well documented in the standard works mentioned earlier. This section will therefore examine areas specific to group work with young abused children. It is, however, worth mentioning a particularly useful theoretical perspective. Tuckman (1965) presented a framework for understanding how groups develop. He identified four stages:

- *forming*, when the group first gathers together;
- *storming*, a testing of boundaries and sorting out of positions and roles;
- *norming*, when members explicitly or implicitly lay down basic ground rules; and
- *performing*, the stage at which the group is able to work on, then meet, its aims and goals.

Each stage will be reached all the more smoothly, and the storming period minimised, if there is careful preliminary planning and preparation. Later, Tuckman and Jensen (1977) added 'adjourning' to refer to the ending phase. It is important to consider this stage as carefully as the other four in therapeutic group work if members are not to feel abandoned and rejected once the group ends or they have to leave the group.

Planning and preparation

The main feature of group work with young children is that it will certainly be noisy and probably messy. Because of this, the room for meetings has to be chosen with care. It is likely that such a group will run during the day, rather than in the evening. This means that either the room has to be soundproof or well away from other people who are trying to work – unless you have remarkably tolerant colleagues. The room should be fairly easy to clean, and time has to be allowed for clearing up any mess. Access has to be considered, to both the group room and other facilities such as toilets, for people using wheelchairs or unable climb stairs.

While adult groups may need little more than a suitable room, chairs, maybe a table, pens and paper, children will require more materials. Toys, paints, modelling clay, a mirror and dressing-up clothes are all likely to be used. As with individual work, toys and materials that are not for use in a session should be kept out of sight, otherwise they can become an irresistible distraction.

The optimum size is probably about six, although two adults may cope with as many as eight children. Usually it is necessary to have two adults present, especially if the children need accompanying to the toilet. One male and one female leader is preferable. Members who have been abused by, say, their mother, will learn through the female worker that women can be kind and caring, while if they have been protected to some extent by their father they may be reassured by the presence in the group of a male helper. The two leaders represent a mother and a father figure and, for children with two opposite sex parents, this may be the first time that they experience this combination of adults communicating and showing respect for each other without either shouting or physical violence.

In groups with small children, the leaders should be directive, ensuring that the sessions do not run out of control and taking the burden of decision-making away from the children. Ruth McKnight (1972), a group worker, writes of her early experience of leading children's groups:

> My first lesson was in direct connection with my role. My experiences hitherto had been of discussion groups with a self-effacing sort of leader who was almost one of the group. The children, in fact, taught me that this was impossible in our setting and moreover it was not what they wanted.
> (p. 136)

Nevertheless, the children should be included in some decision-making – for example, they may express a preference for refreshments at the beginning of the session rather than halfway through, or they may be consulted about the introduction of a new member to the group.

Access to a group work consultant is advisable because young children's groups are fairly boisterous and it is easy for the adults to be distracted from the main issues by particularly demanding or difficult behaviour on the part of one or two members. The consultant needs to be knowledgeable about group dynamics, play work, child abuse and normal child development. The leaders should also be supervised, possibly by the consultant, but preferably by a separate supervisor who will negotiate boundaries of responsibility with the consultant.

Other arrangements to be sorted out before sessions begin are transport, refreshments, recording and timing. An additional issue is the decision as to whether the group is a closed one or whether it will accept new members. Similarly, leaders have to decide whether it will be an open-ended group or, if not, how many sessions will be held. For small children, a closed group with a fairly limited number of sessions is generally the most appropriate.

Another important aspect of planning is liaison and confidentiality. Children attending the group should have their own individual worker, who will help with practical arrangements and may be providing a child with individual therapy. Depending on the circumstances, the worker might be given full details of the child's progress or on the other hand may only be told that the child attended the session. If during a group session the child discloses something that indicates that he/she or any other person is in danger, then the leaders must ensure that a protective agency is informed.

One feature of groups of small children is that there is likely to be an informal group of parents, caregivers and social workers waiting in a nearby room. This occurs because the children are too young to take themselves to sessions and because they have a right to have a reassuring familiar adult to hand in the event of their becoming distressed. If the needs of this informal group of carers are overlooked they may well sabotage the efforts of the leaders by becoming noisy or demanding their attention before and after sessions. Eileen Vizard (1987) and colleagues solved this problem by evolving:

> the practice of having the little children's group and the care-
> takers group amalgamate for part of the last session, in
> order to sit down together and watch extracts from the
> video of the children during the proceeding five weeks. This
> has turned out to be a great success and very popular.
> (p. 18)

Finally, there is nothing more daunting or confusing for a small child than to find that, having been prepared for a group experience, he or she is sitting alone with a couple of equally bewildered group leaders. It is important to ensure that attendances are confirmed and that at least three or four children arrive together to attend the first session.

The first session

With young children, the first group session is of crucial importance. Older clients who disliked their first meeting may be persuaded to return in the hope of matters improving. Small children who do not enjoy themselves on the first occasion often resist any attempt to involve them in subsequent meetings.

It is helpful to familiarise children with the physical surroundings first. They will need to know the whereabouts of the toilet and how to reach their parent/familiar adult if they become distressed. They will also want to play with any toys present.

Once members have satisfied their curiosity about their surroundings they can be introduced properly to the grown-ups and other children in the group. Sometimes name labels are used. Various games can help children learn each other's names. One example is to have several funny hats, which children put on each other's heads. The recipient of the hat says, 'Thank you, I'm Kyle' (or whatever their name is). Once the members know each other's names they can practise by saying, 'Here you are, Kyle' when they put a hat on someone's head. Another idea is a game of catch, where a participant throws a ball of socks or bean bag to another child whose name the thrower remembers and calls out. The leaders will join in these games to ensure that no child is embarrassed due to possessing 'butterfingers', a poor memory or a forgettable name.

The next important part of the first session involves devising a set of group rules and some sharing of why the children are attending. The members need to know what they can expect of the group and what the group expects of them. The children should help in the task of formulating the rules and, as illustrated by the list given by the pair group, they may enjoy the inclusion of a few 'adult' rules such as 'no smoking'.

Suggested activities

The activities of the group will depend largely on its objectives. A group for neglected, understimulated children may start by encouraging children to explore different play materials such as sand, water, clay and finger paints. It will then move on to activities that require a joint effort such as a group collage or building a structure together. For these children, having a meal together, sitting at a table using cutlery and saying, 'Please' and 'Thank you' may be important learning experiences.

A group for those who have been subjected to physical violence will focus on helping them recognise that they should not feel guilty and ashamed. They can be invited to dress up and act out famous stories of children who have been mistreated. They can role-play self-protective behaviours. They may also need to act out angry, violent emotions, through destructive games, mock fights and throwing cushions or bean bags at hated objects. Eventually, through co-operative construction games, a group collage perhaps, they can be shown how much more can be achieved by peaceful means.

Groups for sexual abuse survivors will need to provide outlets for angry feelings. Furthermore, their members may be very bewildered about what has happened to them because, unlike victims of physical abuse and neglect, there are few fairy tales or stories about sexually abused children with whom they can identify. They may need some simple sex education in order to make sense of their experiences. But first they will need to share a vocabulary in order to communicate their experiences. In an early session the members can be encouraged to shout out their own name for the private parts of their body. They learn by this means that everybody uses 'rude' words. The exercise also gives them access to a wide range of terms to describe what has happened to them.

Abused children, whatever the nature of the mistreatment, share many negative feelings. They all have to learn to develop trust and there are games that help in this endeavour. In one game, members close their eyes and allow themselves to fall backwards in order to be caught by other group members. In the case of small children who have limitations of strength and co-ordination it will be advisable for the adults to take the role of catcher, as dropping your partner defeats the object of the exercise!

Activities suggested in the section on individual work can be adapted to group sessions. One example, already described, involves sketching expressions on blank faces, the children are then asked to share their drawings and say what makes them feel sad, happy, angry, ashamed or afraid. Finally, as Piaget's theories demonstrate, young children do not appreciate abstract concepts, so all ideas have to be illustrated in concrete form by the use of dolls, puppets, drawings, stories and games.

Groups for older children and teenagers

Much of the previous section on groups for younger children will also apply to those for older ones. For example, the optimum size will still be six to eight, plus leaders (although there have been a number of successful groups with only three or four members, or up to twelve). This section will therefore simply highlight some of the important features of group work with older abused children.

Planning and preparation

Older children who have been abused for sometime will have had longer than little children to develop a mistrust of adults, longer to adapt to the victim role, and longer to harbour feelings of anger, worthlessness and fear. There is likely to be considerable testing of the trustworthiness of the leaders and of the group boundaries. It is essential to have two leaders, one of whom should be experienced in group work, and both of whom must be emotionally resilient. It is also essential that both workers are supervised and well supported, with both supervisor and group consultant available to give assistance.

It is again helpful to have a therapist of each sex, to present a model of adult men and women working harmoniously together and to provide an outlet for the members' feelings about women/mothers and men/fathers. When helping sexually-abused girls, the male worker is likely to be subjected to periods of severe testing. In one group of four teenage girls, the male leader had to cope with cushions thrown at him, questions about his sexual prowess and 'accusations' of homosexuality when he did not respond to their sexual invitations. In another group, 'The girls were often very angry with the male therapist and expressed suspicion about his motives in running the group' (Furniss *et al.*, 1988, p. 102).

Teenagers can be shy and self-conscious. It will be difficult for them to pluck up the courage to attend the initial meeting by themselves. It may be helpful for them to come to a couple of preliminary meetings accompanied by their social worker, who will stay for the first few informal gatherings. Alternatively, members can meet each other in pairs on a casual basis prior to the initial group session so that when they do arrive for the first meeting they feel they are coming with a 'friend'.

The first session

Older children, in contrast to younger ones, are likely to show more interest in their fellow group members than in their physical surroundings, although soon after their arrival they will need to know where they can put their coats or go to the toilet. But they will be curious about the other participants' names and experiences.

One useful exercise involves finding out the meanings' of members' given names. This helps them to learn both each other's names and also something about themselves. It is fun and flattering for a David to learn that his name means 'beloved', Kumar to hear he is a 'prince', for a Sanjula to learn she is 'beautiful', or a Tammy find out that she is 'perfection'. Those with unusual or less popular names may well be encouraged to learn that it has a pleasant meaning such as Beatrice being 'bringer of joy' or Cyril 'lordly'. The leaders will, however, need to ensure that they do not cause distress to those whose names have less desirable connotations such as Doreen 'sullen', Elvis 'old noise', or Cameron 'crooked nose'.

Suggested activities

Again, activities will depend on the objectives of the group. A group for physically abused, violent teenage boys may concentrate on playing snooker without coming to blows, or learning to trust adults, their companions and their own abilities through an activity such as rock climbing or sailing.

Unless the objective of the group is purely social or narrowly task-focused on an issue unrelated to abuse, members should be helped to find a way to share their experiences. They can be invited to choose how to talk about the abuse to which they were subjected. They may decide to face the wall or window, or try to give an account following the rules of a game such as 'Just A Minute' – without repetition, hesitation or deviation.

Activities with paints, pens and paper prove useful and popular.

A group collage or painting helps participants to express their feelings about themselves and the group without being alone in the spotlight. It also assists in the process of group cohesion. Discussion can be encouraged through paintings and drawings that are then described to other group members.

Filling in a questionnaire is another activity that can help spark-off discussions and often holds an attraction for adolescents. The objective of much group work is a change of attitudes, especially self-denigrating ones. The use of a questionnaire at one of the earliest sessions and again at the last provides a means of evaluating the effectiveness of the group and gives members an insight into their own progress.

Some of the activities, such as role-play, suggested in the section on individual work and on groups for younger children can prove useful in groups for older ones. This includes play and games. So many abused teenagers will have lost the opportunity to play in a happy, carefree environment. Some of the joy of being an irresponsible child can be recaptured by holding the meetings in rooms with toys available, or arranging parties and outings to perhaps fairs or children's films. The members should, however, have a choice in such activities, because adolescents may well resent being treated in a juvenile fashion when they are aspiring towards adulthood.

Finally, the use of video equipment has proved very successful with these groups. Young people are, despite some shyness, eager for feedback on the way they look and behave. Replaying a video film of part of a session provides uncritical, objective feedback. The members may at first express some reluctance to be filmed, in which case persuasion can be tried, but a video should not be used without the group's ultimate agreement. It is also important to clarify the legal situation and issues of disposal of the tapes. There is the risk that if a member gives significant information to the group which is recorded on video, there could be demands for the tape to be shown in court in subsequent care or criminal proceedings.

This chapter and the preceding two all examined ways of working directly with children in different contexts. The next chapter looks at two further interventive, although perhaps less direct, strategies – the provision of substitute care, and the enhancing of children's resilience through the provision of social support.

putting it into practice

Activity 1

Cast your mind back, hopefully not too far, to a time when you joined a new group, perhaps when you started a new job or training course, or became a new member of a sporting or interest club. Can you remember how you felt? Was there enthusiasm tinged with apprehension? Were you 'at home' immediately, or were you made to feel as if you were in alien territory? Can you identify the factors that helped you feel more comfortable, or any that caused discomfort? How important was the physical environment, or was the attitude of other people in the group more significant?

Here the purpose is to encourage you to empathise with children and adults joining a new group. Reflecting on your own experience may help you to understand what makes people more or less comfortable when joining a group. This insight can be transferred to therapeutic practice. However, you need also to bear in mind that the personality and background of the individual, and circumstances causing them to join the group, will also influence their initial experience and maybe result in their experience being very different from yours.

Activity 2

Think back to the children's accounts in Chapter 2 of Marie, Roy, Lloyd, Sarah and Helen. Reflecting on the content of this chapter, determine how group work might have benefited them, assuming that the abuse had been discovered during their childhood. What could they have offered each other had they been in a group together?

The aim of this exercise is to help you to think of the value of group work by applying the ideas to actual cases. You may find that you can identify benefits of group work but can you also identify pitfalls. For example, the children who witness domestic violence by their father against their mother – Roy, Marie and Sarah – may well have difficulty in empathising with Helen, whose father was not abusive to either Helen or her mother.

Further reading

Hough (2001) has produced a clear, readable guide on social group work. Guidance specifically on group work with sexually-abused children is provided by Vizard (1987), Hildebrand (1988), and Leith and Handforth (1988). A major resource, including a chapter on cultural issues by Coward and Dattani, is edited by Dwivedi (1993). Ideas from the books by Smith and Pennells (1995) and Haasal and Marnocha (2000) on groupwork with bereaved children could be transferable to groupwork with abused children.

8 | Care, resilience and social support

Individual, family and group work may not be available or appropriate for some abused children, and insufficient for others. There are two other possible ways of helping abuse victims. The first is to provide substitute care – temporarily during a crisis, or permanently when the physical or emotional risks in the parental home are insurmountable. The second is to develop greater resilience in the child and augment his or her sense of well-being, especially through social support. This is particularly important in those cases of emotional abuse where there are insufficient grounds for enforced intervention but the parents are unable or unwilling to countenance any therapeutic intervention. The earlier part of this chapter explores substitute care and the later sections look at issues of social support.

Substitute care

When children die at the hands of their parents, questions are raised, such as, 'Why wasn't he taken to somewhere safe?' or 'Why was she allowed to go home?' The solution to child abuse seems so simple – children must be rescued from abusive parents and placed with carers who will not harm them. Unfortunately, the answer is not so easy.

This chapter examines issues of substitute care, focusing on the child's perspective. The term 'substitute care' covers the full range of parental alternatives, from short-term foster or residential care or boarding school, to adoption. Nothing in this section will be unfamiliar to specialist home-finding staff. The aim is to help non-specialist workers to understand some of the issues with which children wrestle when being placed in substitute care. It does not aim to cover all aspects of substitute care; there are already comprehensive works on the topic (for example, Argent, 2003; Douglas and Philpot, 2003; Cairns, 2004; Sellick *et al.*, 2004; Thompson, 2004). It does not, for example, address issues – albeit vitally important ones – such as the selection and training of and support for, adoptive parents, foster carers and residential staff. There is also insufficient space to discuss in detail other important issues, including same-race versus trans-racial placements (Zeitlin (2002) provides a discerning discussion of this issue). There are, however, four important principles in such placements.

First, when children are moved from their home, and therefore in a situation of loss and grieving, it is important to maintain as much that is familiar and loved as possible. There are obvious advantages of a child being placed in a home that maintains the same cultural and religious practices and patterns of daily life. This is particularly true of refugee and asylum-seeking children who 'having fled a hostile country and sought sanctuary, can feel socially and psychologically bereft' (Berridge, 2001, p. 171).

Second, according to the Children Act 1989, section 22, 5c, there needs to be genuine sensitivity to the child's 'religious persuasion, racial origin and cultural and linguistic background' (see Masson and Morris, 1992, p. 65). Children are not simply 'black' or 'white', and particular care is required when placing dual- or multi-heritage children. Lau (1991) describes insensitive decisions taken in one instance. This is not a criticism of the professional workers or foster parents, but rather the failure of the system to address the child's cultural needs, particularly bearing in mind Erikson's stage theory and the crucial issues of identity in late childhood and the teenage years:

> An adolescent girl of mixed UK White–Hong Kong Chinese parentage was placed in care following allegations of abuse. The girl was classified as Black, assigned a black social worker and placed with a Black family. In this case the social worker as well as the foster family turned out to be Afro-Caribbean . . . no provision had been made to help her maintain links with the Chinese community or to support her use of the Chinese language.
> (pp. 110–111)

Third, where a trans-racial placement is the only option, children's preferences in terms of diet, dress, grooming, entertainment and other activities should be considered. Sanjula, a young woman with learning disabilities, was the only Asian person in her residential home. Her social worker visited her in care and found she was wearing a tracksuit, despite always wearing a sari at her parents' home. The worker asked Sanjula if she liked wearing a sari. She did but was not allowed to do so in the residential home. The staff explained that Sanjula could not dress herself and no one else knew how to tie a sari. It seems that no one had thought to find out how to do so, or to find someone who could.

Finally, substitute carers and social workers need to be sensitive to the children's concerns about racism, discrimination and their cultural heritage (Banks, 2002), while not assuming that all (and only) black children have a negative self-identity (see Owusu-Bempah, 1994).

Problems of substitute care

Finding an appropriate and stable placement is far from easy, but attachment theory has helped workers to appreciate the damaging nature of frequent changes of carer. Phil Quinn, in his autobiographical account of 'Peter', whose single mother became seriously ill, wrote:

> So began the progression of foster homes for Peter, usually at two- or three-month intervals. He lived in several different foster homes during the two-year period following the break-up of his family . . . Each move became more painful than the last because each convinced the boy that no one loved him or wanted him.
> (Quinn, 1988, p. 47)

The loyalty and attachment many abused children show towards their parents can be explained by reference to both the Stockholm syndrome and to attachment theory. As Bowlby (1969) observed,

> Efforts to 'save' a child from his bad surroundings and to give him new standards are commonly of no avail since it is his own parents who, for good or ill, he values and with whom he is identified.
> (p. 80)

Many abused children do not want to leave their homes; they simply want the abuse to stop and to be loved by their parents. Sarah, it will be recalled, did not see boarding school as an escape.

Instead, she looked forward to each holiday, hoping that 'this time it will be all right'. The strong need of children to belong to their original family was explored in Chapter 3. They live ever-hopeful of 'deserving' their parents' love.

As early as the 1950s, Littner (1956) found that foster children often believed it was because they were bad that they had been 'rejected' by their family. Then Timberlake (1979) demonstrated that the feeling of guilt and responsibility for removal from home is greater in abused children. They were more likely to connect the reason for their placement in care with their own behaviour, whereas non-abused children associated it with a crisis event. The involvement of the police and the use of formal legal processes and the courts, although necessary, all serve to enhance an abused child's sense of wrongdoing.

Even as an adult, Sarah is adamant that she would not have wished to be taken into care. The task of fitting into a new family with its different mores and ways of interacting would have been too difficult for her. Furthermore, when young, she assumed that all fathers beat their children and would have expected any foster parents to do so. Both Marie and Sarah recalled being able to anticipate their father's behaviour and 'keep one step ahead of him'. They felt safer with the 'devil' they knew. Such children feel very fearful of an unknown new situation and will also expect mistreatment and rejection.

When taken into care, each abused child will have his or her own way of adapting to family or residential situations. Some may behave as well as possible, still hoping that by being good they may win a little of their carers' love. Phil Quinn describes what happened to Peter when he was eventually placed with adoptive parents, who started to beat him:

> Peter became hyper-alert to the wants and desires of his adoptive parents . . . He did not blame his [adoptive] mother for losing her temper with him. After all, it only confirmed what he already believed about himself – he was bad and deserved punishment. He tried to atone for his evilness by catering to their every wish.
> (Quinn, 1988, p. 126)

Other children will be withdrawn and retreat to their rooms whenever tension builds. Foster parents have also reported difficulties coping with children who are 'provocative' (McFadden, 1980). The reasons for such apparently difficult behaviour are varied. Some children cannot believe that their substitute carers will not eventually mistreat them, and so test the limits of their carers' patience and tolerance. Some find violence, rejection or molestation so familiar that they feel insecure when given only unfamiliar kindness and protection. Others think they are so wicked that they must be punished, and therefore seek punishment. Many become so used to the role of family scapegoat or seducer that they know of no other way to function. Sexually abused children might have received love only in return for sexual favours; consequently, they believe that their foster carers or residential staff will only care for them if given similar favours.

Some children must feel they cannot win. Zarina, the child who continually played the 'pond' game, had been rejected by one foster carer because she had had tantrums. In the next home she was rejected because she was mute in the presence of the foster carers. She was rejected whether she spoke out or remained silent.

Once in care, children may continue to worry about the rest of the family. Marie stated that she would have resisted being taken into care because she would have been too concerned about her mother and siblings. Jessica Cameronchild (1978) captured some of these fears when she wrote that being an abused child means, 'Hoping maybe you were adopted and that you could find your real parents and convince them you'll be good if only they'll take you back. But worrying about who would take care of your "present" parents if you were rescued'.

Only occasionally can more than two siblings be placed together in the same foster home, yet attachments to brothers and sisters can be stronger than those to parents. Phil Quinn (1988) again describes, through Peter, his feelings when he realised he and his brothers were to be placed in separate foster homes:

As time went by, Peter became more and more interested in his brothers, spending time each day with them . . . Then came the day the welfare workers arrived to take the boys to the [separate] foster homes arranged for them. Without hesitation or resistance Peter had gone with Mr White, not knowing that he was being separated from his brothers . . . It was not until the car began pulling away from the curb

that Peter realised what was happening. Like an animal
caged for the first time, he was suddenly on all fours search-
ing out his brothers through the rear window of the car.
Clawing desperately, he tore at the door trying to get out.
(p. 45)

Serious consideration should be given to trying to recruit substitute carers who are willing to take a group of siblings. Research by
Berridge and Cleaver (1987) has indicated that foster placements
are less likely to break down if siblings are placed together. Judy
Dunn's (1995) research led her to the conclusion that 'in the face of
negative life events . . . most siblings grew closer together and
provided real support for one another' (p. 345).

Fears of violence and feelings of rejection are such that any form
of punishment may provoke an extreme response. Tom O'Neill
(1981) describes his brother's feelings when very caring foster
parents 'had reason to chide him. They ticked him off and sent him
to bed. He went to bed and cried and cried. He cried because they
didn't want him. Admittedly, it was only a temporary banishment
but to him it was a real rejection' (p. 75). Nowadays it is recognised
that corporal punishment of children in care is unacceptable. The
bodies of abused children have been sufficiently degraded in the
past; in care they have the opportunity to learn that their bodies are
worthy of respect. This may cause difficulties in a foster home if the
carers are in the habit of physically assaulting their own offspring.
An additional concern expressed by foster carers relates to caring
for the victims of sexual abuse. Male foster carers in particular may
be unsure about how far they can use touch and cuddling to express
affection.

Finally, although the majority of foster, adoptive and residential
homes provide an excellent environment, there are cases where a
child is abused while in care. Dennis O'Neill was beaten to death
by his foster father. His brother, Tom, describes his end:

He had septic ulcers in his feet. His legs were severely
chapped, a condition for which he had received little or no
medical attention. His chest was extensively bruised and
discoloured. He had recently been beaten on the back with
a stick. His stomach contained no trace of food. He was
dead.
(O'Neill, 1981, p. 68)

Shirley Woodcock (1984, in Appendix) died aged three at the hands of her foster carer, while Christopher Pinder (1981, in Appendix), who was placed for adoption and renamed Daniel Frankland, was killed by his prospective adoptive mother. Victoria Climbié (2003, in Appendix) was killed by an aunt in a private fostering arrangement. A mounting number of inquiry reports (for example, Levy and Kahan, 1991; Kirkwood, 1993; see also Corby *et al.*, 2001) are eloquent testimony to widespread abuse in children's residential homes.

Benefits of substitute care

Although a few children sustain serious injuries or die at the hands of substitute carers, many more would have been killed by their own parents had they not been removed from home. Maria Colwell (1974, in Appendix) and Jasmine Beckford (1985, in Appendix) were killed after being returned home despite the misgivings of their foster parents.

Notwithstanding the problems of substitute care, it can provide children with significant benefits. Lloyd virtually left home from about the age of eleven and lived as best he could. His suicide attempts and total despair in his early teens might have been avoided if he had been accommodated with foster carers or in a residential setting where he could have received counselling, comfort and had someone to turn to for help in his distress.

Some children die because their attempts to escape abuse lead them into danger. The body of eight-year-old Lester Chapman (1979, in Appendix) was found on 26 February 1978, 'Trapped in sewage sludge at a site 50 yards from the river, about a quarter of a mile from his home. He had died of exposure, almost certainly on the bitter night on which he ran away' (p. 1). Lester had been physically and emotionally abused and had run away from home on three previous occasions. Removal to a loving substitute home will usually, in similar cases, save lives.

In spite of the dangers of emotional abuse related to the vagaries of the care system, children frequently thrive when placed with substitute carers. Tom O'Neill (1981) describes the experiences of another of his brothers who, having shared the nightmare of abusing foster carers with Dennis, was then found another home:

From the outset Terry's new foster-family made every effort to give him a real home – not only material benefits but also the one thing that had been missing for many years: love. He was accepted as part of the family. It turned out to be one of the happiest periods in the whole of his lifetime.
(p. 74)

One important benefit given by substitute carers is that they can provide an alternative model of family life. Many foster homes show abused children that instead of violence and recrimination between adult partners there is companionship and respect. The children learn to feel safe and protected by adults. They acquire self-control and discipline through praise, encouragement and gentle correction. They begin to realise that the love of parents for their children should be unconditional. All this will help them to become better partners and parents themselves, if they choose in later life to have their own family.

One of the best therapies for abused children is to be in an environment where they can express feelings without fearing the consequences, where they are helped to feel valued, attractive and capable. Adoptive or foster carers or residential staff can do much to make good the damage to self-esteem caused by maltreatment.

Helping children in substitute care

Whenever possible, children coming into care should be well prepared. Ideally, before being placed they will be helped to understand why they are being removed from home and to appreciate that it is not their fault. Furthermore, when they move from one substitute home to another they need to be told why. Tom O'Neill (1981) describes the experience of three of his brothers:

They had to leave this foster-home. They didn't know why. They had done nothing wrong. Why did no one tell them why they had to go? They were happy there. Could no one have soothed the hurt they were experiencing by just telling them why it had to be as it was?
(p. 61)

Children fear the unknown. Tom O'Neill (1981) again describes how Terry cried out, 'Don't let them take me away, Dad' as he was carried from the foster home where he had suffered savage mistreatment and witnessed the killing of his brother, Dennis. 'He cried out because of the dire consequences that had been instilled into him of being removed' (p. 66). Children can be helped to overcome this fear by being introduced gradually to their new family if circumstances allow. When children have to be removed in haste then they can at least be shown a video or photographs of their new home and/or be provided with a verbal description.

Wherever possible, the parents should also be prepared for the child's removal, with professionals aiming to work in partnership with them. If angered by the actions of protective agencies, they might turn some of that anger against the child and refuse to assist – for example by providing photographs for a life-story book.

Contact

The issue of contact, particularly in adoptions, is a controversial one, and it is hoped that specialist workers will be able to evaluate research findings in this area. There are considerable benefits in maintaining contact between abused children and their families. First, children will worry less about their parents and siblings if they can see them at regular intervals. Second, seeing birth parents and family helps with their sense of identity. Third, they may feel less rejected if the parents wish to continue to see them. But contact with parents is not always positive. For example, a violent father gave the children threatening messages to pass on the their mother: 'Tell the bitch I'll slit her throat'. Parents can give the impression that they are coping well with other siblings who are still with them, so it must be the abused child who is the problem, and not their parenting. Contact can leave a child unsettled, not knowing if they are to remain in care or to return home.

Research by Owusu-Bempah (1995) suggests that when children are not living with a parent they will do better if they have positive knowledge of the absent parent rather than negative or no information. However, information can be obtained from direct or indirect contact with the parent. In some cases a child may be better served by photographs and written information about the parent than acrimonious contact visits or ones that result in further physical, emotional or sexual abuse.

Thought needs to be given to whether contact with parents is essential, or whether there are other people who are more important.

Grandparents, other relatives and family friends can also make a child feel valued and less rejected by being encouraged to keep in touch, remember birthdays and perhaps send presents on special occasions. More controversial and perhaps worthy of further exploration is the need for children to remain in contact with previous foster carers or residential staff. Even more controversial still is the issue of pets. Maltreated children sometimes develop deep relationships with their pets, who become surrogate friends, siblings and even parents. To be wrenched away from these much loved companions can be devastating, and attempts need to be made to ensure pet and child remain in contact.

Another now well-accepted method of helping children to keep in touch with their family and their origins is through a life-story book. While working on their book they can be given answers to why they had to leave home or had several moves in care. They can be reminded of the positives in their lives, such as people who loved them or achievements gained as well as being helped to understand and cope with the more negative aspects.

Kinship care

Kinship care – that is, being placed in care with a relative as foster or adoptive carer – has several benefits. Children's fear of the unknown is minimised, contact can be effortless, and children remain within their cultural and class contexts. In the histories of many families when rates of mortality were greater and parents often incapacitated by ill-health, we find that kinship care was commonplace and unremarkable. In many societies it remains the norm for children whose parents are unavailable.

Nevertheless, there is some need for caution. The case of Victoria Climbié (2003, in Appendix) serves as a warning not to assume automatically that all care by kinfolk is safe care. While non-related foster carers have chosen to provide substitute care, relatives may be more reluctant. Sometimes families are riddled with acrimonious conflict, and the child is likely to be used as a weapon in the warring factions. Some dual heritage children find that the two sides of the family are deeply divided. Placing the child with one side will mean that the culture of the other part of the family, and therefore part of the child's identity, will be derided and demonised.

Another danger with kinship care is that, because it can be viewed as 'natural', the carers are given less support and financial help than non-related carers. Yet often they may need more help, because they may have had fostering or adoption metaphorically 'thrust upon them' when they were least expecting or wanting to be carers. Conversely, as Berridge (2001) points out, 'Anomalies can arise if relatives are paid a significant sum to look after a child, one that was unavailable to the birth parent' (p. 171).

Continuing support

It is tempting for hard-pressed social workers to remove a child from a dangerous household, breathe a sigh of relief and turn attention to those cases where children remain in an 'at risk' situation at home. But this simple rescue is inadequate. However good the new substitute carers, the child will need help in overcoming the negative effects of mistreatment.

As well as direct work with children, the carers will also need support and guidance. Erikson's stage theory and his recognition of the importance of identity issues suggest that it is particularly important that the foster parents and residential staff say nothing derogatory about the children's family of origin within their earshot.

Another area for continuing intervention is when there are conflicts between substitute and original parents about child rearing. This is illustrated by the case of Jasmine Beckford (1985, in Appendix) and her sister, Louise. The foster carers complained about the state in which the girls returned to them after access visits to the parental home; 'There were also frequent complaints about the clothes often being dirty and smelly, and about the greasing of the children's hair. It is normal practice to grease and plait Afro-hair. The social worker felt that the girls were, in fact, returned clean and that their hair had an acceptable amount of grease for the culture involved' (p. 109).

Finally, it is important to keep all parties, including the children, informed of plans for the future. This can be difficult if ongoing assessment means that plans for the future remain uncertain. None the less, children's feelings of powerlessness and insecurity can be moderated by ensuring that they are involved in the decisions made about their own future.

Returning home

The decision will be taken for some children to return to their original homes. Factors indicating that rehabilitation may be viable include a positive change in parental attitudes towards the child, an acceptance that they, not the child, are responsible for the abuse, and an ability to relate to professional helpers as partners in planning for their children's future. If problems such as overcrowding, alcohol abuse, or marital violence were factors that triggered the abuse then assistance to the parents and improvement in these areas will be required before rehabilitation can be considered.

The views of the children

In any plans for rehabilitation, account must be taken of the views of the children. These always have to be taken seriously, as very often children know what is best for them. Nevertheless, some caution has to be exercised in the interpretation of children's verbal and non-verbal communications. Terry O'Neill's, 'Don't let them take me away, dad' could so easily have been interpreted as a real desire to stay with the foster father who had killed his brother, Dennis. Sarah's crying was seen as evidence of her homesickness by the boarding-school staff. Clare Rayner (2003), who was emotionally and physically abused by her mother, describes a similar misinterpretation of her tears; as she was leaving to go to boarding school, her mother 'thought the tears were for her, that I minded going away, but in truth I wept because I *didn't* mind' (p. 88). Furthermore, workers can unwittingly influence their clients, as June Thoburn (1988) warns:

> Often you will become a very important person to the youngster, who will very much want to please you. Since your job is to help prepare a plan which you believe has most chance of meeting the child's needs, there is some risk that your enthusiasm for the plan will communicate itself in such a way that he or she will be reluctant to express any doubts.
> (p. 33)

Other considerations

Social workers are responsible for preparing everyone for the return home. This includes the siblings who have remained at home throughout. They may resent the intrusion of the abused child and the adjustments such as losing a bedroom of their own when rehabilitation takes place. The substitute caregivers and other professionals should also be able to appreciate the reasons for the decision to return the child to his or her home. The child may create problems for the parents simply because both child and family may have difficulties in making the necessary adjustments, and because the child is anxious and insecure. The parents need to be prepared for these eventualities, while the child must be made fully aware of what is happening and be reintroduced at a pace that suits him or her.

Finally, an ability to maintain changes and improvements and to cope with the adjustments required should be monitored once the child is back with his or her parents. It is imperative that the workers involved communicate regularly with the child as well as with the parents; simply *seeing* the child is not enough.

Resilience and social support

Whether children remain at home or return home after a period in care, they need to be helped to cope with the emotional consequences of abuse as well as any undetected emotional maltreatment. Therapy may not be available, possible or sufficient. However, promoting factors that increase resilience is a feasible way of helping.

Emotional abuse

Cases of emotional abuse alone are demanding because of the difficulty of challenging abusive carers. Many physically or sexually abusive acts and physical neglect are illegal, so that police intervention or the threat of prosecution can justifiably be used to protect children. Such threats are no doubt 'oppressive', but this is a lesser oppression compared to the abuse of power by some carers against vulnerable children. But most emotionally abusive behaviour is not proscribed by law, so if parents will not accept intervention it seems that little can be done to help the children. Yet something needs to be offered to the children because research shows that psychological maltreatment, even as the sole form, is one of the most damaging and insidious forms of abuse (Hart *et al.*, 1998; Moran *et al.*, 2004). The way forward is to help children by identifying and strengthening protective factors that help them to cope with the abuse. In emotional abuse cases, these are ones that counter the damage to the self-esteem, the denigration, insecurity and feelings of worthlessness created by psychological maltreatment.

Resilience factors

Researchers have tried to determine which factors promote resilience. In an early study, Lynch and Roberts (1982) identified several factors contributing to a positive outlook for abused children. These included the absence of perinatal problems and early intervention, before any developmental and behavioural problems came to the fore, and the avoidance of both protracted or recurrent legal proceedings and frequent placement changes. High intelligence was also deemed a possible protective factor. Siblings who seemed to do well were those who were born after the identification of abuse, which adds weight to the view that witnessing abuse can be as damaging as being the recipient – the only true non-abused siblings are those who are not in the household during the period of abuse. With reference to Erikson's (1965) theory, children who did well had successfully completed the first development stage and had been able to establish basic trust in themselves and in other people. This enabled them to establish good relationships and these in turn reinforced the children's sense of autonomy and of being valued.

However, one of the problems in identifying resilience factors is that of distinguishing cause and effect. For example, does high intelligence protect children, or are abused children who have greater resilience for other reasons more likely to develop their intellectual potential?

Locus of control and attribution theories

Bolger and Patterson (2003) identify 'two domains with high potential to protect children against the ill effects of maltreatment' (p. 159). The first is perceived internal control. This is based on the theories of attribution and locus of control. Children who believe that they can control what happens to them and attribute any successes and achievements to their own abilities are likely to do better than children who believe that they have no control over events and are subjected to the vagaries of fate or more powerful people.

Locus of control and attribution theories shows why it is essential to include children in decision-making and maximise the control they have over their own lives. This empowerment should be applicable to all children, but special efforts should be made to ensure that abused children are helped to feel in control of themselves and their situation.

Friends and siblings

The second domain is peer friendship. Bolger and Patterson (2003) found that friendships in maltreated children led to a higher self-esteem, less loneliness and a feeling of greater acceptance than those without close friends. This idea of friendship is reflected in the research by Doyle (2001), who found that a key factor in helping abused children is the presence of someone who can give the child unconditional, positive regard, as advocated in the theories of Carl Rogers (1980). In the studies by Doyle (2001, 2003), a 'best friend' was significant. Often these were other distressed children. They could show genuine empathy and understanding, and helped the abused child to realise that maltreatment and misfortune was not 'deserved'. Dogra *et al.* (2002) observe 'Adults often underestimate the support that young people provide for each other' (p. 118). Nevertheless, some abused children will have difficulty making friends because their sense of basic trust (Erikson) has been damaged. In addition, children with certain disabilities 'may have impairments which affect their ability to make friends and many disabled children face particular barriers in establishing and maintaining friendships' (Marchant, 2001, p. 219).

Siblings can also be a source of friendship and support. As noted (Berridge and Cleaver, 1987) children tend to do better in care if they are placed with siblings. But there is no absolute guarantee that siblings will be supportive, Sarah's father used a 'divide-and-rule' strategy, thereby damaging her relationship with her sister.

The role of friendship is such that many abused children will benefit if ways can be found to help them forge and maintain companionship with peers. The only problem to be aware of is that peer groups engaging in high-risk behaviour can be a negative influence (Perkins and Jones, 2004). In some instances, time may be better spent strengthening ties between siblings rather than between child and parents. One of the results of substitute care is that it often results in children being separated from friends and siblings, therefore ways of enabling children to keep in touch with them could usefully be found.

Supportive adults

Another key factor in resilience is a supportive, non-abusing parent (Rutter, 1979; Masten and Coatsworth, 1998) However, in some cases, especially those of emotional abuse, there is no such figure; either both parents are abusive (Lloyd's case), only the abusive parent is present for most or all of the time (Helen's case) or the non-abusing parent is a co-victim (Sarah, Roy, Marie). Four of the five survivors did not have much support from other family members, but Sarah showed how grandparents, aunts and uncles can have a key role. Aunts, whether biologically related or family friends adopted as aunt figures, seem to be particularly important. While they are close to the family, they are not under the same pressure as grandparents, whose loyalties may be divided between their own children and their grandchildren. Many autobiographies of people who had difficult childhoods bear witness to the positive role of aunts – for example, writer Claire Rayner (2003) had 'Aunt Nancy' and, from a Chinese cultural background, author Adeline Yen Mah (2002) had her 'Aunt Baba'. Doyle (2001) found that, of the fourteen survivors of abuse she interviewed, the majority had an aunt figure who had valued and helped them and enhanced their self-esteem.

Helen believes that she owes much of her own ability as a caring parent to a neighbour, Mrs Stevens. Other supportive adults can include non-family members such as youth leaders, voluntary workers, and a variety of helping professionals, including social workers and foster carers. Dogra *et al.* (2002) identify a key protective factor as 'Developing a warm and confiding relationship with a trustworthy and reliable adult (not necessarily within the family)' (p. 118).

Practitioners can encourage other adults in children's lives to offer (in Carl Rogers' terms) 'unconditional positive regard'. It might be as valuable to recruit foster aunts and uncles as it to recruit foster carers so that children can stay at home but obtain emotional support from these alternative figures, especially in cases where the children are not in physical danger but are receiving inadequate emotional nurturing.

Further sources of assistance which should not be underestimated are the counsellors of telephone helplines such as the

Samaritans or ChildLine. The advantage of ChildLine is tha.
dren who are frightened and ashamed can unburden themselve.
a person whom they will not meet; they can decide how muc.
information they disclose and therefore have some control over
events (ChildLine, 1998). If practitioners are unable to intervene in
any other way they can at least remind children of the services of
telephone helplines.

School

Perkins and Jones (2004) found that a positive school climate
helped to enhance resilience. More specifically, Doyle (2003)
explores the key role that teachers play in the lives of abused children. Even teachers only involved with a pupil for a short time can
have a lasting positive impact, as in the case of Lloyd, whose
teacher helped him believe he was special. Dogra et al. (2002) identifies 'Having special skills or a particular talent' (p. 118) as
another protective factor. It is often, as in the case of Lloyd, that
teachers are in a position to identify and help develop these talents.

Other education professionals can also provide key support.
School nurses are not only in a position to recognize abuse but are
often a source of counselling especially for adolescents. Educational
psychologists can help to determine the cause of educational problems and suggest ways in which children can best be helped. Other
people associated with schools, including classroom or lunchtime
assistants, have been, and can be, the supportive adult for some
children.

Religion

'A firm belief and conviction can help survival' (Parkinson, 1993,
p. 95). Perkins and Jones (2004) identified 'religiosity' as a protective factor for adolescents who had been physically abused.
Seidman and Pedersen (2003) also established that religious belief
is a protective factor for children in adverse and oppressive circumstances. Doyle (2001) found that her interviewees identified religion and religious groups as factors in their ability to cope with
their abusive experiences. In many instances, the message 'God
loves you whoever you are' was a powerfully reassuring one,
although no particular religion appeared to have the monopoly in
terms of benefits to children who have been maltreated.

There are concerns that religious 'sects', some religious practices and sexually-exploiting priests can damage young people (Bottoms *et al.*, 1995). But it is probably safe to say that, apart from a consideration of these concerns, there has been scant attention paid by social workers and other helping professionals to the spiritual needs of children unless their cultural background is strongly associated with religion. But perhaps the help that can be offered by spiritual leaders and representatives within the child's community could usefully be harnessed as a source of strength.

Pets

An attachment to a pet, especially an interactive one such as a dog or cat, has been shown to enhance the self-esteem of children in general (Triebenacher, 1998). A study that draws clearly on Erikson's (1965) life stage theory and ecological systems theory demonstrates the key role of companion animals in children's development (Melson, 1998). Doyle (2001) found that pets were another major source of support for children who were emotionally and sometimes also sexually and/or physically abused. As Bodmer (1998) commented, 'Pets are always available and offer their affection to anyone needing it' (p. 245). In addition, Doyle found that when pets were also mistreated by parents, children were relieved of any sense of blame. This was because the children could see that their pets were clearly 'innocent', and so it must be the parents who were at fault and responsible for all the abuse including the child's own.

As with all the other protective factors, there is a negative aspect. Animals are often mistreated in abusing families because either the abuser mistreats everyone and everything over which he or she has power, or because the children displace their anger on to defenceless animals. In households where animals would not be safe, children could be linked to a pet, looked after by someone else but visited regularly by the child. For example, a ten-year-old girl became deeply attached to a horse in the field bordering her garden. She was profoundly distressed when she was taken into care and believed she would not see the horse again.

Generally, while cognitive coping strategies are one aspect of resilience, the other major one is social support, whether from siblings and peers, caring adults including those in schools and religious communities, and even pets. Practitioners can help children, whether in the parental home or in substitute care, to strengthen bonds with any person or animal who can offer the child unconditional positive regard.

This chapter has examined some of the factors that promote resilience in childhood. The next chapter illustrates how these factors, and therapeutic intervention in adulthood, can enable even those children who have suffered multiple and severe maltreatment to have a fulfilling and positive future life.

putting it into practice

Activity 1

Think of a relatively recent occasion when you have been in a new location or accommodation, such as a holiday or conference hotel. Can you remember your feelings? What aspects made the experience more reassuring or positive? Were there any aspects that made the experience negative? Was it, for example, reassuring to have your own distinct luggage, which you packed yourself? Did you pack, or look on arrival for, any 'home comforts'?

This is similar to the exercise on joining a group in Chapter 7. The purpose of this activity is to think about the experience of children coming into care. They are likely to experience very much more emotional turmoil than you experienced. Nevertheless, the activity can help you to think about some of the apparently small factors that can help to alleviate homesickness, confusion and distress. An example might be having bags they identify as 'theirs' rather than their belongings being packed in black bin liners and cardboard boxes.

Activity 2

Review one or more of the cases in Chapter 2: Roy, Sarah, Helen, Marie and Lloyd. Can you identify the social supports and other positive features in their lives that helped to enhance their resilience?

This activity should again help you apply aspects of this chapter to actual cases. As will be seen in the next chapter, all five had a marked degree of resilience; however, can you identify any other supports or factors that might have further enhanced their reliance and made their childhood happier?

Further reading

Useful books on adoption and foster care include Jackson and
Thomas (2000); Kelly and Gilligan (2000); Argent (2003),
Douglas and Philpot (2003); and Sellick *et al.* (2004). The classic,
and still valuable, text is by Fahlberg (1994). Oliver (2000) writes
about supporting adoptive parents of children with special needs.
Issues for minority ethnic children are examined by Kirton (2000)
and Thoburn *et al.* (2000). Thompson (2004) provides a useful
text on children in group care, while Corby *et al.* (2001) review
issues for children abused while in care. Accounts of the
experience of being in care, sometimes with tragic consequences,
are given by O'Neill (1981), MacVeigh (1982) and Quinn (1988).
A useful guide to life story work is provided by Ryan and Walker
(1993). An informative work on aspects of resilience and vulnerability is edited by Luthar (2003). Anthony and Cohler (1987) also
examine resilience factors. Doyle (2001, 2003) explores social
support as a resilience factor.

9 | The effects of abuse – the later years

This chapter looks at the prospects for abused children in later life. The first section examines some of the evidence that exists regarding the long-term effects of abuse. This is followed by accounts of the early adulthood and present situations of Marie, Lloyd, Helen, Sarah and Roy. Their updated stories are retold in the third person because by this means objective observations can be made. The final section examines ways in which workers can help adults who were abused as children.

Evidence of long-term effects

There have been numerous research studies, some of which will be discussed below, that have explored the long-term effects of abuse on children. There are, however, difficulties in collecting and interpreting data which can, if not recognised, give rise to faulty assumptions.

Methodological considerations

Prospective and longitudinal research
Theoretically, it should be possible to compare the development of abused children with non-abused children, tracking them as they grow up. In such 'prospective' research, there are problems in choosing a reliable control group. Helen, Roy and Sarah would almost certainly have found themselves in a control group of apparently non-abused children, with which a group of abused children would have been matched and compared.

A key issue with longitudinal studies is the problem of keeping in contact with the selected children. Lynch and Roberts (1982) noted:

When reviewing the literature we were alarmed by the number of children in other researchers' original samples that were unavailable for follow-up assessment . . . Obviously results which reflect the assessments of less than half the original samples are open to serious criticism as there could be an enormous difference between those families who attend for follow-up assessment and those who do not . . . some of the lost children could be dead.
(p. 4)

Another factor is the difficulty of separating out the negative long-term effects directly attributable to what is construed as 'child abuse' from those that are due to a parenting style that is not construed as abusive (see Hallett, 1995). There is mounting evidence that punitive, authoritarian and critical or emotionally neglectful and inconsistent parenting styles are ultimately more damaging than individual incidents of abuse (Caloustie Gulbenkien Foundation, 1995; Gibbons, Gallagher, Bell and Gordon, 1995). Adorno et al.'s (1950) authoritarian personality theory is also of interest here. However, punitive, authoritarian parenting styles are often not seen as being abusive, and are even warmly endorsed by society – such as those sectors of British society nostalgically demanding a return to 'Victorian values'.

Retrospective research and 'false memory'
Another way of determining the long-term effects of childhood abuse is to evaluate adults who were mistreated as children and compare them with others who were not. Unfortunately, researchers usually have to rely on the subjective assessment of the participants to determine who was and who was not abused, and there is evidence of retrospective under-reporting of abuse (Kendall-Tackett and Becker-Blease, 2004; Dube et al., 2004). A social worker, for example, took a history from a client who declared she had good, although strict, parents, who only 'tapped' her when she deserved punishment. Records revealed that she had been injured by her father's severe beatings on a number of occasions. With the passage of time, abuse can be seen as a minor problem or justifiable chastisement. Sometimes adults simply forget what happened. For example, Williams (1994) asked survivors about their sexual maltreatment twenty years after it

was documented. Over
abuse.

Conversely, a few adults who w
abused as children maintain that they
thy, or because they resented aspects of
Some studies have shown an apparently
Wisdom *et al.*, 2004) but this may be because
totally free of emotional pain, and the memory can e
augment adverse events to explain distress in adulthood.

Another difficulty is disentangling abuse, especially emotio
abuse, from differences in temperament between child and parent.
Morrison's (1993) description of his uneasy relationship with his
father during childhood is attributable to a mismatch between an
ebullient parent's temperament and his son's more reticent one.

Finally, it is difficult to determine which elements are attributable to abuse and which to other influences; other childhood
factors can have an adverse impact on adult functioning. Some of
these may be associated with the family directly, such as poverty,
homelessness, parental illness and bereavement, while others may
be external to the family, such as peer group pressures and bullying, or oppressive school regimes.

Negative consequences of abuse

For a number of children, death is the ultimate negative consequence. For other children there is the burden of multiple disability. One baby, Michelle, was sixteen days old when she was picked
up by the feet by her father and her head smashed against the floor.
She was rushed to a specialist hospital and her life saved. However,
two years later, she was severely mentally and physically disabled,
only able to make a small range of noises and unable to control her
body. She was living in a children's home and there were doubts
about the possibility of finding a foster home for her.

Other children have to live with disfiguring scars from cuts,
burns and scalding. But many more have emotional scars which do
not show so readily. Helen described how, when her memories
came flooding back, she felt as if she had open wounds rubbed raw
by every remembered detail and by the insensitive remarks of well-
meaning acquaintances. Gradually, her wounds healed, although
small scars remained.

recorded
onfidence
depression
, 1987); self-
in academic
(Wolfe, 1987).
childhood and
with people who
ved grief reaction.
ften show develop-
tion to language and
32). Sixty-five per cent
rganic failure-to-thrive'
s, especially in terms of
misuse in a fifteen-year
ker (1992) describes how
red to the extent that people
order.

follo
personality
demonstrate mu

In relation to sexua   ing disorders and psychiatric
problems have been noted (s *et al.*, 2004) as well as 'feelings
of rejection, guilt, unworthiness, inability to cope with normal
sexual relationships and a general distrust of helping agencies'
(Oppenheimer, 1985, p. 27). In a comprehensive study of the long-
term effects of child sexual abuse, Mrazek and Mrazek (1981)
listed twenty-five problem areas, ranging from aversion to sexual
activity and problems with parents or in-laws to masochism and
murder.

Post-traumatic stress

In more recent years, researchers and practitioners (Rowan, 1994)
have been interested in evidence that victims of abuse, especially
where there may have been the use of terror and violence, sometimes suffer from post-traumatic stress (Parkinson, 1993). This was
discussed briefly in relation to children in Chapter 2. The signs of
post-traumatic stress in children and adults take three main forms.

The first is the avoidance of anything connected with the abusive
events. This might also be manifested as a general lack of respon-
siveness to any association with the abuse, or the inability to recall
events. Second, there might be a continual re-experiencing of the
traumatic incidents, including flashbacks, persistent distressing

dreams, intrusive recollection of experiences, or an inability to stop thinking about the events. Third, there might be increased arousal. With adults, this is likely to occur when memories return or if they are in a situation that recreates past abusive experiences. They may have difficulties sleeping, relaxing and concentrating, and hence become irritable. They often display a phobia of apparently innocuous situations, which seems irrational until the associations with past abuse are recognised. For example, someone may refuse to go into the back of a van, or hyperventilate, feel tense and have a racing heart when near the open back doors of a van. This makes sense once it is realised that as a child, the person was regularly assaulted in the back of a van.

Generational cycle of abuse

One of the consequences of abuse that gives rise to considerable concern is the idea of a cycle of abuse from one generation to the next; the idea that people abused as children are more likely grow up to be abusers themselves. Herzberger (1993) argues that there is no sound foundation for these theories. It is also evident that children who have been abused know the warning signs and can protect their own children. On the other hand, being abused as a child does not always help a person develop effective parenting (Cole et al., 1992).

There are sound reasons why abuse in childhood should lead to abusive parenting. A feature of the Stockholm syndrome is that abuse victims interpret parental behaviour as strong, courageous and justified, a model they grow up to emulate: 'In addition to providing models which can be imitated, families, through their use of violence, teach that violence is an acceptable form of expression or problem solving' (Gelles and Strauss, 1979, p. 542). Behavioural theories suggest that violence is learnt. Andrew, a prisoner, commented, 'I didn't like my dad, he was too fond of the belt. He was always laying into me with his belt.' Andrew was serving four life sentences for violent murder (Parker, 1969, p. 205). Children who have been neglected may not know how to cope with household demands and become neglecting parents. Sexual abuse victims may protect their self-image by convincing themselves that there is nothing wrong in sexual relationships between adults and children. Wyre (1986) noted that many men who had raped children had been sexually abused as children and had incorporated their experiences of abuse into their own sexuality.

Some people abused as children become so trapped in their situation that they literally have to blast their way out. Often quiet, introverted people, they collect guns and other weapons as a means of giving them the power and control they had so desperately needed as vulnerable, mistreated children. Then comes the day when they use the weapons to make their bid for freedom, turning them against their family, any innocent passers-by and eventually themselves.

Finally, it perhaps comes as no surprise that Adolf Hitler's father was:

> a drunkard and a tyrant . . . in Hitler's case the love for his young mother and the hate for his old father assumed morbid proportions . . . which drove him to love and to hate and compelled him to save or destroy people and peoples who really 'stand for' his mother and his father.
> (Erikson, 1965, pp. 319–20)

Children who do well

By no means all abused children grow up to be severely damaged or dangerous. Although some may have social difficulties and private sorrows, others become happy, well-adjusted individuals who provide excellent care for their own offspring (Rutter, 1996).

In their examination of the long-term effects of child sexual abuse, Beezley and Mrazek (1981) cite four studies which found no ill-effects in adulthood. In a follow-up study of abused children and their siblings, Lynch and Roberts (1982) noted that 37 per cent appeared to have no particular problems: they could enjoy themselves and were self-confident. They were also healthy, neurologically intact, well-grown, intellectually normal and had no discernible behaviour disturbances. They could form good relationships with both adults and children.

Resilience factors were discussed in the previous chapter and, as noted by Doyle (1996), children benefited from having at least one person who gave them unconditional positive love during childhood. However, there is evidence that, even as adults, victims can be helped, despite having been repeatedly abused as children and despite having no consistent caring figure for much of their early life. Phil Quinn found 'salvation' in the form of acceptance by a group of motor-bikers – 'Satan's Saints' (Quinn, 1988), and Tom

O'Neill met unstinting care, which gave him a sense of being valued, by the staff of a probation hostel (O'Neill, 1981). In the following accounts it will be seen that Marie, Lloyd, Helen, Sarah and Roy were all given significant help in their adult lives.

Marie's account continued

Marie was married early to a man who was violent and sexually abusive. She returned to her parents' home, only to be molested by her father. She realised how inappropriate her father's attitude to his children was when on one occasion during this period he was trying to kiss her, using considerable force. As Marie resisted, he shouted, 'What's the matter? You're a woman and I'm a man.' Marie responded with, 'No, you're my father and I'm your daughter.'

While back with her parents Marie formed a relationship with Glen, a young friend of her father. He was gentle and trustworthy, never showing any anger or swearing. He felt that he was sexually impotent so theirs was a platonic friendship. Marie was able to receive a cuddle from him without feeling dirty and defiled. Glen showed her that not all men were violent and demanding like her father and her first husband.

Marie liked Glen but never loved him. After a while she was able to move on to a relationship demanding more commitment. Her second husband, Luke, was gentle and caring like Glen, but she loved him and was able to have a satisfactory sexual relationship with him. Glen remained in the background for a while and told her, 'I'll always be in the bank for you emotionally.' Marie realised that she was now strong enough to help her husband when he needed support.

The couple had a number of children and when one daughter was molested, Marie immediately sought help for her. Neither parent was responsible for the incident, their daughter was able to tell them what had happened, and they went to great lengths to ensure that all their children were protected in the future.

At the time, Marie was attending a self-help group for adults who had been abused as children. She found that the support of its members was important to her, and they helped her put events into perspective. She also received help during this critical period from a very gentle, caring male social worker who referred her to a psychotherapist. She benefited from the counselling she was given but did not need such intensive help for long. Eventually, she became a 'senior member' of the self-help group, giving assistance to newer members who were at a more vulnerable and painful stage of the healing process.

Marie views her father with a mixture of anger and pity. He is an old man now. When the family visits her parents she ensures that none of her children are left alone with him. Pauline, her elder sister, still has emotional difficulties and cannot communicate with her husband; she will attack him even if he has only one drink. Linda married a violent man who broke her arm; she then found solace in relationships with women. Marie's brother, Barry, followed their father into the Services but he was convicted of causing grievous bodily harm and given a dishonourable discharge. He is still very violent, and in Marie's words 'mixed up and not coping with adult life'.

Marie herself is still sometimes affected by her experiences. She acknowledges that she is a 'worrier'. She 'worries for others' and becomes anxious about potential problems before they arrive. Nevertheless, she is determined that her father, having destroyed her childhood, will not destroy her future. She is a tall, elegant woman who dresses smartly and has an air of confidence and a warm, generous manner. Asked what helped her survive those unhappy earlier years, Marie replied that humour had been her salvation; she would always try to see the funny side of any situation.

Lloyd's account continued

Lloyd was on a generally downward spiral of drink and drugs when at the age of twenty-one he met a group of 'born-again' Christians. He stayed with them for about five years. He found in the group there was total acceptance, 'however bad I was, I was accepted as part of a family'. The reality of what he was doing to himself hit home. He received counselling and the counsellor suggested his experiences were for a purpose. The counsellor also helped him to come to terms with the sexual abuse and understand why it happened and that it was not his fault. He found that he could use his experiences to counsel other abandoned and distressed people. The acceptance of the group and the sense of being of some value to others increased his self-esteem. He eventually left the religious group because he wanted to extend his counselling work and became professionally qualified.

He has now married and has three stepchildren. He has made a conscious choice not to be abusive. He has to check out with his wife about how to respond to the children because he is not sure how to be a good father figure; for example, he did not realise that when the children fell over they needed to be picked up and comforted.

Lloyd occasionally visits his original family. His brothers have fared less well. They are unable to find jobs and have become involved in drugs. While Lloyd is very optimistic about his own future, he is left wondering about the effects on siblings of witnessing abuse rather than being directly abused themselves.

Helen's account continued

During her teenage years Helen concentrated on her academic studies. She wanted to be a doctor but always doubted her ability to achieve this goal and could not believe that a medical school would give her a place. She was frightened of failure. She therefore opted for a career in nursing. Her eating problems meant that although she found the academic work relatively easy, the physical demands of the job nearly defeated her as she had so little stamina. Eventually she managed to complete her training.

During her time as a student nurse she met Hugh. He worked at the nearby university. He was an academic involved in research. He was an idealist committed to fund-raising for Third-World countries. He expressed love for Helen, who now believes that her half-starved, tired appearance appealed to his belief in an ascetic way of life; he rejected any form of indulgence or luxury. Helen became engaged to Hugh. He made no sexual demands, which suited her; he said they would wait until they were married. However, Helen began to find that his coldness, his inability to cuddle her or express any deep affection, and his growing criticisms, were a reminder of her mother's way of relating to her. Despite the fact that she was drawn to him like a magnet, she refused to go with him when he moved to a new job at another university. The engagement was over and Helen was left feeling very lonely but certain that she had made the right decision.

Years passed and Helen became a health visitor. She developed an interest in child neglect. Although contented in her work, she continued to have a bleak time as far as her personal life was concerned. She was unable to relate sexually to any partner and was frequently informed by a string of disenchanted, scornful men that she was 'frigid'.

She then met Jack. In contrast to Hugh, he was outgoing, fun to be with and enjoyed the luxuries of life. He was physically attractive. He helped Helen feel that she too could be attractive. She felt able to put on a little weight and buy fashionable clothes. He was an adept lover and gently reintroduced her to sexual intercourse. For the first time in her life she enjoyed a sexual relationship. She married him, but not long after the wedding discovered that he had been married twice before. She also found that he was an unreliable spendthrift with a fearsome temper, and his sexual demands became more than she could tolerate. One day he walked out and the marriage, somewhat to Helen's relief, was over.

Shortly after this Helen began to recall the sexual abuse of her childhood. She had more or less forgotten about Frank's activities. Suddenly, night after night and day after day, memories came flooding back. Then she started crying and continued to cry whenever she was alone. Occasionally she did so when she was in company, and then she had to pretend she had a cold or an eye infection. She eventually told a colleague, who tried at first to help her but who then began to be intolerant of her moods swings. This made Helen feel even more unwanted, unworthy, a useless person who had a dreary past and a bleak, lonely future. She could see no good reason for not committing suicide.

Then from somewhere deep inside her came a small voice that said that she was worth helping. She sought the help of a female counsellor, who did much to restore her self-esteem. She was also given psychotherapy by a male therapist. He helped her to make connections between her experiences, her behaviour and her relationships. She went through a period of extreme anger and bitterness, but at the same time began to value her own positive features.

Later, Helen met Bill, a kindly, warm-hearted man who, like her father, was involved in business. She had no problems relating to him sexually and they have a number of children. Helen is determined her children will have a mother who cuddles them, spends time with them and takes an interest in what they are doing.

Occasionally, she finds herself copying her mother's offhand manner, and although she quickly checks this, she has to be on constant guard against any seeming coldness, especially when her children are ill. Nevertheless, she is surprised how affectionate she is towards her offspring, and how genuinely interested and concerned about them she is.

Reflecting on her ability to be a loving mother, Helen feels that she owes much to a neighbour, Mrs Stevens. As a teenager, Helen used to visit the Stevens family and began to help with the care of their babies as each arrived. She was trusted to babysit and to take the children for walks. Mrs Stevens was a warm, kindly lady who showed all her children physical affection. She provided a model for Helen, who sometimes still finds herself copying Mrs Stevens' gestures and phrases.

Looking at Helen today, she is an attractive woman with a buoyant self-esteem. There are, however, moments when her face looks sad and thoughtful. She is happy now but feels in someway that she does not deserve happiness, believing that one day it will all be taken away from her. On the other hand, she recognises that the sense of being undeserving is a legacy of her childhood. So she continues to struggle against the feeling of impending disaster and tries to replace it with an optimistic view of the future.

Sarah's account continued

Having left home, Sarah went to live with her aunt and uncle until she felt ready for greater independence. They did not try to stop her leaving; they appreciated the fact that she needed to move on. Living in digs, she met a woman who accepted her and hearing of her experiences commented, 'It isn't fair, why should it have happened to you?' This helped Sarah to appreciate that she was not to blame for what had occurred and there was nothing bad about her, she had not deserved such maltreatment. She learnt about friendship from that woman and was able through her to make other friends. Sarah explained, 'I reached out a little; it worked, so I reached out a little further.'

Sarah then married Mark, a kindly, mild-mannered man. She acknowledges that she almost married a man like her father in the form of the boyfriend to whom she became engaged when she was seventeen. She acknowledged, when she had recovered from the broken engagement, that she did not want to marry a bully. Mark is very similar to her grandfather who, as described by Sarah, was 'the one good man who could love in a giving way, who loved me for myself and who, with his wife, could offer me a safe family'. Sarah's grandparents also loved each other, so she had faith that a loving relationship was possible.

Sarah knows that it has taken her a long time to work through her feelings of worthlessness. She started the work herself. She raised her own family and completed a teacher training course. She reached a position of strength but recognised that she could become inappropriately angry. Furthermore, she would dwell on the deaths of people to whom she was close. She had a profound sense of loss and was stuck in the anger of that loss; in Sarah's words, 'It was beginning to explode.' She knew the anger was inappropriate, so she sought help from a counsellor.

She still had problems over body image and general worth. In therapy, she recalled, amid intense pain, the incident when her father called her a 'pregnant cow'. The counsellor made her understand that what her father had shouted on the beach that day was untrue, emphasising, 'That was a lie, a vicious lie'. Sarah rejoiced in the realisation of the fact that her father was not always right and she was able to lay her burden of anger down.

Sarah also had to cope with a difficult period when a head of department, Mrs A, took a dislike to her and made her life a misery. Sarah realised that the woman felt threatened by her apparent strength and efficiency, therefore she told Mrs A about her childhood in an attempt to demonstrate her vulnerability. After this revelation Mrs A became increasingly vindictive. Perplexed, Sarah went to a colleague for help. The colleague observed that Mrs A was probably even more threatened now because she knew Sarah had the strength to survive such a testing childhood.

Despite the influence of Mrs A, Sarah's teaching abilities were recognised and she is now on the way to having a very successful career. Barbara lives abroad and there is still only a distant, superficial relationship between the two sisters. Their parents divorced and their father emigrated. Sarah has no contact with him. Her mother, while still married, tried to throw herself out of a window, but once divorced could cope no better alone and turned more and more to drink. She eventually died and was lying dead for a fortnight before anyone found her body.

Sarah is a vivacious, attractive woman with a happy marriage, grown-up children, and a fulfilling career. She can readily be described as a warm person with a bright, cheerful expression in her eyes. When asked what helped her to survive she, like Marie, mentioned humour. She recalled how stupid her father looked having an erection in his dressing-gown. She has retained her sense of humour. Sarah also had a much-loved dog and was able to escape the house by taking him for long walks. The countryside around was very beautiful and this sustained her. She felt the mountains belonged to her and she used to 'fill up on the beauty of the mountains'. She found that she was and is creative, with considerable artistic gifts. She won a prize and knew that this was a talent her father could not deny her.

Sarah is now free of the burden of abuse. She once pointed to a photograph of herself as a little girl, saying, 'How could my father have done that to me, I was a lovely child.' She is aware that some of the children she teaches are being abused. She is not sorry that she was abused because she can use her experiences to help others.

Roy's account continued

Roy emerged into adulthood still battling with anorexia nervosa. He continued to eat very little and would do everything to expend energy, such as running round a huge park six times a day. However, the help given to him by staff and fellow patients at the day centre was doing much to restore his self-esteem. As he was recovering from anorexia, he met his wife, who further enhanced his feeling of worth. His mother-in-law, who is a social worker, understood his needs and was, and still is, very supportive. He has three children in whom he delights. Roy's father will not leave Roy or his family alone. But, because of his past violence and his liking for young girls, they will not let him have contact with his grandchildren. He kept pestering them and one day attacked Roy's wife in front of the children in a shopping centre because she would not let him see his grandchildren. He was not charged with assault because there were no visible injuries, but they did get an injunction to ensure that he could not come into contact with the family. This appears to have worked because he has stopped pestering them.

Roy is tall and slim, but not thin, and is happy to eat with the family. There is no sign of the anorexia. He is optimistic about the future and feels he has found a niche in life working with young people. Although his job is poorly paid and they are struggling financially, their home is comfortable. Roy finds he has to work at his marriage as he is not always sure of the best way of overcoming problems. However, there is no question of domestic or emotional violence towards his wife or children. He is an attractive, thoughtful person who is committed to his family.

Helping adult survivors

The phrase 'adult survivor' is used in this section to refer to those abused children who reach independent adulthood. Not all do; some are killed, some commit suicide, some die of preventable diseases – sexually transmitted or as a result of neglect. Others are permanently damaged in such a way that, mentally and emotionally, they remain like dependent children.

As illustrated by the accounts of Marie, Lloyd, Helen, Sarah and Roy it is never too late to attempt to release an adult survivor from the negative feelings and inaccurate perspectives that imprison them. Men and women who were abused over fifty years ago have sought and received assistance. If abused people are not helped during childhood, they may have to live with a lot of pain, but no one should be condemned to lifelong misery. Those involved in child welfare may well have skills that could also help 'grown-up' abused children.

Working with diversity

The following sections examine ways of helping adult survivors. As with children, practitioners know that survivors can come from a range of ethnic and cultural groups, have varying degrees of ability, disability and different abilities, they will have different sexual orientations and be of both genders and a broad age span. This means that care has to be taken to ensure that all intervention is sensitive to this diversity.

Helping the individual

Adults sometimes carry a heavier burden than children, because negative feelings arising from the abuse may have been reinforced over time. They will have an increased number of painful incidents to remember if, like Marie and Sarah, the abuse continued into their late teens or early twenties. One of the most constructive initial steps is to encourage the survivor to recall, when ready to do so, as much of his or her early life as possible. This is often a very painful process and may take several months, especially when the person being helped has suppressed the most difficult incidents. Nevertheless, it is in many cases a necessary journey. Having described events, it is easier to view them from a more accurate perspective. Sarah describes how, during counselling, she was able to recognise that her father had lied about her. Having been relived and reassessed, such incidents can be left behind and the survivor can move on.

However, no one should be forced to recall distressing events. The title of a book by Kathy Evert, who suffered sexual and physical abuse at the hands of her mother, written with her therapist Inie Bijkerk, has the telling and important title *When You're Ready* (Evert and Bijkerk, 1987). If someone prefers never to talk about the past but deals with feelings in the present, then they are entitled to do so and there is no failure in either that person or their helper if past events are not discussed.

As Sarah recognised, anger may need to be dealt with. Often in the wake of recall comes long-suppressed anger, and frequently it is directed towards the survivor, him/herself. Sometimes it is targeted at society in general, or a particular group in society such as men or authority figures like the police. Occasionally it is turned against the therapist – 'You can't know what it felt like'; 'I bet you are enjoying this, hearing the juicy details.' Survivors need to be helped to express anger against the perpetrators of the abuse and those who failed to protect them. They then need to move on to make sense of events, directing their anger into constructive rather than destructive channels. Anger made Marie, Roy and Sarah determined that even though their fathers had ruined their childhoods, they were not going to spoil their future. Anger has spurred people into helping abused children, setting up schemes to prevent abuse, or supporting other adults abused during childhood.

All survivors share a sense of loss. They have lost their only opportunity to be carefree, cared-for children. They need to work through this loss in the same way that bereaved people have to complete the task of mourning. They, like those who are grieving, can be helped to come to terms with what has happened by acknowledging their losses and expressing their feelings, doubts and fears.

Survivors are likely to be most comfortable if they are able to reach a stage when they can look back at themselves as children and can imagine cuddling and comforting their child-self. They will want to tell that child-self that he or she is lovable, was not to blame for the abuse and has done nothing of which to be ashamed. One useful exercise involves the survivors looking at a photograph of themselves when young and describing how they feel about the child they see. Once the mourning and healing process is complete, they will be able to express largely positive emotions about their child-self. Some people will not have any childhood photographs; a drawing or a picture of child resembling them will do instead.

One issue that survivors like Roy have to face is how best to protect their children from possible abuse by their own parents. It is not always easy, as Roy's case illustrates, to keep grandparents away from their grandchildren.

Another related issue with which survivors have to contend are the theories about the generational 'cycle of abuse'. As noted, Herzberger (1993) has challenged these ideas. All five survivor accounts show that abused children do not necessarily become abusive adults. It was Helen who was able to articulate the issue for survivors: 'People who have not suffered abuse as children probably do not have to think about whether they will abuse their own or not. But we have a choice to make. We can make a conscious decision not to be like our own parents.'

Group therapy

Groups for adult survivors can vary in form from relatively short-term projects run by professional workers to open-ended self-help groups. Adults, unlike young children, can take on responsibility for running their own group. One model is that of a self-help group started by experienced group workers who are already skilled in assisting the victims of various situations. These 'facilitators' set up the group in response to a perceived demand. They make the initial practical arrangements such as finding meeting rooms and organising refreshments.

Facilitators also help in the healing process, preventing the group from becoming stuck in a mood of despair or destructive anger. As one or two survivors work through their problems they take over the responsibility for both practical arrangements and for assisting newer or more vulnerable members. Eventually the facilitators withdraw from group sessions, remaining in the background as advisers in case the members need guidance. Workers contemplating setting up such a self-help group should recognise that they will need to commit themselves for at least a year as facilitators, and a further one or two years in an advisory capacity. It is recommended that initially there are two facilitators and a consultant available to the group. However, once the facilitators have withdrawn it may well be possible for only one to remain involved as adviser.

The main benefit of group therapy is that it alleviates the sense of isolation that so many survivors experience. This is particularly important for sexually-abused men, because much of the publicity is directed towards physical abuse and sexually victimised girls. Bruckner and Johnson (1987), who ran groups for such men, write 'Male clients who were referred to the group had reached an impasse in their individual therapy. They continued to perceive sexual abuse as an experience unique to themselves. They viewed themselves as societal oddities, which in turn reinforced their guilt.' (p. 84)

Group work always requires careful preparation. Facilitators need to think and talk through all the problems they can anticipate. If they themselves were abused as children, how will they respond if asked about their own experiences? Are they using the group as a therapeutic tool for themselves? If they were not abused as children, how will they reply to the accusation of failing to understand what it is like to be abused? What action, if any, should the facilitators take if they learn that a member is now abusing a child? What will they do if a member appears to be suicidal?

As with children's groups, it is important that several members should turn up for the first session. Again, it is worth arranging for a few members to arrive together. Meetings are probably best held at least weekly. Often members will feel the need for more frequent contact and will meet informally between sessions. Transport seems to be less of a problem than it is with children's groups, because adults can often drive, and can travel by public transport, walk or cycle in rather more safety than children, or arrange to share a taxi or ask for a lift. However, some potential members will be parents, therefore a crèche may be necessary.

Activities can help to promote or direct discussion. However, adults, more than children, may well want to talk at length because they have much to talk about. Bruckner and Johnson (1987) recommend eliciting specific details of the abusive experiences at the outset. But there is a lot to be achieved in the first session, including clarifying boundaries, agreeing on the purpose of the group and becoming familiar with members' names. It may therefore be more appropriate in the first session for members to introduce themselves with brief details of their experiences; for example, 'I'm Sarah and I've come because my father physically and sexually abused me' – leaving more detailed disclosures for later meetings.

There should be few rules, but it is helpful if members agree to finish promptly. There is a tendency for people to put off bringing up difficult subjects until the last possible moment. This can place other members who have to leave on time in a dilemma. They may be unable to stay any longer, but by going feel they have failed the distressed member. It should be clarified that if participants are to be helped then they must raise problems in good time. In a case of severe distress, a facilitator may have to spend some time after the main session assisting the member with the immediate crisis and helping him or her to bring it to the group on another occasion.

Although planned exercises may often have to be shelved because members want to talk, it is sometimes worth applying gentle pressure to persuade the group to move on with the aid of an exercise. Tried and tested relaxation techniques can be practised, and drawing is useful. At some stage members can be asked to draw what the abuse meant to them then, or perhaps at a later session, be asked to draw the perpetrator or something which symbolises the perpetrator. This helps to focus discussion. Letters can be written to perpetrators, for sharing with other members rather than for posting.

Some members find both exercises and discussions difficult. They should not be made to feel embarrassed if they are unable to participate fully. If maybe they cannot bring themselves to draw the perpetrator, they can be invited to draw a symbol; for example, one participant drew her father's armchair. It is often fellow members rather than the facilitators who give comfort to those in difficulty. However, the facilitators must be sensitive to the needs of different members – encouraging some to talk, allowing others to sit quietly and listen, discouraging some from going over and over events in a unproductive way, and enabling others to repeat what they have said.

Final comment

One aspect of working with abused children that has not been addressed is the need for workers to care for themselves. Child protection work is extremely stressful. Many workers find that they can only engage in direct, front-line work for a limited time before becoming 'burnt out'. This is the draining of emotion because of repeated over-demand on limited emotional resources. Some professionals find that, when they have their own children, the work becomes too emotive. Others are themselves survivors and eventually realise that the scars from their own experiences are being rubbed too raw (Doyle, 1991). The most important advice is for workers to be kind to themselves, be aware of theories relating to the effects of stress and burnout, and to be willing to change to less direct work when the time is right.

Many social workers, other professionals and volunteers striving to help the victims of child abuse may wonder from time to time whether their intervention is effective. It is not unreasonable to assume that people who have been exposed to years of mistreatment will need at least as many years of consistent affection and care in order to be released from the negative effects of abuse.

Nevertheless, from the accounts given by Marie, Lloyd, Helen, Sarah and Roy, it is clear that short-term intervention can create positive change in the courses of victims' lives. All five had, as adults, counselling, psychotherapy or the support of a self-help group. Furthermore, in their teenage years or early twenties they all had someone special to give them direct help. For Marie, Glen opened her eyes to the fact that not all men are violent and demanding. Many male workers give their clients similar assistance, showing sensitivity and caring but not expecting any sexual favours. For Lloyd, members of a religious group and a counsellor gave him unconditional positive regard. Mrs Stevens, Helen's model of someone who could accept her and who demonstrated how to show affection towards other children, can be found among foster carers, residential staff and group leaders. Sarah's female friend whom she met in lodgings has her counterpart in those helping professionals who recognise the injustice of abuse and who prove to be trustworthy helpers. Roy was assisted by hospital staff and fellow patients, plus his wife and mother-in-law.

Many of the survivors' acquaintances – Glen, Lloyd's counsellor, Mrs Stevens, Sarah's fellow lodger, other day-centre patients for Roy – were only involved for a relatively short time. Yet they all played a vital part in the lives of the five. They did much to undo the damage caused by close family members over many years. It is therefore quite possible that through properly focused individual, family or group work, assistance given by committed child protection workers will be effective in helping the victims of child abuse.

putting it into practice

Activity 1

Think back to Activity 2 in the last chapter. Hopefully you will have a list of resilience factors relating to at least one of the children whose accounts were given in Chapter 2. Now that you know the outcomes for Helen, Roy, Lloyd, Marie and Sarah, is there any additional support or assistance that helped to enhance their resilience? Identify any key factors in adulthood that you think were particularly helpful.

This is to help you think more broadly about resilience factors and to recognise that social support and other forms of help can be continued (or introduced) in adulthood to positive effect.

Activity 2

Recall some of the activities suggested in Chapters 5, 6 and 7 for working directly with children. Could you adapt any of the exercises for use when working with adults? For example, could the 'castle' exercise be adapted for adults to help them recognise people, strategies and agencies who could help them when they feel threatened by memories or people from their past, or incidents or people who recreate their experiences of abuse.

The purpose of this exercise is to show that practitioners' repertoire of ways of intervening and helping people therapeutically can be enhanced by adapting activities designed for one group to meet the needs of another. This, however, does take sensitivity, imagination and understanding.

Further reading

Gil (1984, 1988) provides guidance for child abuse victims as well as their siblings and spouses. Adolescent victims of sexual abuse are likely to find Bain and Sanders (1990) helpful. Hall and Lloyd (1989) and Bass and Davis (1990) write for adult female victims, while issues for adult male survivors are addressed by Gonsiorek et al. (1994), Mendel (1994) and Etherington (1995). An appealing book by Evelyn White (1985) is written for black women suffering from domestic violence. Bruckner and Johnson (1987) describe group work with men who were child sexual abuse victims, while Donaldson and Cordes-Green (1994) deal with group work with survivors of both genders.

Appendix: inquiry reports

Published reports into the death or ill-treatment of a child or children are referred to by the children's name. They are listed here in alphabetical order. The exceptions are the inquiry report into child sexual abuse in Cleveland, which is listed under 'Cleveland', because so many children were involved; and the Bichard Inquiry, listed under 'Bichard' because the two unrelated children were not killed by their parent figures or carers. The list does not include the inquiry reports into maltreatment in children's residential or day-care settings. A review of these inquiries is provided by Corby *et al.* (2001). The list was originally compiled with the assistance of Christine Smakowska and David N. Jones.

Auckland (1975) *Report of the Committee of Inquiry into the Provision of Services to the Family of J. G. Auckland*, London: HMSO.

Bagnall (1973a) *Report of the Working Party of Social Services Committee Inquiry into Circumstances Surrounding the Death of Graham Bagnall and the Role of the Council Social Services*, Salop County Council.

Bagnall (1973b) *Report of a Committee of the Hospital Management Committee into the Circumstances Leading up to the Death of Graham Bagnall Insofar as the Hospital Authority was Concerned*, Shrewsbury: Shrewsbury Group Hospital Management Committee.

Beckett (1996) *Overview Sub-committee Report Concerning the Deaths of Tracy and Clare*, Nottingham: Nottingham Area Child Protection Committee.

Beckford (1985) *A Child in Trust: The Report of the Panel of Inquiry into the Circumstances Surrounding the Death of Jasmine Beckford*, London Borough of Brent.

Bichard (2005) *An Inquiry into Child Protection Procedure in Humberside Police and Cambridgeshire Constabulary in the Light of the Recent Trial of Ian Huntley for the Murder of Jessica Chapman and Holly Wells*. Chairman: Sir Michael Bichard. London: The Stationery Office.

Brewer (1977) *Report of the Review Panel Appointed by Somerset Area Review Committee to Consider the Case of Wayne Brewer*, Somerset Area Review Committee.

Brown (1978) *Paul and L. Brown. Report of an Inquiry Held at Wallasey*, Wirral Borough Council and Wirral Area Health Authority.

Brown (1979) *An Inquiry into an Inquiry*, Birmingham: BASW.

Brown (1980) *The Report of the Committee of Inquiry into the Case of Paul Stephen Brown*, DHSS, Cmnd 8107, London: HMSO.

Caesar (1982) *Report . . . on the Involvement of the Social Services Department in the Events Preceding the Death of Jason Caesar*, Cambridge County Council.

Carlile (1987) *A Child in Mind: Protection of Children in a Responsible Society. The Report of the Commission of Inquiry into the Circumstances Surrounding the Death of Kimberley Carlile*, London Borough of Greenwich and Greenwich Heath Authority.

Carthy (1985) *Report of the Standing Inquiry Panel into the Case of Reuben Carthy*, Nottinghamshire County Council.

Chapman (1979) *Lester Chapman Inquiry Report*, Berkshire County Council.

Clark (1975) *Report of the Committee of Inquiry into the Considerations Given and Steps Taken towards Securing the Welfare of Richard Clarke by Perth Town and Other Bodies of Persons Concerned.* Scottish Education Department, Social Work Services Group. London: HMSO.

Clarke (1979) *The Report of the Committee of Inquiry into the Actions of the Authorities and Agencies relating to Darryn James Clarke*, DHSS, Cmnd 7730, London: HMSO.

Cleveland (1988) *Report of the Inquiry into Child Abuse in Cleveland 1987*, Cmnd 412, London: HMSO.

Climbié (2003) [Laming Report] *Inquiry into the Death of Victoria Climbié*. London: The Stationery Office.

Colwell (1974) *Report of the Committee of Enquiry into the Care and Supervision Provided in Relation to Maria Colwell*, London: HMSO.

Colwell (1975) *Children at Risk: A Study into the Problems Revealed by the Report of the Inquiry into the Case of Maria Colwell*, Lewes: East Sussex County Council.

Colwell (1976) *Children at Risk: Joint Report of the County Secretary and Director of Social Services*, Lewes: East Sussex County Council.

Gates (1982) *Report of the Panel of Inquiry into the Death of Lucy Gates, Vol. 1: Chairman's Report; Vol. 2: Report of Other Panel Members*, London Borough of Bexley and Bexley Health Authority.

Godfrey (1975) *Report of the Joint Committee of Enquiry into Non-accidental Injury to Children with Particular Reference to Lisa Godfrey.* Lambeth, Southwark and Lewisham Health Authority (Teaching), Inner London Probation and After-Care Committee, London Borough of Lambeth.

'H' Family (1977) *The H. Family: Report of an Investigation by the Director of Social Services and the Deputy Town Clerk*, Surrey County Council.

Haddon (1980) *Report of the Director of Social Services to the Social Services Committee, Clare Haddon Born 9.12.78*, City of Birmingham Social Services Department.

Henry (1987) *Whose Child? The Report of the Panel Appointed to Inquire into the Death of Tyra Henry*, London Borough of Lambeth.

Howlett (1976) *Joint Enquiry Arising from the Death of Neil Howlett*, City of Birmingham District Council and Birmingham Area Health Authority.

Ismail, Aliyah (1999) *Part 8 Review: Summary Report*. London: Harrow Area Child Protection Committee.

Koseda (1986) *Report of the Review Panel . . . into the Death of Heidi Koseda*, London Borough of Hillingdon.

Mehmedagi (1981) *Maria Mehmedagi. Report of an Independent Inquiry*, London Borough of Southwark, Lambeth, Southwark and Lewisham Area Health Authority (Teaching), Inner London Probation and After-Care Service.

Menhenniott (1978) *Report of the Social Work Service of the DHSS into Certain Aspects of the Management of the Case of Stephen Menhenniott*, DHSS, London: HMSO.

Meurs (1975) *Report of the Review Body Appointed to Enquire into the Case of Stephen Meurs*, Norfolk County Council.

Naseby (1973) *Report of the Committee of Enquiry Set Up to Enquire into the Circumstances Surrounding the Admission, Treatment and Discharge of Body David Lee Naseby, Deceased at Burton-on-Trent General Hospital from February to May 1973*, Staffordshire Area Health Authority.

Neave (1997) *Report on the Professional Judgements and Accountability in Relation to Work with the Neave Family*, London: Bridge Child Care Consultancy.

O'Neill (1945) *Report by Sir Walter Monckton on the Circumstances Which Led to the Boarding Out of Dennis and Terence O'Neill at Bank Farm, Miserley and the Steps Taken to Supervise Their Welfare*, Cmnd 6636, London: HMSO.

Page (1981) *Malcolm Page. Report of a Panel Appointed by the Essex Area Review Committee*, Essex County Council and Essex Area Health Authority.

'Paul' (1995) *Paul: Death from Neglect*, London: Bridge Child Care Consultancy.

Peacock (1978) *Report of the Committee of Enquiry Concerning Simon Peacock*, Cambridgeshire County Council, Suffolk County Council, Cambridgeshire AHA (Teaching), Suffolk AHA.

Piazzani (1974) *Report of the Joint Committee Set Up to Consider Co-ordination of Services Concerned with Non-accidental Injury to Children*, Essex Area Health Authority and Essex County Council.

Pinder/Frankland (1981) *Child Abuse Enquiry Sub-committee Report Concerning Christopher Pinder/Daniel Frankland (Born 19.12.79, Died 8.7.80)*, Bradford Area Review Committee.

Spencer (1978) *Karen Spencer*, Derbyshire County Council.

'Sukina' (1991) *Sukina: An Evaluation of the Circumstances Leading to Her Death*, London: Bridge Child Care Consultancy.

Taylor (1980) *Carly Taylor: Report of an Independent Inquiry*, Leicestershire County Council and Leicestershire Area Health Authority (Teaching).

West (1995) *Part 8 Case Review Overview Report in Respect of Charmaine and Heather West*, Gloucester, Gloucestershire Area Child Protection Committee.

Woodcock (1984) *Report on the Death of Shirley Woodcock*, London Borough of Hammersmith and Fulham.

Bibliography

Abel, G. G., Becker, J. V. and Mittleman, M. (1987) 'Self-reported Sex Crimes of Nonincarcerated Paraphiliacs', *Journal of Interpersonal Violence*, 2(1), pp. 3–25.

Adamson, J. and Warren, C. (1983) *Welcome to St Gabriel's Family Centre*, London: The Children's Society.

Adorno, T. W., Frenkel-Brunswik, E., Levinson, D. J. and Sanford, R. N. (1950) *The Authoritarian Personality*, New York: Harper & Row.

Aguilera, D. (1988) *Crisis Intervention Theory and Methodology*, 8th edn, St. Louis, Miss.: Mosby.

Ahmad, B. (1989) 'Protecting Black children from abuse', *Social Work Today*, 8 June, p. 24.

Ainsworth, M. D. S. (1969) 'Further Research into the Adverse Effects of Maternal Deprivation', in J. Bowlby, *Child Care and the Growth of Love*, Harmondsworth: Pelican.

Ainsworth, M. D. S., Blehar, M., Waters, E. and Wall, S. (1978) *Patterns of Attachment: A Psychological Study of the Strange Situation*, Hillsdale, NJ: Lawrence Erlbaum.

Allen, N. E., Wolf, A. M., Bybee, D. I. and Sullivan, C. M. (2003) 'Diversity of Children's Immediate Coping Responses to Witnessing Domestic Violence', *Journal of Emotional Abuse*, 3, pp. 123–47.

Angelou, M. (1984) *I Know Why the Cage Bird Sings*, London: Virago.

Anthony, E. J. and Cohler, B. J. (1987) *The Invulnerable Child*, New York: Guildford Press.

Arcus, D. and Kagan, J. (1995) 'Temperament and Craniofacial Variation in the First Two Years', *Child Development*, **66**, pp. 1529–40.

Argent, H. (2003) *Models of Adoption Support: What Works and What Doesn't*, London: BAAF.

Argyle, M. (1988) *Bodily Communication*, London: Methuen.

Aries, P. (1962) *Centuries of Childhood* (trans. R. Baldrick), London: Jonathan Cape.

Ayline, V. (1947) *Play Therapy*, New York: Ballantino.

Bahn, C. (1980) 'Hostage Takers, the Taken and the Context: Discussion', *Annals of the New York Academy of Sciences*, 347, pp. 129–36.

Bain, O. and Sanders, M. (1990) *Out in the Open*, London: Virago.

Bandura, A. (1973) *Aggression: A Social Learning Theory*, Englewood Cliffs, NJ: Prentice-Hall.

Banks, N. (2002) 'What is a Positive Black Identity?' in K. N. Dwivedi (ed.), *Meeting the Needs of Ethnic Minority Children*, 2nd edn. London: Jessica Kingsley.

Bannister, A. (2002) 'Group Work in Child Protection Agencies', in K. Wilson and A. James, *The Child Protection Handbook*, 2nd edn, Edinburgh: Ballière Tindall.

Barclay Report (1982) *Social Workers: Their Role and Tasks*, London: NISW/Bedford Square Press.

Bass, E. and Davis, L. (1990) *The Courage to Heal*, London: Cedar.

Bastian, P. (1994) 'Family Care in the United Kingdom', in M. Gottesman, *Recent Changes and New Trends in Extrafamilial Child Care: An International Perspective*, London: FICE.

Beckett, C. (2003) *Child Protection: an Introduction*. London: Sage.

Beezley Mrazek, P. and Mrazek, D. A. (1981) 'The Effects of Child Sexual Abuse: Methodological Considerations', in P. Beezley Mrazek and C. H. Kempe (eds), *Sexually Abused Children and their Families*, Oxford Pergamon.

Ben (Anonymous) (1991) *Things in My Head*, Dublin: Blendale Publishing.

Benedict, R. (1955) 'Continuities and Discontinuities in Cultural Conditioning – 1938', in M. Mead and M. Wolfenstein (eds), *Childhood in Contemporary Cultures*, Chicago: University of Chicago Press.

Bentovim, A. (2002) 'Working with Abusive Families', in K. Wilson and A. James, *The Child Protection Handbook*, 2nd edn, Edinburgh: Ballière Tindall.

Berridge, D. (2001) 'Foster Families', in P. Foley, J. Roche and S. Tucker (eds), *Children in Society*, Basingstoke: Palgrave.

Berridge, D. and Cleaver, H. (1987) *Foster Home Breakdown*, Oxford: Basil Blackwell.

Bettelheim, B. (1979) *Surviving and Other Essays*, London: Thames & Hudson.

Bion, W. R. (1961) *Experiences in Groups and Other Papers*, London: Tavistock.

Blakey, C., Collinge, M. and Jones, D. N. (1986) 'The One-way Screen', *Community Care*, 25 September, pp. 16–17.

Bloch, D. (1979) *'So the Witch Won't Eat Me': Fantasy and the Child's Fear of Infanticide*, London, Burnett Books.

Bodmer, N. M. (1998) 'Impact of Pet Ownership on the Well-being of Adolescents with Few Familial Resources', in C. C. Wilson and D. C. Turner (eds), *Companion Animals in Human Health*, Thousand Oaks, Calif: Sage.

Bolger, K. E. and Patterson, C. J. (2003) 'Sequelae of Child Maltreatment', in S. S. Luthar (ed.), *Resilience and Vulnerability*, Cambridge University Press.

Bolton, F. G. Jr., Morris, L. A. and MacEachron, A. E. (1989) *Males at Risk: The Other Side of Child Sexual Abuse*, Newbury Park, Calif.: Sage.

Bottoms, B. L., Shaver, P. R., Goodman, G. S. and Quin, J. (1995) 'In the Name of God: A Profile of Religion-related Child Abuse', *Journal of Social Issues*, 51(2) pp. 85–111.

Bowlby, J. (1951) *Maternal Care and Mental Health: Report to the World Health Organisation*, New York: Shocken Books.

Bowlby, J. (1969) *Child Care and the Growth of Love*, Harmondsworth: Pelican.

Brabender, V. (2002) *Introduction to Group Therapy*, Chichester: Wiley.

Bronfenbrenner, U. (1979) *The Ecology of Human Development: Experiments by Nature and Design*, Cambridge, Mass.: Harvard University Press.

Brown, R. (2000) *Group Processes: Dynamics Within and Between Groups*, Oxford: Basil Blackwell.

Browne, K. (2002) 'Child Abuse: Defining, Understanding and Intervening', in K. Wilson and A. James, *The Child Protection Handbook*, 2nd edn, Edinburgh: Ballière Tindall.

Bruckner, D. F. and Johnson, P. E. (1987) 'Treatment of Adult Male Victims of Childhood Sexual Abuse', *Social Casework*, February, pp. 81–7.

Butler-Sloss, E. (1988) *Report of the Inquiry into Child Abuse in Cleveland 1987*, London: HMSO.

Cairns, B. (2004) *Fostering Attachments: Long Term Outcomes in Family Group Care*, London: BAAF.

Calder, M. C. and Hackett, S. (eds) (2003) *Assessment in Child Care: Using and Developing Frameworks for Practice*, Lyme Regis: Russell House Publishing.

Caloustie Gulbenkien Foundation (1995) *Children and Violence*, London: Caloustie Gulbenkien Foundation.

Cameronchild, J. (1987) 'An Autobiography of Violence', *Child Abuse and Neglect*, 2, pp. 139–49.

Carpenter, F. (1974) 'Mother's face and the Newborn', *New Scientist*, 21 March, pp. 742–4.

Cattanach, A. (1993) *Play Therapy with Abused Children*, London: Jessica Kingsley.

Charles-Hoon, S. (2003) 'Meeting the Needs of Dual-heritage Children', *Unpublished work study*, University College Northampton.

ChildLine (1989) *I Know You're Not a Doctor But . . .*, London: ChildLine.

Children Act 1989 – London: HMSO.

Children's Society (1995) *Couldn't Care More. A Study of Young Carers and Their Needs*, London: The Children's Society.

Chodoff, P. (1981) 'Survivors of the Nazi Holocaust', *Children Today*, September–October, pp. 2–5.

Cigno, K. (2002) 'Helping to Prevent Abuse: A Cognitive-behavioural Approach', in K. Wilson and A. James (eds), *The Child Protection Handbook*, 2nd edn, Edinburgh: Ballière Tindall.

Cleaver, H. and Freeman, P. (1995) *Parental Perspectives in Cases of Suspected Child Abuse*, London: HMSO.

Cohen, A. J., Mannarino, A. P., Zhitova, A. C. and Capone, M. E. (2003) 'Treating Child Abuse Related Posttraumatic Stress and Comorbid Substance Abuse in Adolescents, *Child Abuse and Neglect*, 27, pp. 1345–65.

Cole, P. M., Woolger, C., Power, T. G. and Smith, K. D. (1992) 'Parenting Difficulties Among Adult Survivors of Father–Daughter Incest', *Child Abuse and Neglect*, 16(2) pp. 239–50.

Colton, M., Sanders, R. and Williams, M. (2001) *An Introduction to Working with Children*, Basingstoke: Palgrave.

Compton, M. (2002) 'Individual Work with Children', in K. Wilson and A. James (eds), *The Child Protection Handbook*, 2nd edn, Edinburgh: Harcourt.

Corby, B. (2000) *Child Abuse: Towards a Knowledge Base*, 2nd edn, Buckingham: Open University Press.

Corby, B., Doig, A. and Roberts, V. (2001) *Public Inquiries into Abuse of Children in Residential Care*, London: Jessica Kingsley.

Coulshed, V. and Orme, J. (1998) *Social Work Practice*, 3rd edn, Basingstoke: Palgrave.

Coward, B. and Dattani, P. (1993) 'Race, Identity and Culture', in K. N. Dwivedi (ed.), (1993) *Group Work with Children and Adolescents*, London: Jessica Kingsley.

Dahl, R. (1997) *The Roald Dahl Treasury*, London: Random House.

Davies, M., Cloke, C. and Finkelhor, D. (1995) *Participation and Empowerment in Child Protection*, London: Pitman.

Davis, P. (1996) 'Threats of Corporal Punishment as Verbal Aggression: A Naturalistic Study', *Child Abuse and Neglect*, 20(4), pp. 289–304.

Dawood, N. J. (trans.) (1990) *The Koran*, Harmondsworth: Penguin.

Dearden, C. and Becker, S. (1995) *The National Directory of Young Carers Projects and Initiatives*, Loughborough: University of Loughborough, Young Carers Research Group.

Department of Health (1995) *Child Protection: Messages from the Research*, London: HMSO.

Department of Health (2000) *Framework for the Assessment of Children in Need and Their Families*, London: The Stationery Office.

Dingwall, R., Eekelaar, J. and Murray, T. (1983) *The Protection of Children: State Intervention and Family Life*, Oxford: Basil Blackwell.

Dobson, C. and Payne, R. (1977) *The Carlos Complex: A Study in Terror*, London: Hodder & Stoughton.

Doel, M. and Marsh, P. (1992) *Task-centred Casework*, Aldershot: Ashgate.

Dogra, N., Parkin, A., Gale, G. and Frake, C. (2002) *Child and Adolescent Mental Health for Front-line Professionals*, London: Jessica Kingsley.

Dominelli, L. and McLeod, E. (1989) *Feminist Social Work*, London: Macmillan.

Donaldson, M. A. and Cordes-Green, S. (1994) *Group Treatment of Adult Incest Survivors*, London: Sage.

Douglas, A. and Philpot, T. (2003) *Changing Families: Changing Times*, London: Routledge.

Doyle, C. (1985) *The Imprisoned Child, Aspects of Rescuing the Severely Abused Child*, Occasional Paper no. 3, London: NSPCC.

Doyle, C. (1986) 'Management Sensitivity in CSA Training', *Child Abuse Review*, 1, pp. 8–9.

Doyle, C. (1987) 'Helping Child Victims of Sexual Abuse Through Play', *Practice*, 1, pp. 27–38.

Doyle, C. (1991) 'Caring for the Workers', *Child Abuse Review*, 5(3), pp. 25–7.

Doyle, C. (1994) *Child Sexual Abuse: A Guide for Health Professionals*, London: Chapman & Hall.

Doyle, C. (1996) 'Psychological Maltreatment: Research Findings and Implication for Practice', Paper presented at the 11th International Conference on Child Abuse and Neglect, University College, Dublin, August.

Doyle, C. (1997a) 'Terror and the Stockholm Syndrome: The Relevance for Abused Children', in J. Bates, R. G. Pugh and N. Thompson (eds), *Protecting Children, Challenges and Change*, Aldershot: Arena.

Doyle, C. (1997b) 'Emotional Abuse of Children: Issues for Intervention', *Child Abuse Review*, 6, pp. 330–42.

Doyle, C. (1998) 'Emotional Abuse of Children: Issues for Intervention', Ph.D. thesis, University of Leicester.

Doyle, C. (2001) 'Surviving and Coping with Emotional Abuse in Childhood', *Clinical Child Psychology and Psychiatry*, 6(3), pp. 387–402.

Doyle, C. (2002) 'Palliative Factors in Psychological Maltreatment of Children', *Research Report for the British Academy*, unpublished.

Doyle, C. (2003) 'Child Emotional Abuse: The Role of Educational Professionals', *Educational and Child Psychology*, 20(1), pp. 8–21.

Dube, S. R., Williamson, D. F., Thompson, T., Felitti, V. J. and Anda, R. F. (2004) 'Assessing the Reliability of Retrospective Reports of Adverse Childhood Experiences among Adult HMO Members Attending a Primary Care Clinic, *Child Abuse and Neglect*, 28, pp. 729–38.

Dunn, J. (1995) 'Studying Relationships and Social Understanding', in P. Barnes (ed.), *Personal, Social and Emotional Development of Children*, Oxford: Basils Blackwell.

Dwivedi, K. N. (ed.) (1993) *Group Work with Children and Adolescents*, London: Jessica Kingsley.

Dwivedi, K. N. (ed.) (2000) *Post-traumatic Stress Disorder in Children and Adolescents*, London: Whurr.

Dwork, D. (1991) *Children with a Star: Jewish Youth in Nazi Germany*, New Haven, Conn.: Yale University Press.

Elliot, M. (ed.) (1993) *Female Sexual Abuse of Children: The Ultimate Taboo*, Harlow: Longman.

Elton, A. (1988) 'Family Treatment – Treatment Methods and Techniques', in A. Bentovim, A. Elton, J. Hildebrand, M. Tranter and E. Vizard (eds), *Child Sexual Abuse within the Family: Assessment and Treatment*, London: Wright.

Ennew, J. (1986) *The Sexual Exploitation of Children*, Cambridge: Polity Press.

Erikson, E. H. (1965) *Childhood and Society*, 2nd edn, Harmondsworth: Penguin.

Etherinton, K. (1995) *Adult Male Survivors of Childhood Sexual Abuse*, London: Pitman.

Evert, E. and Bijkerk, I. (1987) *When You're Ready*, Walnut Creek, Calif: Launch Press.

Fahlberg, V. (1994) *A Child's Journey through Placement*, London: BAAF.

Farmer, E. and Owen, M. (eds) (1995) *Child Protection Practice: Private Risks and Public Remedies*, London: HMSO.

Finkelhor, D. (1984) *Child Sexual Abuse: New Theory and Research*, New York: The Free Press.

Foley, P., Roche, J. and Tucker, S. (eds) (2001) *Children in Society: Contemporary Theory, Policy and Practice*, Basingstoke: Palgrave.

Ford, J. D., Racusin, R., Ellis, C. G., Daviss, W. B., Reiser, J., Fleischer, A. and Thomas, J. (2000) 'Child Maltreatment, Other Trauma Exposure and Posttraumatic Symptomatology Among Children with Oppositional Defiant and Attention Deficit Hyperactivity Disorders', *Child Maltreatment*, 5(3), pp. 205–17.

Foucault, M. (1980) *Power/Knowledge* (papers ed. and trans. by C. Gordon), Brighton: Harvester.

Fraiberg, S. (1952) 'Some Aspects of Casework with Children. 1. Understanding the Child Client', *Social Casework*, 33(9), November.

Francis, J. (1995) 'Stand By Me', *Community Care*, issue 1081, 17–23 August, pp. 18–19.

Franklin, B. (2002) *The New Handbook of Children's Rights*, London: Routledge.

Fraser, S. (1989) *My Father's House*, London: Virago.

Fryer, P. (1984) *Staying Power*, London: Pluto Press.

Furniss, T., Bigley-Miller, L. and Van Elburg, A. (1988) 'Goal-orientated Group Treatment for Sexually Abused Adolescent Girls', *British Journal of Psychiatry*, 152, pp. 97–106.

Gambe, D., Gomes, J., Kapu, V., Rangel, M. and Stubbs, P. (1992) *Improving Practice with Children and Families*, London: CCETSW.

Geiger, B. (1996) *Fathers as Primary Caregivers*, Westport, Conn.: Greenwood Press.

Geldard, K. and Geldard, D. (1997) *Counselling Children: A Practical Introduction*, London: Sage.

Gelles, R. and Cornell, C. (1985) *Intimate Violence in Families*, Beverly Hills, Calif.: Sage.

Gelles, R. J. and Strauss, M. A. (1979) 'Family Experience and Public Support of the Death Penalty, in D. G. Gil (ed.), *Child Abuse and Violence*, New York: AMS Press.

Gibbons, J., Conroy, S. and Bell, C. (1995) *Operating the Child Protection System*, London: HMSO.

Gibbons, J., Gallagher, B., Bell, C. and Gordon, D. (1995) *Development after Physical Abuse in Early Childhood*, London: HMSO.

Gibran, K. (1923) *The Prophet* (annotated edition by S. Bushrui, 1995), Oxford: Oneworld.

Gibson, A. and Lewis, C. (1985) *A Light in the Dark Tunnel*, London: Centre for Caribbean Studies.

Gil, D. G. (1970) *Violence against Children, Physical Child Abuse in the United States*, Cambridge, Mass.: Harvard University Press.

Gil, E. M. (1984) *Out-growing the Pain: a Book for and about Adults Abused as Children*, San Francisco: Launch.

Gil, E. M. (1988) *Treatment of Adult Survivors of Child Abuse*, Walnut Creek, Calif.: Launch Press.

Gittins, D. (1993) *The Family in Question*, 2nd edn, London: Macmillan.

Golan, N. (1978) *Treatment in Crisis Situations*, New York: Free Press.

Gonsiorek, J. C., Bera, W. H. and Le Tourneau, D. (1994) *Male Sexual Abuse*, London: Sage.

Green, A. H. (1978) 'Self-destructive Behaviour in Battered Children', *American Journal of Psychiatry*, **135**(5), May, pp. 579–82.

Greig, A. and Taylor, J. (1999) *Doing Research with Children*, London: Sage.

Gross, R. D. (2003) *Themes, Issues and Debates in Psychology*, 2nd edn, London: Hodder & Stoughton.

Haasal, B. and Marnocha, J. (2000) *Bereavement Support Group for Children*, 2nd edn, London: Accelerated Development.

Hagans, K. B. and Case, J. (1990) *When Your Child Has Been Molested*, Lexington, Mass.: Lexington Books.

Haj-Yahia, M. and Shor, R. (1995) 'Child Maltreatment as Perceived by Arab Students of Social Science in the West Bank', *Child Abuse and Neglect*, **19**(10), pp. 1209–20.

Hall, L. and Lloyd, S. (1989) *Surviving Child Sexual Abuse*, Lenton: Falmer Press.

Hallett, C. (1995) 'Child Abuse: An Academic Overview', in P. Kingston and B. Penhale (eds), *Family Violence and the Caring Professions*, London: Macmillan.

Handy, C. (1985) *Understanding Organisations*, 3rd edn, Harmondsworth: Penguin.

Hardiker, P., Exton, K. and Barker, M. (1991) 'The Social Policy Contexts of Child Care', *British Journal of Social Work*, **21**, pp. 341–59.

Harding, L. (1997) *Perspectives in Child Care Policy*, 2nd edn, Harlow: Longman.

Hart, S. N. (1988) 'Psychological Maltreatment: Emphasis on Prevention', *School Psychology International*, **9**, pp. 243–55.

Hart, S. N., Binggeli, N. J. and Brassard, M. R. (1998) 'Evidence for the Effects of Psychological Maltreatment', *Journal of Emotional Abuse*, **1**(1), 27–58.

Hayes, N. and Orrell, S. (1998) *Psychology, an Introduction*, Harlow: Longman.

Hendrick, H. (1990) 'Constructions and Reconstructions of British Childhood: An Interpretative Survey, 1800 to the Present', in A. James and A. Prout (eds), *Constructing and Reconstructing Childhood*, London: Falmer Press.

Hendrick, H. (1994) *Child Welfare: England 1872–1989*, London: Routledge.

Herzberger, S. (1993) 'The Cyclical Pattern of Child Abuse: A Study of Research Methodology', in C. M. Renzetti and R. M. Lee (eds), *Researching Sensitive Topics*, Newbury Park, Calif.: Sage.

Hildebrand, J. (1988) 'The Use of Groupwork in Treating Child Sexual Abuse', in A. Bentovim, A. Elton, J. Hildebrand, M. Tranter and

E. Vizard (eds), *Child Sexual Abuse Within the Family: Assessment and Treatment*, London: Wright.

Hindmann, J. (1983) *A Very Touching Book*, Durkes, Oreg.: McClure-Hindmann.

Hitchman, J. (1960) *The King of the Barbareens*, London: Putnam.

Hockey, J. and James, A. (1993) *Growing Up and Growing Old: Ageing and Dependency in the Life Course*, London: Sage.

Holt, J. (1975) *Escape from Childhood: The Needs and Rights of Children*, Harmondsworth: Penguin.

Hoover, K. and Donovan, T. (1995) *The Elements of Social Scientific Thinking*, 6th edn, New York: St Martin's Press.

Hough, M. (2001) *Groupwork Skills and Theory*, London: Hodder & Stoughton.

Howe, D. (1995) *Attachment Theory for Social Work Practice*, London: Macmillan.

Howe, D., Brandon, M., Hinings, D. and Schofield, G. (1999) *Attachment Theory, Child Maltreatment and Family Support*, Basingstoke: Palgrave.

Howitt, D. and Owusu-Bempah, J. (1994) *The Racism of Psychology: Time for Change*, Hemel Hampstead: Harvester Wheatsheaf.

Humphreys, C. (2000) *Social Work, Domestic Violence and Child Protection*, Bristol: Policy Press.

Iwaniec, D. (1995) *The Emotionally Abused and Neglected Child*, Chichester: John Wiley.

Iwaniec, D. (1996) 'Emotional Abuse and Growth Failure', Paper presented to the 11th International Conference on Child Abuse and Neglect, University College, Dublin, August.

Iwaniec, D. and Pinkerton, J. (eds) (1998) *Making Research Work*, Chichester: John Wiley.

Jackson, S. and Thomas, N. (2000) *What Works in Creating Stability for Looked After Children?*, 2nd edn, London: Barnardos.

Jennings, S. (1999) *Introduction to Developmental Playtherapy*, London: Jessica Kingsley.

Jones, D. N., Pickett, J., Oates, M. R. and Barbor, P. (1987) *Understanding Child Abuse*, 2nd edn, London, Macmillan.

Kagan, J. (1997) 'Temperament and the Reactions to Unfamiliarity', *Child Development*, **68**, pp. 139–43.

Kellmer Pringle, M. (1974) *The Needs of Children*, London: Hutchinson.

Kelly, G. and Gilligan, R. (eds) (2000) *Issues in Foster Care: Policy, Practice and Research*, London: Jessica Kingsley.

Kendall-Tackett, K. and Becker-Blease, K. (2004) 'Importance of Retrospective Findings in Child Maltreatment Research', *Child Abuse and Neglect*, **28**, pp. 723–7.

Kennedy, M. (1990) 'The Deaf Child Who Is Sexually Abused – Is There a Need for a Dual Specialists?', *Child Abuse Review*, 4(2), pp. 3–6.

Kennedy, M. (2002) 'Disability and Child Abuse', in K. Wilson and A. James (eds), *The Child Protection Handbook*, 2nd edn, Edinburgh: Harcourt.

Kirkwood, A. (1993) *The Leicestershire Inquiry 1992*, Leicester, Leicestershire County Council.

Kirton, D. (2000) *'Race', Ethnicity and Adoption*, Buckingham: Open University.

Kitzinger, J. (1994) 'Challenging Sexual Violence Against Girls: A Social Awareness Approach', *Child Abuse Review*, 3(4), pp. 246–58.

Konopka, G. (1972) *Social Group Work*, 2nd edn, Englewood Cliffs, NJ: Practice-Hall.

Kubler-Ross, E. (1970) *On Death and Dying*, London: Tavistock.

Lahad, M. (1992) 'Story Making and Assessment Method for Coping with Stress: Six Part Story and BASIC Ph', *Dramatherapy: Theory and Practice 2*, London: Routledge.

Lamb, M. E. (ed.) (1987) *The Father's Role: Cross-cultural Perspectives*, Hillsdale, NY: Lawrence Erlbaum.

Lau, A. (1991) 'Cultural and Ethnic Perspectives on Significant Harm: Its Assessment and Treatment', in M. Adcock, R. White and A. Hollows (eds), *Significant Harm*, London: Significant Publications.

Lau, A. (2002) 'Family Therapy and Ethnic Minorities', in N. Dwivedi (ed.), *Meeting the Needs of Ethnic Minority Children*, 2nd edn, London: Jessica Kingsley.

Law, J. and Elias, J. (1995) *Trouble Talking: A Guide for Parents of Children with Difficulties Communicating*, London: Jessica Kingsley.

Leith, A. and Handforth, S. (1988) 'Groupwork with Sexually Abused Boys', *Practice*, 2(2), pp. 166–75.

Levy, A. and Kahan, B. (1991) *The Pindown Experience and the Protection of Children*, Stafford: Staffordshire County Council.

Littner, N. (1956) *Some Traumatic Effects of Separation and Placement*, New York: Child Welfare League of America.

Lorenz, K. (1970) *Studies in Animal Behaviour*, London: Methuen.

Luthar, S. S. (ed.) (2003) *Resilience and Vulnerability*, Cambridge University Press.

Lynch, M. A. and Roberts, J. (1982) *Consequences of Child Abuse*, London: Academic Press.

MacFarlane, A. (1977) *The Psychology of Childbirth*, London: Fontana/Open Books.

MacLeod, M. and Saraga, E. (1988) 'Challenging the Orthodoxy: Towards a Feminist Theory and Practice', *Feminist Review*, 28, pp. 16–55.

MacVeigh, J. (1982) *Gaskin*, London: Jonathan Cape.

Main, M. and Solomon, J. (1986) 'Discovery of an Insecure-disorganized/Disorientated Attachment Pattern', in T. Brazelton and M. Yogman (eds), *Affective Development in Infancy*, Norwood, NY: Ablex.

Maitra, B. and Miller, A. (2002) 'Children, Families and Therapists', in N. Dwivedi (ed.), *Meeting the Needs of Ethnic Minority Children*, 2nd edn, London: Jessica Kingsley.

Marchant, R. (2001) 'Working with Disabled Children', in P. Foley, J. Roche and S. Tucker (eds), *Children in Society*, Basingstoke: Palgrave.

Mascaro, J. (trans.) (1962) *The Bhagavad Gita*, Harmondsworth: Penguin.

Maslow, A. H. (1970) *Motivation and Personality*, 2nd edn, New York: Harper & Row.

Masson, J. (1995) Lecture handout for Session 1 Diploma in Child Protection Studies/Short Course in Child Protection Law, University of Leicester.

Masson, J. and Morris, M. (1992) *Children Act Manual*, London: Sweet & Maxwell.

Masten, A. S. and Coatsworth, J. D. (1998) 'The Development of Competence in Favorable and Unfavorable Environments: Lessons from Research on Successful Children', *American Psychologist*, 53, pp. 205–20.

Mayle, P. (1973) *Where Did I Come From?*, Melbourne: Sun Books.

McFadden, E. J. (1980) 'Fostering and the Battered and Abused Child', *Children Today*, March–April, pp. 13–15.

McKnight, R. (1972) 'Group Work with Children', in Holgate, E. (ed.), *Communicating with Children: Collected Papers*, London: Longman.

Mead, M. (1962) 'A Cultural Anthropologist's Approach to Maternal Deprivation', in *Deprivation in Maternal Care: A Reassessment of its Effects, Public Health Papers*, 14, pp. 9–13, Geneva: World Health Organization.

Melson, G. F. (1998) 'The Role of Companion Animals in Human Development', in C. C. Wilson, and D. C. Turner (eds), *Companion Animals in Human Health*, Thousand Oaks, Calif.: Sage.

Mendel, M. P. (1994) *The Male Survivor*, London: Sage.

Mills, M. and Melhuish, E. (1974) 'Recognition of Mother's Voice in Early Infancy', *Nature*, 252, pp. 123–4.

Milner, J. (1993) 'A Disappearing Act: The Differing Career Paths of Fathers and Mothers in Child Protection Investigations', *Critical Social Policy*, 13(2), pp. 46–68.

Miyake, K., Chen, S. J. and Compos, J. J. (1985) 'Infant Temperament, Mother's Mode of Interaction, and Attachment in Japan: An Interim Report', in I. Bretherton and E. Waters (eds), *Growing Points in Attachment Theory and Research*, Monographs of the Society for Research in Child Development, Serial number 209, 50, pp. 1–2.

Moran, P. B., Vuchinich, S. and Hall, N. K. (2004) 'Associations between Types of Maltreatment and Substance Use During Adolescence', *Child Abuse and Neglect*, 28, pp. 565–74.

Morrison, B. (1993) *And When Did You Last See Your Father?*, London: Granta Books.

Mrazek, P. B. and Mrazek, D. A. (1981) 'The Effects of Child Sexual Abuse: Methodological Considerations', in P. B. Mrazek and C. H. Kempe (eds), *Sexually Abused Children and their Families*, Oxford: Pergamon Press.

National Children's Homes (1994) *Hidden Victims*, London: NCH Action for Children.

Oaklander, V. (1978) *Windows to Our Children*, New York: Real People Press.

Oliver, S. (2000) *Supporting the Adoptive Parents of Special Needs Children*, Norwich: University of East Anglia.

O'Neill, T. (1981) *A Place Called Hope. Caring for Children in Distress*, Oxford: Basil Blackwell.

Oppenheimer, R. (1985) 'Implications for Long-term Treatment', Conference seminar summarized by F. Groves in *Child Sexual Abuse – Report of the Inaugural Conference*, British Association for the Study and Prevention of Child Abuse and Neglect, Midlands Branch.

Orchard, B. and Fuller, R. C. (eds) (1966) *The Holy Bible*, London: Catholic Truth Society.

Orr, R. (2003) *My Right to Play*, Maidenhead: Open University/McGraw-Hill Education.

Owusu-Bempah, K. (1994) 'Race, Self-identity and Social Work', *British Journal of Social Work*, 24, pp. 123–36.

Owusu-Bempah, K. (1995) 'Information about the Absent Parent as a Factor in the Well-being of Children of Single-parent Families', *International Social Work*, 38, pp. 253–75.

Owusu-Bempah, K. (2003) 'Political Correctness: In the Interest of the Child?', *Educational and Child Psychology*, 20, pp. 53–63.

Papalia, D. E., Gross, E. and Feldman, R. D. (2003) *Child Development: A Topical Approach*, New York: McGraw-Hill.

Parker, T. (1969) *The Twisting Lane, Some Sex Offenders*, London: Panther.

Parkinson, F. (1993) *Post-Traumatic Stress*, London: Sheldon.

Parton, N. (1985) *The Politics of Child Abuse*, London: Macmillan.

Payne, M. (1997) *Modern Social Work Theory*, 2nd edn, Basingstoke: Palgrave.

Pennells, M. and Smith, S. C. (1994) *The Forgotten Mourners*, London: Jessica Kingsley.

Perkins, D. F. and Jones, D. R. (2004) 'Risk Behaviours and Resiliency within Physically Abused Children', *Child Abuse and Neglect*, 28, pp. 547–64.

Peters, J. (1966) *Growing-up World, Children in Families*, London: Longman, p. 74.

Phillips, M. (2002) 'Issues of Ethnicity and Culture', in K. Wilson and A. James (eds), *The Child Protection Handbook*, 2nd edn, Edinburgh: Harcourt.

Philpot, T. (1995) Uncertain Ground, *Community Care*, **1067**, 11–17 May, p. 1.

Piaget, J. (1983) 'Piaget's Theory', in P. H. Mussen (ed.), *Handbook of Child Psychology, Vol. 1: Theory and Methods*, New York: Wiley.

Pilcher, J. (1996) *Age and Generation in Modern Britain*, Oxford University Press.

Pizzey, E. (1974) *Scream Quietly or the Neighbours Will Hear*, Harmondsworth: Penguin.

Postman, N. (1983) *The Disappearance of Childhood*, London: W. H. Allen.

Quinn, P. (1988) *Cry Out!*, Eastbourne: Kingsway.

Rayner, C. (2003) *How Did I Get Here From there?*, London: Virago Press.

Reid, W. J. and Epstein, L. (1972) *Task-centred Casework*, New York: Columbia University Press.

Reidy, T. J. (1977) 'The Aggressive Characteristics of Abused and Neglected Children', *Journal of Clinical Psychology*, 33(4), October, pp. 1140–5.

Rickford, F. (1995) 'The Ones Who Get Away', *Community Care*, *1085*, 7–13 September.

Roberts, R., O'Connor, T., Dunn, J. and Golding, J. (2004) 'The Effects of Child Sexual Abuse in Later Life: Mental Health Parenting and Adjustment of Offspring', *Child Abuse and Neglect*, 28, pp. 535–46.

Rogers, C. R. (1967) *On Becoming a Person*, London: Constable.

Rogers, C. R. (1980) *A Way of Being*, Boston, Mass.: Houghton Mifflin.

Rothbart, M. K., Ahadi, S. A. and Evans, D. E. (2000) 'Temperament and Personality: Origins and Outcomes', *Journal of Personality and Social Psychology*, 78, pp. 122–35.

Rothbart, M. K., Ahadi, S. A., Hershey, K. L. and Fisher, P. (2001) 'Investigations of Temperament at Three and Seven Years: The Children's Behaviour Questionnaire', *Child Department*, 72, pp. 1394–408.

Rouf, K. (1991a) *Black Girls Speak Out*, London: The Children's Society.

Rouf, K. (1991b) *Into Pandora's Box*, London: The Children's Society.

Rowan, A. B., Foy, D. W., Rodriguez, N. and Ryan, S. (1994) 'Posttraumatic Stress Disorder in a Clinical Sample of Adults Sexually Abused as Children', *Child Abuse and Neglect*, 18(1), pp. 51–62.

Rowling, J. K. (1997) *Harry Potter and the Philosopher's Stone*, London: Bloomsbury Publishing.

Rutter, M. (1979) 'Protective Factors in Children's Response to Stress and Disadvantage', in J. S. Bruner and A. Garden (eds), *Primary Prevention of Psychopathology, Vols. 3*, Hanover, NH: University Press of New England.

Rutter, M. (1981) *Maternal Deprivation Reassessed*, 2nd edn, Harmondsworth: Penguin.

Rutter, M. (1996) 'Childhood Resilience in the Face of Adversity', Paper presented at the 11th International Conference on Child Abuse and Neglect, University College, Dublin, August.

Ryan, G. (1989) 'Victim to Victimiser: Rethinking Victim Treatment', *Journal of Violence*, 4(3), pp. 325–41.

Ryan, T. and Walker, R. (1993) *Life Story Work*, London: BAAF.

Sapey, R. (1995) 'Why the New Right Reigns Supreme on Ideology', *Professional Social Work*, May, p. 6.

Seidman, E. and Pedersen, S. (2003) 'Holistic Contextual Perspectives on Risk, Protection and Competence among Low-income Urban Adolescents', in S. S. Luthar (ed.), *Resilience and Vulnerability*, Cambridge University Press.

Seligman, M. E. P. (1975) *Helplessness. On Depression, Development and Death*, San Francisco: W. H. Freeman.

Sellick, C., Thoburn, J. and Philpot, T. (2004) *What Works in Adoption and Foster Care?*, Illford: Barnardos.

Skinner, S. and Kimmel, E. (1984) *The Anti-Colouring Book*, London: Scholastic Books.

Smith, M. J. (1998) *Social Science in Question*, London: Sage.

Smith, S. and Pennells, M. (1995) *Interventions with Bereaved Children*, London: Jessica Kingsley.

Solzhenitsyn, A. (1974) *The Gulag Archipelago 1918–56*, London: Collins/Fontana.

Spring, J. (1987) *Cry Hard and Swim: The Story of an Incest Survivor*, London: Virago.

Stainton Rogers, W. (2003) *Social Psychology*, Maidenhead: Open University Press.

Stevenson, O. (1995) 'The Pit and the Pendulum', *Professional Social Work*, February, p. 4.

Stevenson, O. (1996) 'Emotional Abuse and Neglect: A Time for Reappraisal', *Child and Family Social Work*, 1(1), pp. 13–18.

Strenz, T. (1980) 'The Stockholm Syndrome: Law Enforcement, Policy and Ego Defenses of the Hostage', *Annals of the New York Academy of Sciences*, 347, pp. 137–50.

Sunderland, M. (2000) *Using Story Telling as a Therapeutic Tool with Children*, Bicester: Speechmark.

Sunderland, M. and Armstrong, N. (2000) *The Frog Who Longed for the Moon to Smile*, Bicester: Winslow.

Summit, R. C. (1983) 'The Child Sexual Abuse Accommodation Syndrome', *Child Abuse and Neglect*, 7, pp. 177–93.

Sutton, C. (1999) *Helping Families with Troubled Children*, Chichester: Wiley.

Symonds, M. (1980) 'Victim Responses to Terror', *Annals of the New York Academy of Sciences*, 347, pp. 129–36.

Thangam, D. and Mullender, A. (2000) *Child Protection and Domestic Violence*, Birmingham: Venture Press.

Thoburn, J., Norfield, L. and Rashid, P. (2000) *Permanent Family Placement for Children of Minority Ethnic Origin*, London: Jessica Kingsley.

Thomas, A. and Chess, S. (1977) *Temperament and Development*, New York: Brummer Mazel.

Thompson, N. (1991) *Crisis Intervention Revisited*, Birmingham: Prepar.

Thompson, N. (2001) *Anti-discriminatory Practice*, 3rd edn, Basingstoke: Palgrave.

Thompson, N. (2003) *Promoting Equality: Challenging Discrimination and Oppression*, Basingstoke: Palgrave.

Thompson, N. (2004) *Group Care with Children and Young People*, Lyme Regis: Russell House.

Timberlake, E. M. (1979) 'Aggression and Depression among Abused and Non-abused Children in Foster Care', *Children and Youth Services Review*, 1, pp. 279–91.

Triebenacher, S. I. (1998) 'The Relationship between Attachment to Companion Animals and Self-esteem: A Developmental Perspective', in C. C. Wilson and D. C. Turner (eds), *Companion Animals in Human Health*, Thousand Oaks, Calif.: Sage.

Tuckman, B. (1965) 'Developing Sequences in Small Groups', *Psychological Bulletin*, 63, pp. 384–99.

Tuckman, B. and Jensen, M. (1977) 'Stages in Small Group Development Revisited', *Group Organizational Studies*, **2**, pp. 419–27.

Vizard, E. (1987) 'Self Esteem and Personal Safety', *ACPP Newsletter*, 9(2), pp. 16–22.

Von Ijzendoorn, M. H. and Kroonenberg, P. M. (1988) 'Cross-cultural Patterns of Attachment: A Meta-analysis of the Strange Situation', *Child Development*, **59**, pp. 147–56.

Vygotsky, L. S. (1978) *Mind in Society*, Cambridge, Mass.: Harvard University Press.

Walker, M. (1992) *Surviving Secrets*, Buckingham: Open University Press.

Walton, P. (2002), 'Safeguarding and Promoting Children's Welfare: A Question of Competence', in K. Wilson and A. James (eds), *The Child Protection Handbook*, 2nd edn, Edinburgh: Harcourt.

Waters, E., Vaughan, B. E., Posada, G. and Kondo-Ikemura, K. (eds) (1995) 'Caregiving, Cultural and Cognitive Perspectives on Secure-Base Behavior and Working Models', *Monographs of the Society for Research in Child Development*, **60**, pp. 27–48.

Watson, F., Burrows, H. and Player, C. (2002) *Integrating Theory and Practice in Social Work Education*, London: Jessica Kingsley.

Whitaker, D. S. (1985) *Using Groups to Help People*, London: Routledge & Kegan Paul.

White, E. C. (1985) *Chain, Chain, Change*, Seattle, Washington: Seal Press.

White, M. and Gribbin, J. (1992) *Stephen Hawking: A Life in Science*, London: Penguin.

Williams, L. M. (1994) 'Recall of Childhood Trauma: A Prospective Study of Women's Memories of Child Sexual Abuse', *Journal of Consulting and Clinical Psychology*, **62**, pp. 1167–76.

Wilson, J. (1992) *The Story of Tracey Beaker*, London: Random House.

Wilson, K. and James, A. (eds) (2002) *The Child Protection Handbook*, 2nd edn, Edinburgh: Harcourt.

Winton, M. A. and Mara, B. A. (2001) *Child Abuse and Neglect: A Multidisciplinary Approach*, Boston, Mass.: Allyn & Bacon.

Wisdom, C. S., Raphael, K. G. and DuMont, K. A. (2004) 'The Case for Prospective Longitudinal Studies in Child Maltreatment Research', *Child Abuse and Neglect*, **28**, pp. 715–22.

Wolfe, D. A. (1987) *Child Abuse: Implications for Child Development and Psychopathology*, London: Sage.

Wolfe, D. A., Sas, L. and Wekerle, C. (1994) 'Factors Associated with the Development of Posttraumatic Stress Disorder among Child Victims of Sexual Abuse', *Child Abuse and Neglect*, **18**(1), pp. 37–50.

Wyre, R. (1986) *Women, Men and Rape*, Oxford: Perry.

Yen Mah, A. (2002) *Chinese Cinderella*, Harlow: Longman.

Yule, V. C. (1985) 'Why are Parents Tough on Children?', *New Society*, 27 September, pp. 444–6.

Zeitlin, H. (2002) 'Adoption of Children from Minority Groups', in N. Dwivedi (ed.), *Meeting the Needs of Ethnic Minority Children*, 2nd edn, London: Jessica Kingsley.

Index